Clinical Counselling in Primary Care

More counsellors than ever before are being employed in medical settings. Yet existing literature on primary care counselling contains insufficient examination of its complexities, and of the variety of its therapeutic applications.

Clinical Counselling in Primary Care fills this gap. In the light of the current professionalization of counselling, it looks at the variety of original and creative solutions that practitioners have developed to meet the challenges of this setting. Whilst highlighting the fact that there are still considerable differences between practices, it takes the view that, if the counsellor can work with the healing power inherent in the setting, then s/he has an important tool for therapeutic change.

The book examines the broader conceptual framework of clinical counselling in primary care, taking a differentiated postmodern outlook, and establishes a distinction between the different ways of seeing clinical practice in this setting. A range of important clinical issues – such as the therapeutic framework, seeing the clinical work as part of the greater whole, and the need to develop suitable therapeutic models – are discussed. In addition to this, the book looks at possible developments in the future and argues that, with careful professionalization and a well thought out academic base, counselling can be a sophisticated activity which is not just the poor neighbour of psychotherapy.

John Lees is Senior Lecturer in Counselling and runs the post-graduate training course in counselling at the University of Greenwich. He is a UKRC registered independent counsellor and works as a counsellor and supervisor in a variety of settings. He is a member of the British Association for Psychoanalytic and Psychodynamic Supervision and is also editor of the journal *Psychodynamic Counselling*.

Contributors: Anna Bravesmith; Roslyn Corney; Mary Costello; Annalee Curran; Sue Davison; Richard House; John Launer; David Mann; Marilyn Miller-Pietroni; Jonathan Smith; Peter Thomas; Jonathan Whines.

...cal Counselling in Context
Series editor: John Lees

This series of key texts examines the unique nature of counselling in a wide range of clinical settings. Each book shows how the context in which counselling takes place has profound effects on the nature and outcome of the counselling practice, and encourages clinical debate and dialogue.

Clinical Counselling in Context
An introduction
Edited by John Lees

Clinical Counselling in Primary Care
Edited by John Lees

Clinical Counselling in Further and Higher Education
Edited by John Lees and Alison Vaspe

Clinical Counselling in Primary Care

Edited by John Lees

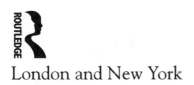

London and New York

First published 1999 by Routledge
11 New Fetter Lane, London EC4P 4EE

Simultaneously published in the USA and Canada
by Routledge
29 West 35th Street, New York, NY 10001

Editorial matter © 1999 John Lees;
individual chapters © 1999 the contributors

Typeset in Goudy by Keystroke, Jacaranda Lodge, Wolverhampton
Printed and bound in Great Britain by Clays Ltd, St Ives PLC

British Library Cataloguing in Publication Data
A catalogue record for this book is available from the British Library

Library of Congress Cataloguing in Publication Data
Clinical counselling in primary care / [edited by] John Lees.
       p.   cm. — (Clinical counselling in context series)
     Includes bibliographical references and index.
     1. Health counseling. 2. Primary care (Medicine) 3. Clinical
psychology. I. Lees, John, 1951– . II. Series.
     [DNLM: 1. Primary Health Care—methods. 2. Counseling.
3. Psychology, Clinical.   W 84.6 C641 1999]
R727.4.C56   1999
616.89—dc21
DNLM/DLC
for Library of Congress   98–29005
       361. O6 LEE   CIP

ISBN 0–415–17953–X (hbk)
ISBN 0–415–17954–8 (pbk)

Contents

Figures and tables

Figures

Tables

Contributors

Anna Bravesmith (B.Ed, Diploma in Psychotherapy) took her degree at London University in 1975 and has a background in teaching and community work. She trained as an Analytic Psychotherapist at the Institute of Psychotherapy and Social Studies, graduating in 1987. She has worked in private practice as a psychotherapist for ten years, as a teacher of psychodynamic counselling and as a supervisor and trainer of psychotherapists. Between 1996/7 she worked as a GP counsellor for The Forest Healthcare Trust in a research project funded by London Implementation Zone and based at Thorpe Coombe hospital in Walthamstow. Research was carried out by an all-Jungian team. She is a trainee Jungian Analyst at the Society of Analytical Psychology.

Roslyn Corney is Professor of Psychology at the University of Greenwich. She has undertaken a number of research studies on mental health issues in general practice and has developed a special interest in the role of counsellors in this setting. She edited *Developing Communication and Counselling Skills in Medicine* in 1991 and co-edited *Counselling in General Practice* with Rachel Jenkins in 1993; both published by Routledge.

Mary Costello (B.Med Sci, MBBS, DA) has been a full-time general practitioner in a three-partner, inner-city practice for the past six years. Her interest in psychotherapy developed during her vocational training psychiatric attachment, where she worked in both small and large groups. She has attended the Institute of Group Analysis general course in groupwork. She is currently also a GP tutor to medical students and conducts small group teaching seminars.

Annalee Curran is a practice counsellor in an inner-London GP surgery where she has worked for the past twenty years, first as a National Childbirth Trust antenatal teacher and then, since 1985, as a counsellor.

She is also a psychotherapist, supervisor and trainer in Cognitive Analytic Therapy (CAT) and is a founder member of the Association of Cognitive Analytic Therapists. Training and supervising CAT has taken her to many parts of Britain and to Finland and Greece. She has done work for the Department of General Practice and Primary Care at Kings College Hospital and with Professor Roger Higgs has given a number of presentations on counselling in primary care and related issues. They co-authored a chapter in *Counselling in Primary Care* (Routledge, 1993, ed. Corney and Jenkins). Annalee Curran also wrote a chapter on 'The use of CAT in primary care' in *Cognitive Analytic Therapy: Active Participation in Change* (Wiley, 1990, ed. Ryle). She has been a member of a project team for the Open University working on a course entitled 'Mental Health and Distress: Perspectives and Practice'. Currently she has a small private psychotherapy practice.

Susan Davison (PhD, MRCP, MRCPsych.) is a psychoanalyst and a consultant psychotherapist to the Bethlem and Maudsley NHS Trust.

Richard House is a counselling practitioner and a Steiner Waldorf teacher-trainee (Norwich). An NHS GP counsellor since 1990, he is also Group Supervisor for Waveney Counselling Service (Westminster Pastoral Foundation affiliate). He has published widely in the literature, and is co-editor, with Nick Totton, of *Implausible Professions* (PCCS Books, 1997).

John Launer has been a GP in London for fifteen years. He is a trained family therapist, and since 1995 he has also been a part-time consultant in general practice and primary care at the Tavistock Clinic.

David Mann is a psychoanalytic psychotherapist and a member of the London Centre for Psychotherapy. He works in primary care and private practice. In addition he teaches, lectures and runs workshops around the UK and has extensively published in leading national and international psychotherapy journals. He is author of *Psychotherapy: An Erotic Relationship – Transference and Countertransference Passions* (Routledge, 1997) and is editor of *Erotic Transference and Countertransference: Clinical Practice in Psychotherapy* (Routledge, 1999).

Marilyn Miller-Pietroni is a counsellor and psychotherapist at Marylebone Health Centre and Principal Lecturer in Primary Health and Community Care at the University of Westminster. She qualified first as a psychiatric social worker, was a founder member of staff of Hill End Adolescent Unit and worked in community and mental hospital services. She qualified as an adult psychotherapist at the Tavistock

Clinic in 1974. She was for many years a member of the teaching staff of the clinic and of the London Centre for Psychotherapy. She is a member of the British Association for Counselling and the British Confederation of Psychotherapists and the author and editor of a number of publications which draw on psychodynamic thinking.

Jonathan Smith (LLB, CQSW, Diploma in Psychotherapy) studied law at Warwick University, and then went on to train in social work at Sheffield University. He worked for twelve years as a social worker for the London Borough of Hounslow, and during this time he trained in psychodynamic psychotherapy at the Institute of Psychotherapy and Social Studies. He currently works as a trainer in psychodynamic counselling and counselling skills at Birkbeck College and at the Westminster Pastoral Foundation. He supervises trainee counsellors at the St Marylebone Healing and Counselling Centre. He is book reviews editor for the journal *Psychodynamic Counselling* and works as a counsellor in two GP practices in Wandsworth for Pathfinders NHS Trust.

Peter Thomas (MSc., P/G Diploma in Counselling, SRN, NDN, PWT, UKRC Reg. Ind. Counsellor) has been working as a counsellor in general practice for eleven years, conducting bereavement and therapeutic groups as well as individual short-term therapy. He also works as a counsellor for Lambeth Healthcare Community NHS Trust, conducting staff development and supervision groups. He is a freelance supervisory consultant in private practice.

Jonathan Whines originally became interested in holism through the study of yoga in India. He subsequently gained a Masters in Literature in Kent and qualified as a Masseur and Traditional Acupuncturist. He is an experienced Gestalt Psychotherapist, holding a Masters in Gestalt Psychotherapy from Metanoia Institute. He works for a variety of organizations including two general practices and has a busy private practice in Norwich. He is currently Chair of the Norfolk Association of Professional Surgery Counsellors which represents forty counsellors in general practices.

Acknowledgements

Several people have provided help and encouragement in the process of assembling this volume. In particular, however, I would like to thank all those who helped to review the chapters, as well as the contributors for doing what was needed and in meeting deadlines. Finally, I wish to thank Ellen Noonan and the counselling training staff at Birkbeck College who first planted the idea of the contextual nature of counselling in my mind.

Most of the contributions to this volume appear for the first time, with the exception of the following two chapters:

Chapter 9: 'Working with different models: adapting to the context', by John Launer, is a modified version of a paper which appeared in 1994 as 'Psychotherapy in the General Practice Surgery: Working With and Without a Secure Therapeutic Frame' in the *British Journal of Psychotherapy* 11, 1: 120–7.

Chapter 10: 'Inter-disciplinary collaboration for group therapy' by Peter Thomas, Mary Costello and Susan Davison, is a modified version of a paper which appeared in 1997 as 'Group work in general practice' in *Psychodynamic Counselling* 3, 1: 23–33.

Introduction

John Lees

This book is based on the notion that there is a complex inter-relationship between clinical work and the context in which it takes place – that the context is inextricably bound up with the work and is an important force for therapeutic change. Building on this notion, it also takes the view that if we work with the healing power inherent in the context itself – whilst also being aware of its potentially negative influences – then we have an important tool for therapeutic change at our disposal. Furthermore it is felt that counsellors have a special expertise in this area since much counselling work takes place in organizational settings and consequently some of its originality lies in its contribution to thinking and technique in the contextual field. Indeed it is felt that 'clinical counselling in primary care' is a sophisticated and complex clinical activity, quite distinct from 'clinical counselling' in other settings. The pure theory of therapeutic work is transformed and metamorphosed by the unique characteristics of the primary care setting.

The book aims to present a picture of what actually goes on in the consulting room – what counsellors do and the rationale behind this. So it will include a substantial amount of case material and accounts of actual experience, and will show how this can be illuminated by theory. It will show how different practitioners have responded to the needs of the primary care setting in a variety of ways. Each contributor has found a way of responding and understanding their experience in keeping with their theoretical preferences and the uniqueness of their primary care situation. For, even though there are some common characteristics within the primary care sector – the ubiquity of the medical model, the busyness, the huge range of presenting problems – there are still considerable differences between practices. The primary care sector as a whole consists of a differentiated variety of sub-cultures, probably numbering as many as there are surgeries. Ultimately, each situation is unique and each chapter of this book reflects this characteristic inasmuch as each looks at clinical counselling in primary care from the unique standpoint of the chapter contributor.

The heterogeneity of primary care counselling lends itself well to the principles of adaptation, homeostasis and growth (see Lees, 1997, for a discussion of this). In the first place we adapt our clinical technique to the needs of the setting. Rather than running against the flow, so to speak, we go with it. Secondly, we can try to create a balance between the potentially conflicting demands of the culture of the setting and our own clinical practices. If we were to give up our clinical principles completely then we would simply create a situation where the blind lead the blind. On the other hand, if we work in isolation from the setting we fail to harness its healing potential. So a middle way is sought in which there is a creative tension between the culture of the setting and our clinical principles and practices. Finally, by adopting such an approach, it is felt that we are able to make a contribution to the ongoing growth and development of clinical practice and technique. Indeed these three principles of clinical practice inform most of the chapters in the book to varying degrees (with the exception of the final chapter which is research, rather than clinically, based and is concerned with standing back and giving an overview of some developments in this setting). The chapters show how the different practitioners have adapted their technique to the primary care setting, have struggled with the tensions inherent in it in order to establish a balanced and coherent way of working, and have come to a synthesis which has created a new and original perspective on clinical counselling in primary care.

The book can be divided into three parts. Chapter 1 looks at the broader conceptual framework of clinical counselling in primary care. Chapters 2 to 10 look at a range of clinical issues which the counsellor has to negotiate in this setting, and chapter 11 examines the importance of research and discusses some possible developments in the future.

Chapter 1, entitled 'The postmodern context of counselling in general practice' by Marilyn Miller-Pietroni, provides a general introduction to clinical counselling in general practice in the 1990s. Taking a differentiated, postmodern outlook, it establishes distinctions between the different ways of seeing clinical practice in primary care: the traditional bio-medical model which sees therapeutic work in terms of curing illness; the psychosocial model, with its emphasis on the complexities of the interactions between human beings; and the market model, which has arisen out of the National Health Service and Community Care Act (1990).

The clinical part of the book covers several overlapping themes. Chapters 2 and 3 both examine the therapeutic framework. In 'The culture of general practice and the therapeutic frame', Richard House gives a broad introduction to the peculiarities of the setting of general practice counselling and, in particular, examines the therapeutic framework and its relevance to clinical practice in this setting. Surveying some of the theory on the subject he comes to the conclusion that a flexible approach to the therapeutic framework is the most desirable in this setting. In chapter 3, entitled 'Holding the dance: a flexible approach to boundaries in general practice', Jonathan Smith comes to much the same conclusion. However, he approaches the matter from the point of view of clinical practice, with several case examples, and so complements the ground covered in chapter 2.

There is a common theme running through chapters 4 to 7; namely, the issue of holism. Much of the basic theory of clinical counselling has traditionally been presented in a discrete manner isolated from the setting in which the work has taken place. However, in different ways, all of these chapters present new ideas based on seeing the work in the consulting room as part of the whole setting. In chapter 4, for example, Annalee Curran examines 'Counselling within a time limit in general practice'. Apart from making the obvious point that counselling in general practice needs, of necessity, to be time limited she also looks at such issues as the notion of 'intermittent counselling' and shows how this is entirely in keeping with the culture of the setting as a whole where the patients are seen intermittently over a period of time – in some cases for the whole of their lives. In chapter 5, entitled 'A holistic approach to working in general practice', Jonathan Whines presents a different view of holism. The setting itself, with its emphasis on the medical model, is viewed as fostering a fragmentary view of the human being which encourages dependency rather than autonomy. In contrast to this, an approach to clinical counselling is presented that attempts to see the client in a more holistic way, which is empowering rather than disempowering. Chapters 6 and 7, in different ways, also adopt a holistic perspective in that they see the counsellor's interventions and clinical techniques as closely linked to the dynamics of the whole setting rather than as cut off behind the doors of the consulting room. In 'The matrix at work: a post-Jungian approach to general practice counselling' Anna Bravesmith refers to the matrix of the setting as a whole, as opposed to the therapeutic dyad. She describes the symbolic aspect of therapeutic work and the way in which this can affect the way clients and other practice staff use symbolic imagery. In 'The generalized transference in general practice', meanwhile, David Mann develops an approach to the transference which sees it in terms of client fantasies towards the members of the staff team as a whole rather than just to the therapist. He describes how the therapist's capacity to interpret these generalized transferences can have significant healing power.

Chapters 8, 9 and 10 form the final sub-group of the clinical part of the book. They all, in different ways, show that, in their particular general practice settings, one model of practice (say six individual counselling sessions each lasting 50 minutes) proved to be too narrow and limiting. In 'Counselling for patients with severe mental health problems in the general practice setting' Marilyn Miller-Pietroni describes a range of counselling services on offer – one or two sessions, brief work of up to ten sessions, fortnightly sessions, sessions once every four to six weeks on an open-ended basis, and short emergency sessions. She shows how such a degree of flexibility can offer some meaningful therapeutic work to a wide range of clients with many different presenting problems, including those with severe mental health problems. John Launer, in the chapter entitled 'Working with different models: adapting to the context', describes a three-level model of counselling ranging from counselling proper (or 'Big-C counselling') to the use of counselling skills by health professionals (or 'Little-c counselling') to one or two sessions with either an individual or a family (or 'Middle-C counselling'). Finally, Peter Thomas, Mary Costello and Susan Davison, in 'Inter-disciplinary collaboration for group therapy' show how instituting a psychotherapy group in general practice enabled them to meet client demand and avoided the necessity of referring clients on, instead building on the trust which had already been established with the counsellor. The model also describes the possibilities of inter-disciplinary co-operation; in this case between a counsellor, a consultant psychiatrist and a GP.

The final chapter in the book, 'Evaluating clinical counselling in primary care and the future' by Roslyn Corney, examines the importance of evaluating counselling services in primary care in view of its increased availability over the last few years and the fact that there is very little evidence to prove its clinical effectiveness. Whilst acknowledging the difficulties in obtaining definitive evidence she nevertheless also acknowledges that it is here to stay and looks to a future where there is greater integration and co-operation between counsellors and other health professionals working in this setting.

Each of these chapters describes a unique way of working which each contributor has arrived at on the basis of his/her experience. Each shows the creative and innovative solutions that were developed in the light of the challenges of primary care counselling. Yet the book is not meant to be prescriptive. As previously discussed, one of its fundamental principles is the notion of differentiation and heterogeneity. It is felt that there are as many ways of working as there are practitioners. Ultimately we all have to find our own synthesis, whatever our theoretical persuasion.

REFERENCES

Department of Health (1990) *National Health Service and Community Care Act*, London: HMSO

Lees, J. (1997), 'An approach to counselling in GP surgeries', *Psychodynamic Counselling*, 3(1): 33–48

1   The postmodern context of counselling in general practice[1]

Marilyn Miller-Pietroni

Introduction

This chapter provides a conceptual framework in which to view the recent changes in the National Health Service and their implications for counselling in general practice, in particular the impact of the National Health Service and Community Care Act (Department of Health 1990). The ideas and theories of postmodernism are taken as a starting-point for consideration of the new professional categories and languages that have developed. Specific examples are drawn from a counselling service in one inner city GP practice to illustrate how some postmodern concepts can facilitate thought about the paradoxes that abound in this setting, in which the GP's patient is the counsellor's client and the Health Authority's customer. Using case histories and drawing upon current thinking in the literature and training for counsellors working in primary care, some of the advantages and the question marks relating to an interprofessional approach to primary care are identified. The chapter concludes with the proposal that it is necessary, in a mixed economy of care, to recognize the implications of living and working in a postmodern world.

The contextual approach and the need for a meta-theory

The literature on counselling in general practice in the UK has been expanding rapidly (Corney and Jenkins 1994, Keithley and Marsh 1995, Jenkins 1994). Debate has centred on the need for outcome studies related to the dramatic increase in counselling activity and expenditure in this front-line setting (Parry 1994, Sibbald et al. 1993, Le Fanu 1995, Harris 1994). Evidence for the efficacy of specific counselling approaches e.g. Gestalt, cognitive, psychodynamic is also under review (Parry 1994, Jenkins 1995). The fruits of these debates have been used to propose a national curriculum for training in this field (Jenkins 1994).

COUNSELLING IN GENERAL PRACTICE

Front-line work

|

NEW MARKET FORCES – POLICY FRAMEWORKS

Professional world views under fire

|

PREVAILING CULTURAL BELIEFS AND VALUES

Current theories and models
e.g. bio-medical, psycho-social

|

META-THEORIES/CONTEXTUAL THEORIES

e.g. postmodernism

Figure 1.1 A contextual approach: use of a meta-theory

This chapter seeks to contextualize these debates within a broader conceptual framework, or meta-theory, borrowed from the field of cultural studies, namely postmodernism. This perspective has been extensively applied to widely varying fields of academic enquiry and professional practice, e.g. architecture, electronics and literary criticism. These applications have been made extensively in the USA and Europe; the UK has however, been slower to realize the contribution postmodern interpretation can make to understanding rapidly changing fields of knowledge and practice.

Some recent exceptions are the work of Parton (1994), Rustin (1991), Richards (1994), Hoggett (1992) and Pietroni (1995). These authors demonstrate the case for a contextual theory that is capable of transcending the terms of debate used in one part of the system, and locating those terms within the broader intellectual frameworks of the day. They also demonstrate that a postmodern perspective can usefully relate theory and practices of all kinds to their cultural and historical context (see Figure 1.1).

To the two models traditionally applied to counselling in general practice, the bio-medical and psycho-social, will be added a third, the market model . The chapter will apply each of these three models to counselling in general practice. Key terms selected from these models will be used to explore typical referrals to the counselling service, namely 'patient', 'client', and 'customer'. The first and second terms are used conventionally within the field: GPs refer to 'patients', counsellors to 'clients'; the third term however contextualizes the other two within the

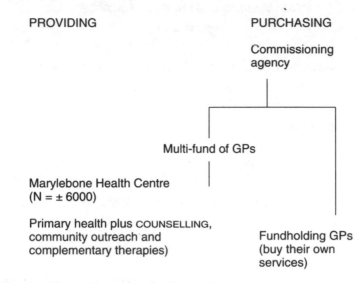

Figure 1.2 The purchaser/provider framework

new order of complexity brought about by the NHS and Community Care Act (Department of Health 1990), with its market framework, costed episodes of care, and purchaser/provider split. This market of care signifies those who use services as 'customers, users or consumers'. From these, the term 'customer' has been chosen because it relates most explicitly to the idea of the market, and thus signifies the policy context.

The three key terms, 'patient', 'client', 'customer' will be used as different perspectives from which to examine in detail four case studies. This multi-perspective approach exposes ambiguities and contradictions which are at the heart of counselling in general practice, and which, in the authors' view, outcome studies or methodological debate can only go so far to illuminate.

The specific context

A diagram of the purchasing and providing framework of one counselling service is provided in Figure 1.2. This illustrates how the counselling service is part of an established general practice model of integrated health and social care, otherwise known as a holistic approach. The practice in question[2] is a provider of health and social care services with a list size of around 6,000, at one point twinned with another practice for fund-holding status.

The overall profile of this counselling service was first described by Webber et al. (1994), and is typical of a city with high rates of unemployment, refugees and other mobile populations, isolated single and elderly people, and ambitious young families.

What is postmodernism?

Postmodernism is a theoretical perspective with a set of core concepts that have been used in different ways in different fields, but about which there is an international consensus. It is called a meta-theory because it subsumes a range of other theories; these are drawn particularly from sociology and linguistics and are most frequently applied to the field of cultural studies.

The conceptual building blocks of postmodernism, hammered out internationally over the last fifty years, will be identified (Table 1.1). Sufficient consensus has now been reached for a series of overviews to be written, from which these are drawn (Natoli and Hutcheon 1993, Smart 1993, Bertens 1995). It can be seen that the idea of a rapidly changing, global market (similar to the one emerging in the UK on the edge of public sector health and welfare) is central to the postmodern perspective.

The concepts are drawn from primary sources on postmodernism such as Jameson (1991), Lyotard (1984) and Eco (1987), and the overviews referred to above. The concepts are illustrated with indicative examples drawn from the field of health and social care: some from the broader social context, others from changes in policy and practice which have occurred since the introduction of the GP contract and the *NHS and Community Care Act* (Department of Health 1990). Although more debate of the examples would be useful, at this stage the intention is only to indicate the broad conceptual framework of postmodernism, and its potential for wide application to the field of health and social care.

In summary

> The terms and ideas of postmodernism were founded on a disillusionment with radical politics and the socialist promise of the early twentieth century. . . . Loss of certainty, the acceptance of a relativist philosophy and the fragmentation of values, thought and beliefs . . . have been identified as the normal features of postmodernism. . . . The nearest there are to facts are the constructivist nature of knowledge, the dizzy pace of change, the babel of professional languages, and the continuous erasure of categories of thought and formal structures of all kinds.
>
> (Pietroni 1995: 45)

Table 1.1 The conceptual building blocks of postmodernism

---

1 Commodification and the global market

- Expanding international market in independent consultancies, information networks, and health and social care provision
- Commissioning of 'care' and the contract culture
- The purchaser/provider split and associated change to the language of the market
- Emphasis on cost, volume and specified outcomes or products; short-term output; time-based and tariff-based services e.g. clinical 'episodes' or 'packages' of care, and referrals to secondary care services

2 Complexification in relation to critical change

- Fundamental changes in policy, philosophy and organisation: repeated reorganisations, rewriting job and person specifications, rewriting job titles, reselections of staff
- Mixture of clinical and market criteria in front-line decision-making
- Increased inter-agency and inter-sector collaboration bringing a 'jangle of jargons'
- Increased complaints promoted by consumer charters
- Complex relations with a wide range of information technology, via audit, and quality or performance measures
- Versatility on the 'front-line' required by the 'cultural melting pot' of the inner cities
- The breakdown of family life and increase in poverty and mobility
- Ideologies of political correctness: a persecutory culture which inhibits debate and is intolerant of differences of view and language
- The contested nature of the concept of 'normalcy' at a time of high profile 'normalisation' policies e.g. in fields of mental health, disability, learning difficulties, homelessness, parenting etc.

3 The global city and 'a new Medievalism' (Eco 1987)

- Fundamentalist conflicts across racial, religious, political and ideological groups
- Increased violence at work, at home and on the street
- Extreme distress of refugees and torture victims presenting in general practice
- The illicit drugs market and associated sub-culture
- International client/patient/refugee populations import distant wars and cultural issues into local practice e.g. female circumcision, Bosnian/Serb conflicts etc.
- Language and interpretation issues
- Cultural practices in conflict e.g. female circumcision, gender roles, marital conventions

4 Crisis in authority and leadership

- Conflicts between managerialist and professionalist values and approaches in all agencies; rise of anti-professional lobbies

continued

- Clumsy restructuring: dismantling of old 'centres of excellence'; closure of newly commissioned units; severe shortages of basic facilities e.g. in-patient beds, home aids and equipment
- Privileged new generation of 'non-professional' manager/leaders with high-tech skills/denigration of old-style 'experienced clinician'
- Increase in 'early retirements' and 'redundancy packages' leading to rapidly changing leaders and leadership systems
- Cost, volume and output-led decision-making competes with clinical decision-making

5 Superficial language games: a crisis in meaning and representation

- Contested terms: patient, client, consumer, user; counsellor, counselling psychologist, psychotherapist; needs-led assessment, user-centredness, eligibility criteria, care management; increased 'choice'; quality measures and performance indicators
- Care in the community when equated with de-institutionalization
- Philosophy and language of 'partnership' in 'conflict of interest' situations e.g. child protection, mental health, care of elders
- Policy taboo on the individualized recording of 'unmet need' at needs assessment stage of care management in social services

6 'Banalization': an amalgam of sentimentality, parody and pastiche

- Buzz words with a hollow, public relations quality : 'user-centredness', 'seamless service', 'quality'
- Bizarre new jargon: 'social bathing', 'health bathing'
- Buzz phrases that normalize radical and untested ideas: the 'market of care'/'mixed welfare economy'
- Simplistic colour matching of client and practitioner e.g. in fostering and adoption, ignoring race, ethnicity, class and religion
- Care 'packages', care 'plans' where eligibility criteria and other local policies supercede the meeting of individual need
- The name 'key worker': often applied to part-timers or others low in power and status in the multidisciplinary/multi-agency team
- Partnership policies in conflicted areas of practice that can promote fudged compromises and undermine independent critical thinking

7 Impact of new technology and rapid information exchange

- Threats to confidentiality from inter-agency databases
- Reception desks: interaction with computers competes with and often super-cedes interaction with human beings
- Improved information provides opportunity for regulated, targetted innovations e.g. home bathing services, home repairs, putting to bed services
- Audit and information systems associated with the purchaser/provider split and monitoring of service contracts introduces year-by-year regulatory changes and associated instability in the workplace

Counselling in general practice: four case studies

The following case studies are examined in the light of key terms from the bio-medical, psycho-social and market perspectives. The case studies were selected as representatives of key groups of patients that use the counselling service in general practice: Mary, a depressed young mother; Jeffery, a single man in middle life who has been made redundant; Naina, a female immigrant from Africa with multiple problems including bankruptcy; and Yana, a female refugee from Europe with a history of severe mental illness. The female/male ratio of three to one is average for this service. In terms of ethnic mix, again this is average for the practice, and reflects the 'global city' described by writers on postmodernism.

The brief case study allows some human depth and complexity to be conveyed, and demonstrates how everyday ambiguities in practice and language have profound structural and policy roots. The term 'patient' used here in relation to the bio-medical model reflects the perspective of the general practitioner, the term 'client', associated with the psycho-social model reflects the view of the counsellor, and the term 'customer' signifies the commodification of care, aptly described by postmodern theorists.

Case study 1: Mary – a 'straightforward' case?

Medical model

A female middle-class *patient* of 29 years presents frequently with minor ailments, contraceptive needs, pregnancy and baby-care issues, stress related to marital problems and the impending death of her father. A fairly normal picture contradicted by an unusually high use of the practice. Needs to talk to someone.

Psycho-social model

A young anxious female *client*, with developmental problems related to conflicts in her roles as wife, mother and daughter, especially as she has never really separated emotionally from her family of origin. Harsh sibling rivalries and strong paternal attachment interfere with her capacity for marital and sexual relationship. Offered ten fifty-minute sessions over period of one year, given the strong developmental issues which will not be touched if seen on a shorter, more frequent basis. Crisis work on weekly basis additionally offered, however, during period of grief after father's death. Total: 10 + 6 sessions over 15 months.

Market model

A responsible *customer* or a conspicuous *consumer*? Expensive referral to secondary services avoided by use of counsellor on site. Reduced attendance at GP's surgery follows counselling referral. Economy of preventive work in sustaining parenting, preventing use of drugs and avoiding longer term mental ill-health.

Case study 2: Jeffery – a 'deceptive' case?

Medical model

A male *patient*, older than he seems at 41, with vague symptoms: seems retarded and lacking in energy. He may be clinically depressed, but does not want to take drugs. He fears redundancy but dislikes his job, is single but has a long-term girlfriend. Please see and assess.

Psycho-social model

Unusual *client* who finds it difficult to talk, is hard to assess, and seems empty and hollow. Initial contract of six weekly sessions offered; in last ten minutes of last session reveals major sexual problem easily satisfied in capital city and from videos and internet, but hidden from long-term girlfriend and GP. High risk of psychotic breakdown and/or proscecution. Referred to specialist clinic for long-term work. Seen monthly while waiting for a vacancy. Responds well and with relief when accurately assessed and referred. Total: 6 + 6 sessions over 9 months.

Market model

Undemanding *customer* in general practice and counselling services. Potential for psychiatric hospital admission or jail would increase cost to national care budget; cheaper as out-patient, although secondary care specialist referral expensive for practice budget. Patient makes use of inner city and modern technology markets to meet sexual needs and desires.

Case study 3: Naina – a 'heartsink patient'?

Medical model

A female *patient*, aged 56, who presents frequently with unresolvable minor and major complaints eg severe back pain, hormonal disturbances, hypertension, depression, stress associated with bankruptcy and family problems, unresolved grief from family accident causing deaths of siblings. Pleads poverty and draws benefits but is expensively dressed and by-passes NHS frequently with private health care (uninsured). Makes regular formal complaints about GP. Non-compliant with prescribed treatments. Regular night calls.

A 'heartsink' patient, can you do anything with her?

Psycho-social model

A glamorous and talkative *client* with many unfocussed problems. Generated sympathy in first instance but repeated, random complaints are not amenable to limited counselling help. Tried cognitive, structured approach after assessment but it was ignored. No continuity of sessions from week to week. Dreadful history has been adapted to by 'wheeling and dealing' between different staff of the practice and from private sector whom she frequently plays off against each other. *Patient* was referred to counselling to give GP a break and contain behavioural excesses. Seen weekly for 10 weeks then monthly for 6 months to support GP. No change to client although she was appreciative of the time and listening which she does not get elsewhere.

Market model

A complex picture. Sees herself as a *customer* who wants much more from the service than she is getting. Uses complaint systems frequently. Is dissatisfied. Very expensive to practice because of high investigation rates across a range of changing and recurring complaints. A dissatisfied customer.

Case study 4: Jana, a refugee

Medical model

A female *patient* of 38 with a history of severe mental illness: differential diagnosis manic-depressive psychosis/schizophrenia. Strict drug regime but has had no severe episodes for last four years. Drugs could be slightly reduced to try and improve her quality of life. Unemployed and lives in bed and breakfast. Family are alive in peaceful region of war-torn country and in telephone contact. Patient does not want to return because she was regularly hospitalized in primitive institutions with little drug treatment, suffered terrible hallucinations and poor physical care. Possibility for partnership approach with counsellor while drugs are gradually reduced to optimal level?

Psycho-social model

Referrals of this kind are usually contraindicated. Agree to see and assess only, following which however, I accept *client* for monthly to six-weekly sessions based on my prior experience of good psychiatric out-patient clinics. Close liaison with GP. Contrary to expectations, client is a real pleasure to see, recognises the delicacy of the gradual drug reduction, accepts advice from GP and observes appointments meticulously. Dramatic improvement over two-year period from near zombie-state sleeping all day and doing little, to resuming her artistic activities, an active social life and taking up a steady sexual partner. Begins to present 'ordinary' relationship and living problems rather than 'extraordinary' problems of severe mental illness. Collaboration with community mental health team after one and a half years destabilizes her: too many activities and reidentifies with mentally ill clients at the day centre she now attends; starts to demand cigarettes, money, argues with partner. Interagency review organized on a day that I cannot as a part-timer attend. Work continues: about 30 sessions over three and a half years: pragmatic mixed approach taken.

Market model

Counselling in partnership with GP monitoring and reduction of drugs have reduced costs and may even have avoided further severe and therefore expensive episodes. *Customer* is highly satisfied and at one point tries to resume work, which would have taken her off benefits. For a period, low cost and quality are co-terminous. International market of care is present: patient is actively shopping for best UK care now she is well enough to do so, but she is finding multiple agencies and approaches indigestible and is at risk of relapsing. Some tension between general practice and specialist services is likely on professional grounds although they are at risk of being seen as cost issues.

Discussion

This rich mixture of presentations from the serious to the banal, the worrying to the incredible, the needy to the greedy is characteristic of general practice. The complex relationship between professional and market issues is however fairly new. It brings a new aspect to professional risk management, when cost and complaint systems impinge on complex clinical management. The GP and counsellor are not only required to incorporate the bio-psycho-social aspects of assessment and provision, but also to consider the market and its back-up complaints systems, at every step. In the midst of this complexity, there are new ethical pressures and research-mindedness is more than ever necessary, if decision-making is to rise above simple reaction to everyday pressures.

The three perspectives overlap, sometimes in a complementary way and sometimes in a conflicted way. The perspectives on Mary are difficult to assess because the question of whether she is a 'satisfied customer' or a 'conspicuous consumer' hinges upon the efficacy of the preventive work undertaken by the counsellor, which is not amenable to proof in the short term. Marital conflict, parenting problems and grief are core issues in counselling in general practice, and indeed counselling in other settings too, but as yet there is no research to demonstrate that the work undertaken can be justified in patient, client or customer terms.

The market perspective on Jeffery conflicts with the bio-medical and psycho-social: the referral to secondary services is necessary on clinical grounds but expensive. Professional values are in conflict with those of the market and high ethical standards are essential to place the 'patient' and 'client's' needs first. Similarly, good relations with local community mental health providers that need ' business' if local services are to be maintained, could be threatened by the practice counsellor's different, more individualized approach to Jana. The pressure on the counsellor to provide a short-term service in the general practice setting tends to support the use of a second community service; so also does the prevailing professional view of counselling with severely mentally ill people that generalizes it into an 'inappropriate category' which is at odds with the views of user groups such as MIND. Counselling however, is above all else focused on the unique needs of individuals and experienced counsellors should be able to assess when, if, and how such work is appropriate.

Naina, on the other hand, can work her way through private and public sector services around the clock, and still the complaints system put in place by The Patient's Charter (1991) will offer her another route for pressurising demands on the professionals. In the mixed welfare economy each episode is a 'new episode', and as a customer she is not held accountable for the range, and frequency of her complaints, nor for their impact on the professionals, nor the opportunity cost to other patients, clients and customers of her abuse of the system.

In conclusion

It has been argued that a postmodernist perspective has something to contribute to understanding the complexity of counselling in general practice. It has also been suggested that the conceptual framework of postmodernism could offer a useful reorientation to the experience and nature of everyday practice in the field of health and social care more generally. A postmodern perspective emphasises the policy and philosophical context of practice and indicates that the terms of professional debate need redefining into a framework that is capable of representing multiple points of view in a variety of overlapping but different languages (Pietroni 1992).

Ambiguity and contradiction have always been at the heart of professional knowledge and practice. They are heightened however, by the intrinsic complexity of an activity which takes place on the boundary between two professional fields (counselling and general practice), and within a national policy framework cast into virtual free-fall by the NHS and Community Care Act (1990).

REFERENCES

Bertens H. (1995) The Idea of the Postmodern: a history. London and New York: Routledge.

Corney R. (1995) The researcher's perspective. In Keithley J. and Marsh G. (eds) Counselling in Primary Health Care. Oxford: Oxford University Press pp. 286–95.

Corney R. and Jenkins R. (eds) (1994) Counselling in General Practice. London:Tavistock/Routledge.

Department of Health (1990) National Health Service and Community Care Act. London: HMSO.

Eco U. (1987) Travels in Hyper-reality. London: Picador.

Harris M. (1994) Magic in the Surgery: counselling and the NHS. London: Social Affairs Unit.

Hoggett P. (1992) Partisans in an Uncertain World: the psychoanalysis of engagement. London: Free Association Books.

Jameson F. (1991) Postmodernism or the Cultural Logic of Late Capitalism. London/New York: Verso.

Jenkins G. C. (1994) Diploma in Primary Care Counselling. London: Counselling in Primary Care Trust.

Jenkins G. C. (1995) 'The complete guide to counselling in general practice'. *Pulse* 3 June pp. 65–73.

Keithley J. and Marsh G. (eds) (1995) *Counselling in Primary Health Care*. Oxford: Oxford University Press.

Le Fanu J. (1995) 'Counselling: a luxury we cannot afford'. *Daily Telegraph*, 3 May.

Lyotard J.-F. (1984) *The Postmodern Condition: a report on knowledge*. Manchester: Manchester University Press .

Natoli J. and Hutcheon L. (eds) (1993) *A Postmodern Reader*. Albany: State University of New York Press.

Parry G. (1994) 'Department of Health psychiatry services: advice to purchasers'. Paper given at *Third St George's Counselling in Primary Care Conference: collaboration in care*; London, 17 June.

Parton N. (1994) '"Problematics of government", (Post)modernity and Social Work'. *British Journal of Social Work* 24 pp. 9–32.

Pietroni M. (1995) 'The nature and aims of professional education for social workers: a postmodern perspective'. In Yelloly M. and Henkel M. (eds) *Learning and Teaching in Social Work: towards reflective practice*. London and Bristol: Jessica Kingsley, pp. 34–50.

Pietroni P.C.P. (1992) 'Towards reflective practice: the languages of health and social care'. *Journal of Interprofessional Care* 6: 1 pp. 7–16.

Richards B. (1994) *Disciplines of Delight*. London: Free Association Books.

Rustin M. (1991) *The Good Society and the Inner World: psychoanalysis, politics and culture*. London: Verso.

Schon D. (1992) 'The crisis of professional knowledge and the pursuit of an epistemology of practice'. *Journal of Interprofessional Care* 6:1 pp. 49–63.

Sibbald B., Addington-Hall J., Brennneman D. and Freeling P. (1993) 'Counsellors in English and Welsh general practices: their nature and distribution'. *British Medical Journal* 306:2 Jan pp. 29–33.

Smart B. (1993) *Postmodernity: key ideas*. London and New York: Routledge.

Webber V., Davies P. and Pietroni P. (1994) Counselling in an inner city general practice: analysis of its use and uptake. *British Journal of General Practice* 44 pp. 175–8.

NOTES

1 Thanks are due to Professor Patrick Pietroni who developed with me some of these ideas for our joint presentation at the annual meeting of the Counselling in Medical Settings Section of the British Association of Counselling in 1995. Also I am grateful to Alison Vaspe for help on developing the first full text, supported by a grant from the University of Westminster.

2 Marylebone Health Centre in Central London.

2 The culture of general practice and the therapeutic frame

Richard House

Introduction

In this chapter I intend to present a wide-ranging introduction to the context within which general practice (GP) counselling typically occurs, and to the associated stresses that obtain in that setting. My main vehicle for this discussion will be a close consideration of what is commonly referred to as 'the therapeutic frame' (Langs 1988; Gray 1994) within which GP counselling takes place.

The structure of the following discussion will reflect my own emerging views about the importance or otherwise of a preoccupation with 'boundaries' and 'the frame' in GP counselling work. I find myself in increasing agreement with the feminist psychotherapist Laura Brown, who has written: 'One myth is that of the universal frame for psychotherapy, with concomitant universal boundaries. . . . [A]ppropriate boundaries in therapy are a reflection of [*inter alia*] . . . the specific and unique relational matrix among and between the human beings in the therapy room' (Brown 1994: 30, 31). And writing specifically about Robert Langs' work, she questions his assumption that there is one and only one 'appropriate, non-invasive approach to creation of boundaries in psychotherapy' (ibid.: 30–1). In what follows, then, I will focus closely on the utility or otherwise of a 'therapeutic frame' focus in GP counselling.

The discussion will also take account of issues relating to the increasing professionalization of counselling and therapy (Mowbray 1995; House and Totton 1997), and the associated process by which arguably misguided attempts are increasingly being made to render the therapeutic experience 'scientific' and objective, and in principle predictable and controllable. These trends have particular relevance to the GP counsellor, who works within a medical setting where the modern totems of 'cost-effectiveness' and 'objective' evaluation increasingly hold sway. In turn, this leads into quite fundamental questions about the *ideological* tensions that exist with any form of counselling in scientific-medical contexts (House 1994, 1996a); for if the therapeutic experience is an indissolubly (inter)subjective process of human relationship, quite possibly in principle ineffable and beyond the ambit of rational scientific discourse (Spinelli 1996; House 1996b, 1997a, 1997b), then there must be considerable doubt about the extent to which non-mechanistic approaches to counselling can comfortably subsist within the exclusively medical environment of general practice (Totton 1997).

The remainder of this chapter takes the following form. First, I will briefly describe the general context within which GP counselling takes place and its impact upon the GP counsellor. This will serve as a prelude to the main body of the chapter, which will address the question of the GP 'frame', and its various characteristics and vicissitudes. The chapter concludes with some challenges to conventional thinking about the GP counselling frame and the GP counselling experience more generally.

The culture of general practice

Before moving on to the main discussion on the therapeutic framework within which GP counselling unfolds, I will briefly set out some more general contextual characteristics of the GP setting.

A medical setting

The setting is of course an explicitly *medical* one, predominantly focused on the so-called 'biomedical model' of diagnosis and treatment (Engel 1977). This in turn has crucial implications in terms of both the working and organizational milieu, and the counsellor's case-load. Thus, for example, GP-referred clients are probably more likely to be taking psychotropic medication of some sort, with knock-on implications for the nature of the counselling relationship (Hammersley and Beeley 1992). The GP-referred case-load is also typically very wide-ranging, with a very wide variety of presenting problems and rapid client 'turn-over' rates, in a setting which is typically dominated by time-limited contracts. This is important because the greater the scope of presenting difficulties in the counsellor's case-load, the more likely it is, *ceteris paribus*, that the counsellor's own unworked-through difficulties will be activated, in turn leading to greater levels of experienced counsellor stress than might be the case in other settings. Sussman's excellent book *A Curious Calling* (1992) sets out in great detail the various unconscious dynamics that can underlie motivations to become counsellors, and is for this reason a very useful handbook for counsellors working in this demanding setting.

Medical settings typically exhibit an atmosphere dominated by 'physical' ill-health and dis(-)ease, with all the associated levels of anxiety (often collusively denied) (Stein 1985, 1990; Menzies Lyth 1988); for 'Illness and anxiety are as inseparable as winter and wet weather' (Higgs and Dammers 1992: 27). A significant number of GP-referred clients are likely to be suffering somatic symptoms; and some of these will be so-called 'psychosomatic' patients. Such clients are likely to present a major challenge to the counsellor, not least because (quoting Alexander and Szasz 1952: 286), 'whenever it [the psychological approach] attempts to penetrate behind the ego's defenses and uncover aetiological factors, it is likely to activate emotional tension *and cause an exacerbation of somatic symptoms*' (my emphasis; see also McDougall 1989: 11) – with the associated likelihood of client resistance to, and possible subversion of, the counselling process. If, as is often the case, such a client is receiving medical attention from her or his GP concurrently with counselling, then there is the very real possibility of a conflict between the holistic, healing-orientated approach typical of counselling, and the doctor's biomedical/ diagnostic, cure-oriented approach to the client's/patient's worsening somatic symptoms . . . not to mention the splitting of the therapeutic relationship into the so-called 'therapeutic triangle' of doctor–patient/ client–counsellor. This kind of inter-professional conflict will have significant effects on the unconscious dynamics of the doctor–counsellor relationship, with all the frustrations and anxieties that can ensue.

It is also widely recognized in the literature (see Strain 1978: chapter 2 for an excellent review) that physical illness precipitates anxiety and *regression* in patients, with a consequently greater likelihood that the patient/client will develop a strong regressive transference relationship with her or his doctor and counsellor; and as Nemiah (1961: 299) writes, 'In the regressive reaction brought about by illness, transference colored by infantile needs and impulses may make the doctor's [counsellor's – RH] task a very difficult one'. Thus, given that the counsellor is more likely to have clients with somatic/physical symptoms in a GP setting, it follows that she or he will probably have a greater exposure to difficult regressive transferences, and the associated countertransferential stresses to which this gives rise.

Psychosomatic ways of being are seen by McDougall (1989: 10) as constituting 'an archaic form of mental functioning that does not use language', and as such, the possibility of short-term counselling even scratching the surface seems at best remote.

Finally, Holmes (1992: 8) has discussed 'the psychodynamics of commercialism' that are currently dominating the National Health Service (cf. House 1996b), and which must inevitably impinge upon the environment and culture within which the GP counsellor must subsist. Holmes's useful discussion highlights how 'the commercial atmosphere of the Health Service is likely to reinforce [a] servicing ethos', whereby things are expected to be 'done to' clients, as opposed to the 'being with' values of therapeutic counselling at its best (ibid.: 9–10). Clearly, GP counsellors need continually to contain and manage the ideological tensions and dilemmas that are intrinsic to their working in the GP medical setting (House 1996a).

Demand factors

Another feature of the setting is the very high level of demand for counselling in general practice which far outstrips the supply. This of course has all kinds of implications, not just the obvious one of length of counselling contracts and waiting-list pressures. The following quotation, although describing another type of institutional setting, throws some light on the tensions operating in a GP setting:

> The administration thinks the counselors spend too much time with each client and therefore see too few of them; the counselors think they have to spend too little time with each client and are unable to help clients get truly rehabilitated. The administration wants to see more clients treated and more completed 'successful termination' forms; the counselors feel the number of terminations is meaningless . . . . This recurrent clash of goals places an extra emotional burden on the . . . counselors, since they are caught between the competing demands of their clients and of their superiors.
>
> (Maslach 1982: 49)

Organizational dynamics

The medical GP setting is of course by definition an organizational one. This has implications for the unconscious group and organizational dynamics that will inevitably obtain in a setting fraught with anxiety, with the associated effects upon the well-being of staff. Of course, there will tend to be strong collusive forces mobilized to deny the primitive anxieties that are inevitably present in any medical setting (Menzies Lyth 1988; Shur 1994). Stein's (1985) important though much-neglected work provides an extremely illuminating perspective on the psychodynamics of the medical setting (see also Sher 1992). Thus, for Stein, 'the utopian character of family medicine invites massive transference from patients above and beyond what arises in the medical encounter' (1985: 53). With medicine being the target of a very strong social transference, Balint's reference to 'the special psychological atmosphere of general practice' (1964: chapter 13) comes into sharp focus.

For Sher (1992: 10), 'In general practice . . . *there are anxious substances about* . . . – the pain, both physical and mental, the anxiety and the stress that both the patients and the difficulty of the work bring to the situation' [his emphasis]. He continues, 'Counsellors and psychotherapists [within general practice] have become bearers of the unconscious state that is intended to *shield us from unhappiness*, rejection and abandonment' [his emphasis]. Integral to such a system is the requirement that counsellors be omniscient, and 'Counsellors and therapists themselves foster this belief and fall victim to it, often at great personal cost' (ibid.: 6).

Frame particularities

Finally and most pertinent to the current discussion, there are manifold problems with the 'security' of what Robert Langs (1988) calls the 'therapeutic frame' in the GP setting. To take just one example, the basic physical aspects of the setting are commonly less than fully secure, regarding room space, confidentiality and record-keeping, and with a lack of clarity about who precisely has ultimate responsibility for the client in the GP setting. Phillips (1991), for example, has applied Langs' Communicative approach to compromises of confidentiality in a counselling centre. The current consensus seems to be that the referring GP has ultimate clinical responsibility for her or his GP-counselled patients (Higgs and Dammers 1992: 33).

The impact of the setting on the counsellor

There has been much research into the stressful and burn-out experiences of people working as psychotherapists and counsellors in general (Guy 1987: 249–68), but there are very few studies in the literature specifically devoted to the stresses of mental health professionals working in medical settings – though several studies do exist which consider the incidence of stress in health care professionals more generally (e.g. Maslach and Jackson 1982; Margison 1987). From the perspective of social psychology, Maslach and Jackson (1982: 236–9) argue that lack of control of the working milieu and role ambiguity are particularly important environmental contributors to stress. They argue that feedback about the value of one's work from others is crucial; and in jobs where pay increases and promotion are not part of the institutional structure of recognizing worth (GP counselling falls into this category), such affirming feedback is much less common. Health professionals are also said to overestimate the importance of dispositional factors relative to environmental influences in the aetiology of experienced stress (ibid.: 239), which might well have a lot to do with the unconscious motivations of carers and the common patterns of personality dynamics of people working in the caring professions.

The implications of these various distinguishing features of the GP setting for the stresses experienced by the surgery counsellor will be developed in the remainder of this chapter.

The therapeutic framework

Frame insecurities of the GP setting

Earlier I introduced the notion of the 'therapeutic frame' (Gray 1994), and its importance for the safety and 'holding function' of the counselling relationship. In the 'Communicative psychotherapy' literature (e.g. see Smith 1991: chapter 7), discussions of the 'insecure' or so-called 'deviant' frame invariably place emphasis upon its deleterious effects for the *client* (or 'patient'); what seems to be neglected are the effects of a deviant frame on the *counsellor* or therapist – both in terms of direct effects upon the counsellor's working milieu, and indirect effects to the extent that the counsellor is affected by the client's negative responses to a deviant frame. I maintain here that, in some circumstances, deviant frames can be at least as stressful for the counsellor as they are for the client. (In passing it should be noted that there are significant philosophical difficulties with the notion of a 'deviant' or 'ideal' relationship frame; for it can be argued that such an ontology is an example of what might be called an ideology of normality, or what Buck (1992) has called 'the myth of normality'.)

What is it, then, about the so-called deviant frame that is alleged to resonate with clients' (and counsellors') personality dynamics in an unhelpful way? Smith (1991: 173) argues that the 'patient' (his term) has 'deep unconscious expectations about a secure, safe therapeutic frame', for such a framework provides for the patient, *inter alia*, a sense of basic trust, clear interpersonal boundaries, 'a healthy therapeutic symbiosis' and 'a powerful sense of being held well and of appropriate containment' (ibid.). It can be argued that psychodynamically, these are basic human needs for all of us, not just for our clients; and to the extent that the security of the frame is not 'good enough', the counsellor's anxieties around insecure boundaries will tend to be triggered, as well as those of the client, these processes being essentially unconscious, only the *products* of which will be experienced as anxiety and stress at the conscious level.

There are a number of ways in which the therapeutic frame in the GP setting is often less than secure. Thus, of the eleven components of the secure frame listed by Smith (ibid.: 174–91), at least five are compromised at various times and to varying degrees in the GP setting – namely, total privacy, total confidentiality, consistency of the setting, the question of a fee, and the client's responsibility for termination of the counselling. Hoag (1989, 1992) has given extended consideration to frame difficulties in a GP setting. Clearly, shortcomings in frame 'safety and security' could significantly compromise the effectiveness of a counsellor's work, with expected associated impacts on self-esteem via doubts about professional competence, levels of motivation, and so on. I will now examine some of these common GP setting frame deviations.

Privacy

For Smith (1991: 182), 'To the deep unconscious system it is vital that the analysis be restricted to two people – the analyst and the patient – with no third parties present'. Within the GP setting, there is the problem that clients have to wait in a public waiting-room, perhaps with known members of the local community (e.g. neighbours); it is very difficult for the counsellor to fetch the client for the session without drawing special attention to her or him (other surgery patients are typically summoned over the intercom). In addition, the presence of receptionists dealing with the clients can clearly compromise privacy, particularly when receptionists reside in the local community and may know at least some of the practice's patients personally. In some cases, appointments are made by the surgery receptionists rather than by the counsellor, but according to Langs, the counsellor or therapist alone should make all appointments throughout the counselling relationship: 'Failure to do so is an abdication of basic responsibilities to the patient, invites splitting of reactions in the patient, and undermines the therapeutic alliance and the therapy' (Langs, quoted in Phillips 1991: 93). Finally, in any community-based clinical setting, previous clients often tell their neighbours and friends about it if they have benefited from counselling, and so the counsellor may often end up working with clients who are friends or acquaintances of ex-clients, with all the well documented complex dynamics that can ensue.

Confidentiality

With regard to the related issue of confidentiality, Irving (1993: 62) notes that the referral process is unlikely to work smoothly all the time. For Irving, there is a very difficult balance to strike in terms of 'the need to keep communication between [doctor and counsellor] open without affecting the confidential nature of the counselling work'. Irving sets the following guidelines: that 'the doctor . . . should be kept informed by the counsellor of any treatment or progress in the patient's condition. The counsellor, too, should be kept informed of any changes the doctor makes in the patient's treatment programme' (ibid.). With regard to the issue of frame security considered here, such a view has severe problems, as will become clear below.

Apart from the related issue of privacy, there are the problems of referral letters from GPs (who sometimes insist on such a procedure), record-keeping in the client's surgery notes, and the ambiguities of the so-called 'therapeutic triangle' of the counsellor, the client and the referring GP (Pickvance 1993). Regarding referral letters, it can be a real dilemma whether or not to read them, as there may be crucial medical information in them which would make a general, principled decision *not* to read any referral letters quite inappropriate and potentially damaging to the referred client.

With regard to the so-called 'therapeutic triangle', GPs often have very intimate and long-standing therapeutic relationships with their patients over many years, and this raises questions not only about the implications of this for counselling relationships with such referred clients, but also whether knowing this fact might affect the degree to which the counsellor feels able to be congruent with her or his clients – for example, being firm with a client who fails to keep appointments, knowing that the client may well 'report back' to her or his GP on what s/he thinks of the counsellor – with the GP, of course, being the counsellor's employer! This appears to be a classic example of a difficulty arising directly from the insecurity of frame boundaries.

Hatwell (1992: 7) also sees confidentiality as being a difficult area: 'you are responsible *to* your client but the doctor is responsible *for* his patient and you in turn have a responsibility to the doctor. You need to make this clear to your client' (her emphasis). As Abel Smith, Irving and Brown (1989: 130) put it, 'The counsellor may be party to one of the dilemmas of the concept of "shared care" '; and 'Once the relationship between doctor and patient has been opened up to include a third party, whose responsibility should it be to set the new boundaries?' (ibid.).

In addition, in a GP setting where there is commonly only one counsellor, and where whole families are commonly registered (and thus in principle should have equal access to the service), the counsellor often either finds her/himself counselling a member of a family, a member of which s/he has counselled before, or is faced with the difficult decision of what to do if s/he notices that there is such a client on the waiting-list.

The Langsian, Communicative view on confidentiality is that 'It is probably impossible to overestimate the importance that patients unconsciously attach to confidentiality issues' (Smith 1991: 183); and even if this is seen as an exaggeration and a rather fetishized view of the unconscious, there can be no doubt that the *spirit* of confidentiality, and where the counsellor is 'coming from' in dealing with its complexities, are extremely important.

Setting consistency and the fee issue

Some counsellors find that they work in a different room each week (and even have to change rooms in the middle of the day), depending on the number of doctors' surgeries being held that day (cf. Green 1990: 28). Irving (1993: 60) also refers to the fact that because counsellors tend to work in GPs' consulting rooms, it is hard for the counsellor to present a role which differs from that of the doctor. In addition, in the vast majority of surgeries, no fee is charged, the service being free at the point of delivery under the National Health Service; but according to Smith (1991: 185), 'There should be a single, fixed fee paid by the patient. . . . The fee should . . . not [be paid] by third parties'; and he points out that the majority of commentators believe that free treatment has a deleterious effect on analysis (whether similar arguments can transfer to the case of counselling is obviously an open and debatable question). For Smith (ibid.: 186), the patient might feel that she 'must be grateful for what she is given, but unconsciously would prefer not to be dependent on free therapy. . . . The absence of a fee makes it difficult for the patient to express her negative feelings towards the therapist'. It seems likely that these psychoanalytically informed concerns, which focus on the resolution of the so-called 'transference neurosis' and the importance of the 'negative transference', are likely to be far less relevant to GP counselling, which is typically short-term and cannot be expected to work at the level of a typical psychoanalytic relationship.

Time limit and termination

According to Smith (ibid.: 188–9), writing with regard to the client's responsibility for the termination of counselling, 'the patient should be the one to decide when and how the therapy is to be terminated . . . any attempt by a therapist to unilaterally set a date for the therapy to terminate is a violation of the secure frame and generates tremendous unconscious distress'. It is well known that there is often an enormous demand for counselling within general practice which far outstrips its supply, and under these conditions many counsellors are forced, much against their better judgement and preference, to work to a time-limited contract – with all the implications this has for triggering often very primitive psycho-dynamic reactions around abandonment, loss, and so on. De Zulueta (1993: 148) refers to a case in which an 'arbitrary time-limit' was set for therapy, which some might describe 'as an abusive experience for the patient, a professionally condoned re-enactment of earlier abuse now taking place between the therapist and the patient'. And as mentioned above, there will also be an indirect effect on the counsellor, to the extent that she or he is adversely affected by the client's anxious responses to a deviant frame.

It should be noted that the way in which the existence of time-limited counselling affects the counsellor will be an important function of the particular counselling philosophy of the counsellor. Thus, *ceteris paribus*, it might be expected that the cognitive-behavioural counsellor will be happier working within a time-limited framework than a more dynamically or humanistically inclined practitioner. Thus, the statement of Curran and Higgs (1993: 82) that 'offering time-limited counselling or therapy to a patient means that it is vitally important to get to the core of their pain and work at a deep level, rather than just offering a tiny and, perhaps, superficial bite of something which is actually meant to be much longer', seems far more applicable to the cognitive-behavioural practitioner than it does to someone working with a developmental relationship focus in a more psychodynamic-humanistic modality. I have argued forcefully elsewhere (1997c) that a time-limited framework is not of itself necessarily inconsistent with a 'humanistic-dynamic' way of working.

It might be thought that in time-limited counselling there could be insufficient time for the normal transference and countertransference dynamics posited by dynamically inclined practitioners to develop, but according to Maroda (1992: 8), although in short-term work 'both the transference and countertransference are less rich . . . the patient's need for insight and understanding of his emotional impact on others remains the same'. And later, she argues that 'the same basic stages of treatment will occur in an analytic therapy of shorter duration'; she quotes Schlessinger and Robbins (1983) in maintaining that it is 'possible for comprehensive mini-transferences to surface and be worked through in a matter of days. *It seems likely that the patient will present the transference as best he can in whatever time he is allowed to do so*' (ibid.: 113, my emphasis). With such a 'telescoping' of the transference and countertransference dynamics,

> a therapist [or counsellor – RH] has less of a margin of error and cannot afford to be overcautious The objective is to work fast, while working *well*, and therapists in this [time-limited] setting must be not only

astute but decisive in order to deal effectively with both the transference and the countertransference.

(ibid.: 68, her emphasis)

It is also clear that a time-limited counsellor will have to deal with far more endings in the course of her or his work than the counsellor who is not so limited; and to the extent that the counsellor has significant unresolved issues around separation (ibid.: 167–71), this again will lead to increased levels of stress for the counsellor. Finally, while there is perhaps some very limited truth in the maxim that at least some clients will fit their 'work' into whatever time is available, it is also the case, certainly from a dynamic perspective, that many clients' difficulties need far more time to work with than is provided by the typical time-limit of six or eight sessions.

Qualitative research on framework particularities

In 1994 I conducted a detailed questionnaire survey of GP counsellors in Norfolk (House 1995), with sixteen completed questionnaires being returned out of twenty-two (73 per cent response). Below I set out those responses relevant to the current discussion, together with other qualitative evidence from the literature. Of the sixteen respondents to the survey, a majority (ten counsellors, constituting 62.5 per cent) mentioned matters directly related to the therapeutic frame.

Privacy

Five counsellors (31 per cent) specifically mentioned privacy-related issues. Three (19 per cent) mentioned counselling sessions being interrupted, some by staff, doctors, or even surgery patients walking into the counselling room by mistake during a session, or internal phone calls from staff or doctors urgently wanting a piece of medical equipment, or simply having dialled the wrong number. (Because counsellors typically work on only one day or half-day a week, there is perhaps a tendency for staff not to get used to the presence of the counsellor in the surgery, particularly when there are part-time staff working irregular hours.) One counsellor refers to feelings of unease when in the course of his work in the surgery, he bumps into ex-clients, not quite knowing whether to acknowledge them openly, discreetly, or even to pretend that he hasn't noticed them (cf. Dryden 1993!). Finally, one respondent referred to 'the poor handling of potential clients' by surgery staff, and another to the difficulty of clients making any kind of loud noise during sessions because of proximity to the waiting-room.

Confidentiality

One respondent wrote of her concern that the GP referral of clients 'is a vital part of the dynamic', and another mentioned her concerns about what to record, if anything, and where. Another mentioned feeling uncomfortable when receptionists start chatting or gossiping about their own experience of clients whom the counsellor is seeing.

The feasibility study of counselling in primary health care conducted by Green (1990) found that there was a general view that there should be good communication between doctors and counsellors about the progress of clients: one Leeds GP is quoted as saying: 'It is good to have feedback and know how patients are getting on; we often don't hear anything when they go to other agencies' (ibid.: 12). In the same study a counsellor is quoted as saying, 'my code of confidentiality is slightly different to the doctors and the others'; and a Health Visitor: 'I never get as much information from the counsellor as I do from other professionals; I understand why but it can seem difficult' (ibid.: 26). Clearly, there is scope here for conflictual dynamics within the Primary Health Care Team over different approaches to the confidentiality question, with perhaps some envy of the counsellor's seemingly 'special status' with regard to confidentiality issues – which some could even perceive as 'precious' or inflated.

Finally, and *contra* the Langsian view about confidentiality, Green's report contains quotations from some clients and potential clients arguing for the *benefits* of close doctor–counsellor collaboration: one patient said that 'Confidentiality should be shared between the doctor and the counsellor. Often ill health goes together with other problems' (ibid.: 46). The Communicative, Langsian response would be that what clients say they want on a manifest, conscious level is by no means necessarily what they want at a deep unconscious level – so this remains a matter of debate, and a difficult question to which there is probably no decisive resolution. As so often in counselling and psychotherapy, the position one takes on these questions will depend upon one's own particular counselling philosophy.

Setting consistency and the fee issue

The consistency of the setting specifically concerned four survey respondents (or 25 per cent). One put 'suitability of room for counselling' first on her list of stresses, and another made the general comment that the surgery is 'not an ideal setting for counselling'. One counsellor wrote of 'lack of suitable accommodation – I have been "put" in all sorts of places'. Another still often finds himself working in a different room each week, which he experiences as disruptive both for himself personally and to his work with clients. Baws (1992: 11) suspects that the reality for most surgery counsellors is 'a room with a couch, sink, autoclave and reminders of illness rather than health. . . . [so] the client is reminded, by the surroundings, of the medical setting' (cf. Totton 1997). Being a surgery counsellor herself, she writes forcefully that 'I cannot totally lose sight of the surroundings: it cannot help but unconsciously shape my own thinking about the "task" I am there for' (ibid., her emphasis).

Just two respondents, who work privately as well as in surgeries, mentioned the issue of the fee, one writing that 'The private clients want to come (usually) and there is a sense of their paying and therefore wanting to get something for their money! A number of GP clients are there "because they were sent" '. The other respondent wrote that 'in private practice, clients cancelling still pay, so they are taking full responsibility – this makes it easier for me'.

Time limit and termination

Finally, by far the greatest level of response was around the issue of time-limited working (to which the question of termination is obviously implicitly related), mentioned specifically as a stressful part of their work by five respondents (or 31 per cent). Others mentioned the related issue of burgeoning waiting-lists, with some having only just started time-limited working very recently. In Green's feasibility study referred to above, all of the surveyed practices had waiting-lists for counselling, and "swamping" of the service was a problem acknowledged by all parties' (Green 1990: 27). For Maslach (1982: 40), a situation in which there are too many clients and too little time adequately to serve their needs is a situation ripe for the development of emotional burnout – and these characteristics certainly seem to be typical of GP counselling. I would add, however, that it is only when the counsellor has her or his own personal issues around 'needing to help', and associated feelings of guilt or helplessness with regard to burgeoning waiting-lists as symbolic of the unmet needs of others, that substantial stress is likely to be experienced.

It is also commonly argued in the literature that 'the practice of psychotherapy is difficult, slow work. . . . most therapists admit that few therapy patients will experience significant changes over a short period of time' (Guy 1987: 261). Given that the aims of counselling are at least to some extent similar to those of psychotherapy (and indeed, that 'GP practices hire "counsellors", regardless of the fact that the person doing the actual work may consider him or herself a psychotherapist' (Hoag 1992: 417), it follows that the indiscriminate imposition of time-limited working is likely to be a significant source of dissatisfaction, frustration, stress and associated 'feelings of inconsequentiality' (Farber 1983) for the counsellor to the extent that she or he is unable to offer the client the length of counselling relationship that s/he might think appropriate.

Of course, the presence of a time limit implies a forced and essentially non-negotiable termination of the counselling, which violates one of the secure-frame conditions described earlier. The following quotation from one respondent sums up graphically the general feeling of most respondents: '[There is] a long waiting-list with pressure sometimes from doctors and clients that the counsellor see people as soon as possible. Balancing this need with that of giving clients a reasonable series of sessions – without terminating at a bad time for them – can be stressful'. One counsellor placed this matter third on her list of stresses, having recently changed to time-limited working, writing: 'I think this will cause me considerable stress and will probably be at the top of my list but I don't know this yet'. She added later that 'I may feel constrained to presenting problems rather than underlying causes, but I'm not sure I can work like that'.

Another counsellor referred to the stress of having to '[decide] on priority cases and how long to see existing clients'; and a bit later, 'I feel the time issue does affect my work in that I find it hard to determine when to stop seeing someone and feel I can't offer the sort of intensive and/or long-term therapy needed by some/many clients'. Yet another counsellor wrote that 'the presenting problem is often the tip of the iceberg'; and for another, while she has personally found time-limited counselling 'exciting and rewarding . . . There is a danger of falling into a "fix it" or "band-aid" type of counselling, which can fail to address the underlying needs and difficulties of the client' (cf. Maslach 1982: 49).

One respondent reported finding time-limited working 'very intense and exhausting – I feel as exhausted after two sessions as I do after four at "Relate" or elsewhere'. Another reported that she had just had her contract terminated because the practice 'wished to introduce a time-limited contract which I felt was unethical (it involved discussion which I felt might breach confidentiality, and also disempower the client)'. Finally, several respondents reported stressful conflicts resulting from burgeoning waiting-lists and the associated demand for time-limited working, on the one hand, and the way in which this conflicted with their model of counselling on the other. Thus, for one counsellor, 'Coming from an integrative perspective with strong psychodynamic influences, I believe that clients sometimes need long-term counselling with a relationship-oriented focus. . . . But I am severely constrained in doing long-term work by the nature of the setting'. One respondent reported 'a personal difficulty in having to end my work with clients just when they are beginning to trust me . . . and when they seem to sense that they could get something very important from our relationship if only we could find a way to continue'.

To set against these concerns, however, is the argument that time-limited counselling does not necessarily have to be inferior to longer-term work (e.g. Coren 1996; House 1997c).

Concluding comments

In conclusion, while frame-related issues clearly do matter, I believe that a preoccupation with the security or otherwise of the therapeutic frame can be unhelpful, and that what is far more important to the efficacy of counselling is the overall *quality* of the therapeutic relationship, which is a phenomenon over and above the technicalities of frame management. I am also aware that the Communicative literature is relevant to a particular form of psychoanalytic psychotherapy, which, it might be argued, is very different in nature from face-to-face time-limited counselling. Notwithstanding these cautionary remarks, however, I would argue that the effects of so-called 'deviant-frame' counselling, and all that goes with it in terms of activated unconscious psychodynamics and their associated anxieties, must inevitably be felt by the counsellor as well as by the client within 'the bipersonal field' (Langs 1976) of the therapeutic relationship. Psycho-dynamically, there can be nothing that the client experiences that does not at some level affect the counsellor (as well as vice versa, of course), so any client anxieties around frame insecurities cannot also but affect the counsellor's levels of experienced stress.

Flexibility and 'boundary-mindedness'

Freud's depiction of psychoanalysis as 'the impossible profession' is arguably more widely ascribable to therapy in general. Strupp and Binder (1984: 40) capture the difficulty well: 'the psychotherapeutic relationship is a highly personal relationship within a highly *impersonal* framework' (my emphasis). The enormous task facing each and every counsellor and therapist is to find a professionally appropriate yet maximally humane and effective stance in their work, given the very considerable peculiarities complexities, paradoxes – and ultimate ineffableness (Spinelli 1996) – of every therapeutic relationship. Clearly this is no easy task, and must be a life-long journey; but it is crucial for counsellors to be open to the significant anxieties that must be consciously and unconsciously aroused in them because of the inherently 'impossible' nature of their chosen 'profession' – *and as far as possible not to act out from those anxieties.*

In a personal communication (1998), David Kalisch has written that 'most therapeutic systems create some kind of defence for therapists against the sometimes intolerable openness of the therapeutic encounter'. It may well be that the over-professionalized, so-called 'defensive psychotherapy' (House 1997e: 327–8) that seems to be taking an increasing hold in the therapy field may be a *therapist-driven*, acted-out reaction to *therapist* anxieties, and much less an appropriate response to the genuine needs of clients, as is routinely claimed by the professionalizers and the proponents of 'boundary-mindedness'. The increasing preoccupation with boundary-mindedness, which seems to be spreading rapidly, and largely uncritically, into the counselling field, does, I believe, require very careful and critical consideration, to the extent that it represents a corporate acting-out within the culture of therapy from the anxieties mentioned above (cf. Hermansson 1997). At its worst, perhaps boundary-mindedness might even constitute a self-serving consequence of the commodification and 'marketization' of counselling and therapy (House, forthcoming a, b).

On this view, then, what some might see as the rigidity towards boundaries and frame issues of the Communicative approach might say more about the deep anxieties triggered in *the therapist* by this work than it does about the provision of an appropriate and humane healing milieu for the client (cf. Brown 1994: 36). To this observer, the Communicative literature sometimes has the feel of a rather *self-punitive* therapist-centredness, and an over rigid or precious preoccupation with 'the frame' and its boundaries. Thus, there is a predominant focus on the *therapist's* errors or mistakes (typically called therapist 'madness' by Langs – Langs 1988), and on the client's assumed unconscious need for the security of the therapeutic frame, *and* on the necessity that this need (given its existence) be met for successful therapy to occur.

There are, of course, enormous assumptions being made in all this – and there is the added problem that clients/patients may well unconsciously fit themselves into the Communicative (or any other) ideology, using whichever belief system the therapist relates to and experiences her or his client! Vlosky (1984) is an interesting example of a writer who applies Communicative insights to the 'frame deviations' inherent in a US community health centre (which, along with Hoag's (1989, 1992) and Launer's (1994) work, provides a clear example of the application of Communicative ideas in a GP-like setting). For Vlosky, all his patients 'responded to breaks in the frame with a sense of disruption and distress' (263), and 'inconsistent framework management can ruin psychotherapy' (260).

Contrast this negative preoccupation with the therapist's errors with the approach of Strupp and Binder (1984). For them, time-limited therapy creates special hazards (192), and 'the therapist is bound to commit involuntary errors . . . [which] *are an integral part of the fabric of therapy* . . . [being] *inevitable* responses to the patient's self-protective maneuvers in the face of misperceived interpersonal dangers. . . . *[T]he therapists errors may further rather than hinder the progress of therapy*' (my emphases). The implication is that the GP counselling process is likely to be more creative and client-centred to the extent that the counsellor can remain open, from moment to moment, to the co-created intersubjective experience of the therapeutic relationship, rather than taking into their work pre-conceived, anxiety-driven notions about the ideal-typical structure that the counselling relationship should take. (I return to this crucial issue in the final section.) And perhaps the very notion of a 'mistake' might benefit from a healthy dose of ontological deconstruction – but this is beyond the scope of the current discussion.

For this writer it is most refreshing to find recent examples in the literature where writers are questioning the current emphasis being placed on boundaries and 'the frame' in the culture of therapy. Thus, Lees (1997) has dared to challenge some conventional psychodynamic wisdoms when he writes about the need for flexibility in the GP setting. Lees advocates a Winnicottian flexibility to the GP therapeutic framework, appropriate to the unique features of the setting. With one of his clients he describes try-ing 'to establish balance in regard to the therapeutic framework – between the pole of elasticity and the pole of inelasticity, between flexibility and rigidity' (43) – which has a much more open, enabling, creative and, above all, humane feel than does the technical preoccupation that can so easily dominate in a culture of boundary-mindedness. An explicitly flexible approach to boundary management in counselling is also strongly advocated by Laura Brown, for whom 'a boundary which will work and facilitate treat-ment with one person may . . . be experienced as engulfing and invasive with another, or cold and punitive with a third' (1994: 31).

In fact, Lees is following a long lineage in the therapy field, stretching back, for example, to the innovative (and, until recently, neglected) work of Sándor Ferenczi and the radical innovations in technique of Franz Alexander (Alexander and French 1946; Alexander 1971), who questioned the assumption that prolonged treatment was a necessary precondition of therapeutic change and that rigid therapeutic boundaries were necessary, and who championed flexibility and a more interpersonal focus in analytic work (Strupp and Binder 1984: 10–11). The book by Alexander and French, though written fifty years ago, is still a veritable goldmine for the time-limited GP counsellor struggling to make sense of time-limited work, and to resist the mounting pressures for ever more symptom preoccupied cognitive-behavioural or solution-focused approaches to counselling in general practice.

Hermansson (1997) has recently written a highly perceptive paper on boundaries, and takes a view similar to the one favoured here. He approvingly quotes Lazarus's view (1994) that the growing conservative thrust towards ever more stringent boundary-mindedness may be under-mining clinical effectiveness – with the result that 'risk-management principles are in danger of taking precedence over humane interventions' (Hermansson 1997: 139). Hermansson himself pulls no punches in his challenging of the boundaries shibboleth:

> there is in some quarters an excessive zeal about boundary control which can lead to stances that seem overly precious and at times even arrogant in relation to clients and to colleagues in the profession. . . . [J]ust tightening boundaries is also over-simplistic and has the added danger of possibly setting off from involvement the very qualities that make counselling therapeutic. What is left can be a pseudo-professional stance that is controlling in its effects and barren in its essence.
>
> (1997: 140)

Sobering words indeed for those who aspire to creating a conventional 'profession' of counselling and psychotherapy.

All in all I believe that the GP setting provides a wonderfully creative crucible that could easily place it at the forefront of the therapy field with regard to flexible, pioneering, progressive innovations in 'technique' (which might well include the privileging of 'being-centred' over 'technique-centred' values). My hunch is that there is almost certainly a significant amount of path-breaking therapeutic work quietly being done in GP settings up and down the country, and that such innovations will in time diffuse into and benefit the therapy field as a whole in quite unforeseeable ways.

Discussion and conclusions

In contradistinction to a strict, 'precious' approach to the frame, I would argue that clients (and human beings in general) are, potentially, infinitely creative, and will very often 'use' (in the Winnicottian sense) *whatever* 'good enough' experience is available for their own healing. A strict frame-mindedness can all too easily result in treating the client as a relatively helpless 'victim' of her or his therapeutic environment (Hall 1993) – with the attendant danger that such an approach, along with its assumptive preconceptions, self-fulfillingly 'creates' the client in precisely the image which the counsellor assumed from the outset. As McDougall (1995: 235–6) has poignantly written, 'We discover only what our theories permit us to find. . . . Our cherished concepts appear to be continually self-confirming'.

The concept of 'normality' – such a prevalent notion in therapeutic and in cultural discourse more generally – has been thoroughly deconstructed and criticized by a number of feminist, postmodernist and transpersonal writers; and I see the currently fashionable notions of 'boundaries' and 'the frame' as constituting ideological shibboleths of comparable proportions. Taken-for-granted theoretical assumptions about 'normality', 'boundaries' and 'the frame' necessarily entail profound and typically unarticulated ontological assumptions about the nature of 'reality'; and their invocation may well tell us more about the wish to control the therapeutic process, about the fear-driven roots of knowledge construction and about the professionalization of therapy as a cultural phenomenon than it does about the 'realities' which these concepts purport to describe and illuminate. As House and Totton (1997: 336) have recently written, 'Trying to control "what psychotherapy *is*" may well end up preventing it from being anything worth having'. And it is refreshing that at least a few commentators are beginning to pose quite fundamental questions about the very relevance of 'theory' itself, from both psychodynamic and philosophical perspectives (Craib 1987; Spinelli 1996; Genosko 1998).

On this view, then, and following earlier discussions, it is far more productive and creative to adopt an open, non-rigid and flexible approach to the therapeutic framework of GP counselling – one which engages with the ineffable and paradoxical space or edge between order and chaos (Stacey 1997) wherein I believe most if not all true healing actually occurs. Here is van Deurzen-Smith (1997: 192): 'What is needed is optimal challenge, not total security or absolute chaos'.

These views are consistent with those of Bohart and Tallman (1996), whose powerful advocacy of 'the active client' brings home so clearly the inherent resourcefulness of most clients, referred to earlier in this section (cf. House, 1997d).

In sum, perhaps the GP counsellor's task is to be as fully aware as possible of the particular (and sometimes peculiar!) characteristics of the GP counselling frame in which they work, and to be as open as possible to monitoring from moment to moment, and then responding appropriately and creatively to the complex interplay between the setting, the counsellor's and the client's personality dynamics. In this way, GP counselling becomes an alive, creative, emerging experience entered into by two co-creating subjects (Orbach and Eichenbaum 1995), rather than a programmatic, mechanistic process which self-fulfillingly fits clients into a preconceived theoretical framework which may say far more about the *counsellor's* 'neurotic' need for security than it does about the unconscious security needs of the client.

I have written elsewhere (1994, 1996a) about the profound ideological tensions that exist between the medical treatment model typical of general practice, and the 'healing' model of change that humanistic and some dynamic approaches to counselling typically embrace. All those working within GP settings must be all too aware of the increasingly strident demands for so-called 'scientifically proven' (essentially cognitive-behavioural) modes of treatment which privilege symptomatological, problem-focused, programmatic approaches to counselling (Fahy and Wessely 1993); yet it *is* possible to work within the constraints of a time-limited GP framework without necessarily sacrificing holistic ways of working on the altar of mechanistic medical-model ideologies (House 1997c; for a different view see Totton 1997).

The foregoing discussion has relevance to the question of counsellor stress. I believe that for some GP counsellors, it will be far more stressful – at least initially – for them to stay as open as possible to the emerging co-created direction of the work than it would be to enter it with comparatively rigid preconceived, audit-driven assumptions (House 1996b) about the form that the therapeutic framework or relationship should take. (Cf. Wilfred Bion's famous remark that the therapist should as far as possible enter a therapeutic relationship without memory, desire or understanding – Smith 1984.) It follows from this that counsellors need to be aware of their own issues around the need for security, fixed boundaries and professionalized structures more generally (House and Totton 1997).

It may be high time for us to move away from the 'professional' and ideological view that there is some 'normal' or 'correct' way to 'do' counselling and psychotherapy, which the professional counsellor should attempt to impose upon her or his clientele, or assume that his or her clientele should fit into. Rather, whatever 'counselling' is (Spinelli 1996) is a decidedly peculiar and certainly unique form of relationship, the nature of which should, I contend, always be *something to be collaboratively co-constructed by the client and the counsellor* in as open, demystified and relatively undefended and non-rigid a way as each can manage, given their respective personalities and the way those personalities intersubjectively 'meet' (Crossley 1996; Josselson 1996).

If GP counsellors can, non-mechanistically, take this sincere *intention* and *love* into their work, I believe that *healing will very often quite naturally happen*; and under such conditions it will assuredly happen despite, rather than because of, any mechanistic or consciously 'scientific' attempt to control or secure the client's healing process (House 1996c) – even though we may in reality, if we can dare to be really honest, have very little idea of how, precisely, such healing and change occur, or of what 'change' actually consists (Spinelli 1996). Perhaps the brilliant Indian philosopher J. Krishnamurti (1984) was right when he ceaselessly maintained that it is only through a jettisoning of thought, memory and the conceptualization process itself that we can directly experience the real (Falconar 1997) – and discover thereby the *instantaneity* of the change process (House, forthcoming).

REFERENCES

Abel Smith, A., Irving, J., and Brown, P. (1989) 'Counselling in the medical context', in W. Dryden, D. Charles-Edwards, and R. Woolfe (eds) *Handbook of Counselling in Britain*, London: Routledge, 122–33.

Alexander, F. (1971) 'The principle of flexibility', in H.H. Barton (ed.) *Brief Therapies*, New York: Behavioral Publications, 28–41.

Alexander, F. and French, T.M. (1946) *Psychoanalytic Therapy: Principles and Applications*, New York: Ronald Press.

Alexander, F. and Szasz, T.S. (1952) 'The psychosomatic approach in medicine', in F. Alexander and H. Ross (eds) *The Impact of Freudian Psychiatry*, Chicago, IL: University of Chicago Press, 260–91.

Balint, M. (1964) *The Doctor, His Patient and the Illness*, 2nd edition, Edinburgh: Churchill Livingstone, 1986 [orig. Pitman Publishing].

Baws, H. (1992) 'Is counselling properly located in primary care?', in British Association for Social Psychiatry, *Counselling in Primary Care? – Conference Proceedings*, London (November), 8–15.

Bohart, A.C. and Tallman, K. (1996) 'The active client: therapy as self-help', *Journal of Humanistic Psychology* 36, 3: 7–30.

Brown, L.S. (1994) 'Boundaries in feminist therapy: a conceptual formulation', *Women and Therapy* 15, 1: 29–38.

Buck, L.A. (1992) 'The myth of normality', *Social Behavior and Personality* 20: 251–2.

Coren, A. (1996) 'Brief therapy – base metal or pure gold?', *Psychodynamic Counselling* 2: 22–38.

Craib, I. (1987) 'The psychodynamics of theory', *Free Associations* 10: 32–56.

Crossley, N. (1996) *Intersubjectivity: The Fabric of Social Becoming*, London: Sage.

Curran, A. and Higgs, R. (1993) 'Setting up a counsellor in primary care: the evolution and experience in one general practice', in R. Corney and R. Jenkins (eds) *Counselling in General Practice*, London: Routledge, 75–88.

Dryden, W. (1993) 'Oi, Windy! Over here', in his *Reflections on Counselling*, London: Whurr Publishers, 66–8.

Engel, G.L. (1977) 'The need for a new medical model: a challenge for biomedicine', *Science* 196, 4286: 129–36.

Fahy, T. and Wessely, S. (1993) 'Should purchasers pay for psychotherapy?', *British Medical Journal*, 307 (September), 576–7.

Falconar, A.E.I. (1997) *How to Use Your Nous*, Maughold, Isle of Man: Non-Aristotelian Publishing [orig. 1986].

Farber, B.A. (1983) 'Dysfunctional aspects of the psychotherapeutic role', in B.A. Farber (ed.) *Stress and Burnout in the Human Services Professions*, New York: Pergamon, pp. 97–118.

Genosko, G. (1998) *Undisciplined Theory*, London: Sage.

Gray, A. (1994) *An Introduction to the Therapeutic Frame*, London: Routledge.

Green, A.J.M. (1990) *A Feasibility Study into the Use of Counsellors in Primary Health Care Teams*, Leeds: MIND (157 Woodhouse Lane, Leeds LS2 3ED).

Guy, J.D. (1987) *The Personal Life of the Psychotherapist*, New York: Wiley.

Hall, J. (1993) *The Reluctant Adult: An Exploration of Choice*, Bridport: Prism Press.

Hammersley, D. and Beeley, L. (1992) 'The effects of medication on counselling', *Counselling* 3, 3: 162–4.

Hatwell, V. (1992) 'Counselling in general practice', *CMS News (Quarterly Journal of the Counselling in Medical Settings Division of the BAC)* 32, August: 6–7.

Hermansson, G. (1997) 'Boundaries and boundary management in counselling: the never-ending story', *British Journal of Guidance and Counselling* 25, 2: 133–46.

Higgs, R. and Dammers, J. (1992) 'Ethical issues in counselling and health in primary care', *British Journal of Guidance and Counselling* 20, 1: 27–38.

Hoag, L. (1989) 'Psychotherapy in the general practice surgery: considerations of the frame', unpublished MA dissertation, Dept Psychology, Regent's College, London.

—— (1992) 'Psychotherapy in the general practice surgery: considerations of the frame', *British Journal of Psychotherapy* 8, 4: 417–29.

Holmes, J. (1992) 'Psychiatry without walls: some psychotherapeutic reflections', *Psychoanalytic Psychotherapy* 6, 1: 1–12.

House, R. (1994) 'Counselling in general practice – a conflict of ideologies?', *The Therapist* 4, 1: 40–1.

—— (1995) 'The stresses of working in a general practice setting', in W. Dryden (ed.) *The Stresses of Counselling in Action*, London: Sage, 87–107.

—— (1996a) 'General practice counselling: a plea for ideological engagement', *Counselling* 7, 1: 40–4.

—— (1996b) 'Audit-mindedness in counselling: some underlying dynamics', *British Journal of Guidance and Counselling* 24, 2: 277–83 [also appearing as Chapter I/6 in House and Totton 1997].

—— (1996c) 'Love, intimacy and therapeutic change', *Self and Society* 24, 1: 21–6.

—— (1997a) 'The dynamics of professionalisation: a personal view of counselling research', *Counselling* 8, 3: 200–4 [also appearing as Chapter I/5 in House and Totton 1997].

—— (1997b) 'Therapy in new-paradigm perspective: the phenomenon of Georg Groddeck', in R. House and N. Totton (eds) *Implausible Professions*, Ross-on-Wye: PCCS Books, 225–40.

—— (1997c) 'An approach to time-limited humanistic-dynamic counselling', *British Journal of Guidance and Counselling* 25, 2: 251–62.

—— (1997d) 'Training: a guarantee of competence?', in R. House and N. Totton (eds) *Implausible Professions*, Ross-on-Wye: PCCS Books, 99–108.

—— (1997e) 'Participatory ethics in a self-generating practitioner community', in R. House and N. Totton (eds) *Implausible Professions*, Ross-on-Wye: PCCS Books, 321–34.

—— (forthcoming a) 'Limits to counselling and therapy: deconstructing a professional ideology', *British Journal of Guidance and Counselling.*

—— (forthcoming b) *Limits to Professional Therapy: Critical Deconstructions,* London: Free Association Books [in preparation].

House, R. and Totton, N. (eds) (1997) *Implausible Professions: Arguments for Pluralism and Autonomy in Psychotherapy and Counselling,* Ross-on-Wye: PCCS Books.

Irving, J. (1993) 'Practical and training issues', in R. Corney and R. Jenkins (eds) *Counselling in General Practice,* London: Routledge, 56–66.

Josselson, R. (1996) *The Space Between Us: Exploring the Dimensions of Human Relationships,* London: Sage.

Krishnamurti, J. (1984) *Mind Without Measure,* Madras: Krishnamurti Foundation.

Langs, R. (1976) *The Biopersonal Field,* New York: Jason Aronson.

—— (1988) *A Primer of Psychotherapy,* New York: Gardner Press.

Launer, J. (1994) 'Psychotherapy in the general practice surgery: working with and without a secure therapeutic frame', *British Journal of Psychotherapy* 11(1): 120–6.

Lazarus, A.A. (1994) 'How certain boundaries and ethics diminish therapeutic effectiveness', *Ethics and Behavior* 4: 255–61.

Lees, J. (1997) 'An approach to counselling in GP surgeries', *Psychodynamic Counselling* 3, 1: 33–48.

McDougall, J. (1989) *Theatres of the Body: A Psychoanalytic Approach to Psychosomatic Illness,* London: Free Association Books.

—— (1995) *The Many Faces of Eros: A Psychoanalytic Exploration of Human Sexuality,* London: Free Association Books.

Margison, F.R. (1987) 'Stress in psychiatrists', in R. Payne and J. Firth-Cozens (eds) *Stress in Health Professionals,* Chichester: Wiley, 107–24.

Maroda, K.J. (1992) *The Power of Countertransference: Innovations in Analytic Technique,* Chichester: Wiley.

Maslach, C. (1982) *Burnout: The Cost of Caring,* Englewood Cliffs, NJ: Prentice-Hall.

Maslach, C. and Jackson, S.E. (1982) 'Burnout in health professions: a social psychological analysis', in G.S. Sanders and J. Suls (eds) *Social Psychology of Health and Illness,* Hillsdale, NJ: Lawrence Erlbaum, 227–51.

Mawardi, B.H. (1983) 'Aspects of the impaired physician', in B.A. Farber (ed.) *Stress and Burnout in the Human Service Professions,* New York: Pergamon Press, 119–28.

Menzies Lyth, I. (1988) 'The functioning of social systems as a defence against anxiety', in her *Containing Anxiety in Institutions: Selected Essays, Volume 1,* London: Free Association Books, 43–85.

Mowbray, R. (1995) *The Case Against Psychotherapy Registration: A Conservation Issue for the Human Potential Movement,* London: Trans Marginal Press.

Nemiah, J.C. (1961) *Foundations of Psychopathology,* New York: Oxford University Press.

Orbach, S. and Eichenbaum, L. (1995) 'From objects to subjects', *British Journal of Psychotherapy* 12, 1: 89–97.

Phillips, M. (1991) 'Violations of the ground rules of confidentiality in a counselling centre: the contribution of Langs', *Counselling* 2, 3: 92–4.

Pickvance, D. (1993) 'Sheffield GP counsellors' conference: the therapeutic triangle', *Counselling* 4, 1: 92.

Schlessinger, N. and Robbins, F. (1983) *A Developmental View of the Psychoanalytic Process: Follow-up Studies and Their Consequences*, New York: International Universities Press.

Sher, M. (1992) 'Dynamic teamwork within general medical practice', in British Association for Social Psychiatry, *Counselling in Primary Care? – Conference Proceedings*, London (November), 50–63.

Shur, R. (1994) *Countertransference Enactment: How Institutions and Therapists Actualize Primitive Internal Worlds*, Northvale, NJ: Jason Aronson.

Smith, D.L. (1984) 'On the psychoanalytic listening process', *Self and Society* 12, 4: 213–16.

—— (1991) *Hidden Conversations: An Introduction to Communicative Psychoanalysis*, London: Routledge.

Spinelli, E. (1996) 'Do therapists know what they're doing?', in I. James and S. Palmer (eds) *Professional Therapeutic Titles: Myths and Realities*, Division of Counselling Psychology, Occasional Papers Volume 2, Leicester: British Psychological Society, 55–61.

Stacey, R. (1997) 'Excitement and tension at the edge of chaos', in E. Smith (ed.) *Integrity and Change: Mental Health in the Marketplace*, London: Routledge, 176–95.

Stein, H.F. (1985) *The Psychodynamics of Medical Practice: Unconscious Factors in Patient Care*, Berkeley, CA: University of California Press.

—— (1990) *American Medicine as Culture*, Boulder, CO: Westview Press.

Strain, J.S. (1978) *Psychological Interventions in Medical Practice*, New York: Century–Appleton–Crofts.

Strupp, H.H. and Binder, J.L. (1984) *Psychotherapy in a New Key: A Guide to Time-Limited Dynamic Psychotherapy*, New York: Basic Books.

Sussman, M.B. (1992) *A Curious Calling: Unconscious Motivations for Practicing Psychotherapy*, Northvale, NJ: Jason Aronson.

Totton, N. (1997) 'Inputs and outcomes: the medical model and professionalisation', *Self and Society* 25, 4: 3–8 [also appearing as Chapter II/3 in House and Totton 1997].

van Deurzen-Smith, E. (1997) *Everyday Mysteries: Existential Dimensions of Psychotherapy*, London: Routledge.

Vlosky, M. (1984) 'Community mental health, clients' rights, and the therapeutic frame', in J. Raney (ed.) *Listening and Interpreting: The Challenge of the Work of Robert Langs*, New York: Jason Aronson, 255–65.

Zulueta, F. de (1993) *From Pain to Violence: The Traumatic Roots of Human Destructiveness*, London: Whurr Publishers.

3 Holding the dance: a flexible approach to boundaries in general practice

Jonathan Smith

Introduction

Most of the literature on the nature and function of boundaries in the counselling relationship has focused upon the classical situation of the client who visits a counsellor in private practice and who pays a fee for the counsellor's services. Within the Psychodynamic model of counselling, which is the one that guides my own practice and the one that I will be addressing in this chapter, authors such as Anne Gray (1994) have articulated the purpose of these boundaries and the connections that they have with the infant's experience of early maternal or primary care. In such a context emphasis is placed upon the importance of maintaining firm and clear boundaries, in providing a safe place from which the client can begin to explore their experience, much as a toddler needs safe boundaries in order to explore its environment and learn from this experience (Noonan 1983). Elaborating upon this theme, and drawing from the theoretical framework of attachment theory, Jeremy Holmes (1994) has identified the role of the counsellor as providing a secure base for the client, just as a primary carer provides a secure base for the toddler; a relationship to which the infant can return when facing the risks of exploration of the external world. The counsellor needs to provide a similar relationship for the client in their exploration of their inner world. Violations of the frame or the boundaries of the counselling relationship have been regarded as undermining the establishment of this secure base and therefore of the process of counselling, and as lessening the likelihood of the client engaging in the difficult and uncertain task of exploring their experience. In Winnicott's (1960) view, the primary carer's provision of a holding environment for the infant, in the earliest stages of development, includes their protection of the infant from external impingements which would otherwise disrupt the infant's 'continuity of being'. The counsellor's management of the frame is seen as fulfilling a similar function, enabling the client to experience a dependence upon the counsellor, or a regression in a safe space protected from external intrusions, in which the parts of the client that may have been hidden as a consequence of early external impingements can gradually be found and expressed, with a restored 'continuity of being'. The firmly held frame can also be seen as providing the client with the space in which their experience is contained in the service of understanding, and in which feelings such as anger or hatred can emerge in relation to the counsellor, evoked by the inevitable frustrations that the boundaries impose upon the client (arising, for example, from the unavailability of the counsellor outside the time of the counselling session itself). In this way, the frame can be seen as representing the frustrations of reality. Earlier childhood experiences in relation to the experience of similar frustrations, such as, for example, the absence of a parental figure when the child wanted their attention, can be evoked in the counselling relationship; the feelings can be expressed and reflected upon. That feelings can be evoked in relation to the frame, thought about and linked to earlier childhood experiences, forms a central and defining feature of the Psychodynamic approach to counselling (Gray 1994).

I have restated this classical position in outline form, though it will no doubt be familiar to many readers, for two reasons. Firstly, it is this conceptual framework in relation to boundaries that many counsellors, including myself, have brought to their work when they have begun practising as counsellors in primary care and which therefore influences the way in which they will endeavour to establish the boundaries for the work in this setting. Secondly, where deviations from this classical frame occur, the meaning and interpretation that the counsellor makes of these deviations will be shaped by this very same conceptual framework.

The frame in the context of the GP setting

The frame of the counselling relationship becomes much more complex, of course, once the counsellor enters the organisational context of primary care. It has been noted that the culture of primary care is one in which confidential information is shared amongst the members of the team, and that therefore the boundary of confidentiality is conceived as one that surrounds the surgery as a whole (East 1995). The counsellor arriving in such a setting immediately faces a problem: how far do they accommodate to the culture of the setting in which they work, and share information with other professionals as a collaborative member of the team, and how far should they stand firm, defending the secure base of the counselling relationship, of the client's right to have a confidential and private space, alone with the counsellor, in which their anxieties can safely unfold?

I have been struck by the way in which the polarities of this dilemma were reflected in two recent articles concerning the practice of counselling in this setting. In the first of these articles, Linda Hoag (1992), drawing from Langs' perspective on the importance of the maintenance of the therapeutic frame, argued that the counsellor should aim to maintain the boundaries of confidentiality as far as possible, just as they would in a private setting, and that the sharing of information with GPs and other health care professionals should therefore be kept to the barest minimum. Hoag went on to suggest that the counsellor should aim to give only generalized information about clients in their feedback to GPs rather than discuss the progress and development through counselling of specific individuals whom they have seen in the practice.

In marked contrast to this, another article by a group of counsellors working in an inner-city GP practice (Jones et al. 1994) described their own highly collaborative work with GPs where it was recognized that clients experience powerful transferences to both the counsellor and the GP, who could be experienced in phantasy as a parental couple. The authors suggest that a client will always experience some transference to the doctor, arising in part from the dependency that is evoked in the person seeking assistance with a health problem. It was this transference that Balint (1964) used in his psychotherapeutic work as a doctor with his patients. A client will therefore form transference relationships, of greater or lesser intensity, with both the doctor and the counsellor. A further possible outcome of this is that the client, knowing of the relationship between the doctor and the counsellor, represented by the referral, will experience this as an Oedipal triangle, and that Oedipal phantasies in relation to their own parents will be projected onto the relationship of the doctor and the counsellor in the form of a transference. Communication between the counsellor and GP in this context becomes an essential and intrinsically therapeutic part of the work, representing the experience of a parental couple communicating well, and holding potential splits and projections which can then be internalized by the client, to positive therapeutic effect.

It has seemed to me that both of the positions so far articulated have serious limitations in their application to counselling work in a GP setting. Hoag's position has several disadvantages. Firstly, it raises the question of the relevance of the counsellor working within the setting itself, when so little is communicated to other professionals about the work that is under-taken. Would it not be just as appropriate for the counsellor to work in another separate counselling clinic and visit the practice periodically in order to give the doctors limited, generalized feedback? Secondly, it can be considered that the counsellor has a very significant function in primary care, assisting doctors and other professionals to think about the emotional and psychological difficulties and needs of their patients, and that some direct feedback on the clients that are referred to the counsellor is a necessary part of this process and of the counsellor's role. Counselling in primary care owes its very existence partly to the reduction of the doctor's ability to provide a relationship in which patients' emotional, relationship and psychological difficulties can be aired and articulated. The pressures upon doctors arising out of the changes in the NHS and the imperatives of financial efficiency have contributed to a widening of the split between the attention that is paid to the patient's soma, and that which is paid to the psyche, in the patient's relationship with the doctor. Communications to health care professionals concerning the emotional needs and difficulties of individual patients provides a means of reducing that split within the practice as a whole, feeding back into the general practice system an awareness of the emotional and psychological components of patients' problems.

The other polar position, one that promotes a very full collaboration and communication between the counsellor and the doctor, and one where the boundary of confidentiality is placed around the surgery as a whole, for counselling just as for any other activity in the setting, also has disadvantages. Firstly, there are few GPs who have a sufficiently sophisticated understanding of psychodynamic processes to be able to work alongside the counsellor in the ways that are described in this article. Most GPs have time for only limited feedback and discussion of their patients with the counsellor, and concepts such as transference or projection have little meaning for them, so that the counsellor's agenda in terms of communication, feedback and collaboration needs to be set with more limited goals in mind, ones that can be more realistically achieved. An over ambitious attempt to engage GPs in therapeutic work, where they may have little wish or inclination to do so, may result in a greater resistance to the development of the counsellor's role within the setting. General practices, as organizations, need to develop at their own pace in their acquisition of psychodynamic or psychological perspectives on their patients. Secondly, patients waiting to see doctors will often see patient notes lying around the reception area, or being passed from one area of the practice to another. The degree of perceived safety of the boundaries of the surgery as a whole is therefore frequently limited, and I would suggest is too insecure for some patients to feel that they can safely divulge their difficulties to the counsellor, unless a more secure boundary is drawn. For some patients, as I will demonstrate, there may be specific reasons for their wish for a more secure boundary with the counsellor, one that excludes the doctor from access to some of the material that they share.

The analogy of a dance: a flexible approach to boundaries

Lees (1996) applied the concept of the Extended Clinical Rhombus, first articulated by Szecsody, to the context of the counsellor working in a primary care setting. It reflects a need for flexibility, a degree of elasticity with regard to the boundaries whilst at the same time having a sound and firm structure, one that can hold the client, and yet move with them. I would suggest that the analogy of a dance, applied to the boundaries of the counselling relationship in this setting is a useful one, as it captures what I would consider to be a necessary movement and a delicacy of poise that the counsellor needs to maintain, and provides a framework and a metaphor for articulating the nature of the boundaries in the primary care setting. But the principles upon which this dance takes place need further elaboration. In what circumstances should the counsellor share information with colleagues? What routine information about this should be given to clients? When and how should the counsellor maintain a firmness of structure and boundaries?

In order to establish the development and elaboration of these principles a little further I will give some case illustrations, but before I do this, I will outline how I personally introduce the counselling frame to clients. This process is an important aspect of counselling generally, and part of structuring the counselling relationship and developing a sound working alliance (Bordin 1979), but it is particularly important when working in primary care, because many of the clients who come to see a counsellor do so knowing little about the nature or purpose of counselling, or may arrive simply because the doctor, relatives or others have advised them to do so.

I am employed to work as a counsellor in General Practices by an NHS Trust that provides Mental Health Services in both Primary Care and Community Mental Health Teams. There are specific agency guidelines with regard to the limits of confidentiality where issues concerning the abuse of a child are raised by a client or where the client is judged to be at risk of seriously harming themselves or another person. In such circumstances the counsellor may be required by their supervisor and manager to contact other agencies such as Social Services or to refer the client to the Community Mental Health Team for a full psychiatric assessment. A client who is seen by a counsellor in a GP setting, within such an agency context, needs to be made aware that there are significant limits to the confidentiality of the counselling relationship. So early in the initial session I mention the issue of confidentiality, and add that later in the session, after they have had an opportunity to tell me something about their difficulties, I will discuss this with them in some detail. Towards the end of this first session I will then explain that the sessions are confidential, with the overriding exception, which I emphasise, that if it emerges during counselling sessions that a person is a danger to themselves or someone else, that I might in such circumstances need to discuss this with another professional, in order to establish how we could be of help to that person. In this way I convey both the agency and the professional limitations to confidentiality so that clients are aware from the outset that it is not an absolute privilege in this setting. It is also a requirement of the Mental Health Service that the counsellor gives a short written report to the referring GP, which goes into the patient notes held by the surgery, at the end of each client's counselling. So I go on to tell the client that at the end of a series of counselling sessions I will give some feedback to the GPs about their experience of the counselling and how it may have been of help to them. I explain that such feedback will be agreed with the client concerned, and will very generally describe how they will have used the sessions, and what they will have discussed with me. Additionally, I tell the client that if there are any details that they wish to remain confidential just to me, that this would be respected, and that they can tell me at any point during the counselling sessions if there is any matter that they may wish to remain confidential to me as their counsellor, and which they would not wish to be shared with their doctors in the feedback I give at the end of their counselling. Finally I will add that there is a wider confidentiality offered by the surgery as a whole. By describing confidentiality in this way, I endeavour to create the conditions for a safe and holding dance, but one where there is sufficient flexibility to meet the needs of the setting, including those that are required by the Mental Health Service. I should add here that the doctors are made fully aware of these boundary limitations and structure.

That this dance with the client needs to be flexible and that there are times with the very same client when a firm holding of the boundaries is required and other times when a loosening of them is necessary is illustrated by the following case examples.

Case examples

Sharon

Sharon was referred to me by her doctor following a violent assault by her husband upon her nineteen-year-old daughter, Angela. Sharon had long-standing difficulties manifesting themselves in anxiety and depression. This had been significantly exacerbated by the attack upon her daughter, which she had witnessed, and which had resulted in her feeling deeply distressed. As a consequence of these events Sharon had filed for divorce, and had also been granted an order excluding her husband from the home. The complex dynamics of this situation began to emerge in the initial interview when Sharon told me that her husband denied many of the details of the assault upon her daughter and that several of her neighbours had sided with her husband, believing his account of the events, in which he had claimed that Sharon was 'mad' and had fabricated much of what had happened. Additionally, both her husband and her daughter were registered with doctors in the same practice. The doctor who referred her to me had been providing her with both medication and a supportive relationship in the weeks immediately following the assault. He had also provided some initial medical treatment for her daughter. Another doctor in the practice was meanwhile providing support for Sharon's husband, and Sharon was aware of this. That this was creating strain within the practice was evident from the doctor's referral letter.

Sharon raised the issue of the confidentiality of the sessions with me during the initial assessment. Each of the factors that I have described combined to leave Sharon feeling very anxious about the safety of the boundaries of the counselling relationship, and this was reflected in her expressed wish that no information that she divulged to me be shared with any other members of the practice. This left me facing a dilemma because I was clear that the structure of my work in the surgery was such that some degree of feedback to the GPs was part of my role, notwithstanding the tricky details of this particular case. The boundaries of the counselling relationship were important, and I was acutely aware of the need to provide a secure base for Sharon, but so were the boundaries of my role with the doctors in the practice. I therefore carefully considered my response to her request. I first let Sharon know that I could see how important the question of the confidentiality of the counselling sessions was to her, in view of all that had happened, and in view of the fact that her husband was still receiving support and assistance from one of the doctors in the surgery. There was also an outstanding court case, and Sharon was understandably worried that information could be passed on to her husband which he might then use to his advantage in court. I recognized this factor too, but firmly stated that I would be giving feedback to the GPs at the end of the series of counselling sessions. I emphasized however that I realised how much care I would need to take in providing that feedback, and that its contents would be very fully discussed and agreed with her before being made to the GPs. This straightforward maintenance of the boundaries of my role, and the care and clarity with which I discussed the question of confidentiality with Sharon provided her with sufficient reassurance of the safety of the counselling relationship for her to engage in the counselling.

Sharon attended every session of the twelve that I was able to offer her, and used them very fully to discuss the emotional impact upon her of her husband's assault upon her daughter. Anxieties about the safety of the counselling relationship and the boundaries of confidentiality remained, and at appropriate times I would interpret them. I was later to discover that the support of the counselling sessions relieved the doctor who was seeing her regularly of considerable strain, as the demands that she made upon his time diminished appreciably and continued to do so long after the counselling sessions had ended. Significantly, some months after the counselling had finished Sharon requested to see the written feedback report that I had given to the doctors. I had told her that she could do so if she wished. Before giving her the report the doctor had some discussion with me about this, and after Sharon had seen it, it was evident that she was quite satisfied with it. During her final session of counselling she had been able to tell me that the question of confidentiality and the discussion that we had had about this had been very important in enabling her to make use of the counselling sessions, but also that the limited confidentiality and the fact that the counselling sessions took place in the setting of a GP practice meant that there were some of her experiences, and the more vulnerable parts of herself, that she had felt unable to share with me. This seemed to accurately reflect the fact that meaningful and significant work can be undertaken within the context and boundaries of the GP setting but that it is important for the counsellor to be aware of, and to be thinking about, its limited nature, and how the limits of confidentiality are to be conveyed and discussed with the client. In this case it seems clear that the boundaries provided a base that had limited security and one in which the client's true feelings and vulnerability could emerge from being protectively hidden within, but to only a limited extent. This would further appear to confirm both the classical position concerning the importance of the frame as described by Winnicott (1960) and Holmes (1994) and a position that recognizes that adaptions to the frame to meet the requirements of the setting can still result in useful therapeutic work.

Jane

A somewhat different difficulty concerning the boundaries of working in a GP setting emerged with another client, Jane, who was referred for counselling because she was suffering from panic attacks, following unsuccessful treatment for infertility. She used the sessions well, focusing upon her feelings about the infertility itself, as well as the links between the onset of the panic attacks, the infertility treatment, and the death of her own mother in her adolescence, giving birth to a sibling. Jane had also become very attached to an aunt who had contributed significantly to her care during her childhood, and who died at about the same time as the panic attacks and the infertility treatment began. Exploring the links between these experiences, and other significant childhood losses and separations seemed to afford Jane some relief, but from about the third session Jane began arriving late for her appointments. She talked about her doubts about the extent to which the counselling sessions would really be of help to her in relieving her panic attacks, and I interpreted a link between these doubts and her lateness in arriving for her appointments. However, her lateness continued. In a subsequent session Jane found it particularly difficult to begin talking. After exploring the difficulty itself a little she went on to tell me that her husband had at one time been involved in some petty fraud at work and she had only found out about this when a friend of her husband inadvertently revealed this to her. She clearly felt ashamed and embarrassed about this. Later in the session she told me that she intended to miss the following one, due to a difficulty concerning her work commitments, but I linked this difficulty and the possibility of missing the next session with the difficulty she had experienced in telling me about her husband's past illegal activities and in sharing other experiences with me in the counselling sessions.

Significantly, she was able to alter her work commitments so that she attended the next session but nonetheless she arrived ten minutes late once again. It was evident that Jane was able to take in and make use of the interpretations that I was making, but it was also clear that I was missing something significant reflected in her continued lateness. I therefore encouraged her to tell me more about her ambivalence towards attending the counselling sessions. She explained that after each session she would feel somewhat anxious about what she had shared with me. She was then able to tell me that she had experienced some feelings of being let down by the doctors in the practice where I saw her, in relation to her infertility treatment. She believed that they had not taken up some options for treatment that they should have done. She went on to tell me that she was left at the end of each session wondering what I had told the doctors and that this added significantly to the strain that she experienced in coming to see me. At this point I clarified again that I would very carefully discuss the feedback that I gave to the doctors with her at the end of the series of counselling sessions, that this feedback would be agreed between us, and that if there were matters that she wanted to remain confidential to me, then this would be respected. This restatement of the nature of the boundaries of the sessions came as a real relief to her, and she was able to tell me more about the difficulties that the setting caused her.

In the practice where I was working at the time I did not have my own counselling room, because of the limited amount of space in the building. During the week prior to this particular session, my client had had to make an appointment to see one of the doctors for a medical matter. Unfortunately the doctor had seen her in the very same room in which the counselling sessions took place. Jane had experienced this as being very uncomfortable and it had exacerbated her anxieties that the boundaries of the counselling session would become muddled with those of the doctors. She was also able to tell me that the toys in the room, which were left there so that children could play with them whilst a parent had a discussion with the doctor, had been a very painful reminder to her of her infertility. Finally, she was able to tell me that some years previously one of the doctors in the surgery had admitted her sister to the psychiatric ward of the local hospital, and Jane herself had been actively involved in her care at that time. When she came to see me at the surgery she was worried about the possibility that this doctor would see her, and think that she was coming to the counselling sessions because she too was 'mad', just like her sister. It was evidently a great relief for Jane to be able to tell me about this, and, significantly, she arrived on time for the next session. She had grown up in a family where issues were generally not talked about, so that within the 'family' of the surgery there were for her a number of parallels and difficult transferences. At the very end of the counselling, she told me that the only detail that she particularly wished to remain confidential to myself, was that her husband had been involved in petty fraud, and the process of agreeing the overall feedback to the GPs was one which we completed comfortably and to the satisfaction of both of us.

In the setting in which this work with Jane took place, there were a number of deviations from the classical frame, arising directly from the context of Primary Care in which the counselling took place. It became evident that these deviations in the frame limited the extent to which I was able to provide her with a secure base, and that this in turn evoked anxieties which lessened Jane's ability to use the setting to explore her inner world. However, interpreting her resistances arising from these deviations in the frame, and clarifying the boundaries of confidentiality, clearly lessened her transferential anxieties, which were impeding the working alliance, and enabled her to explore her inner experience more deeply and with greater confidence. There were also some indications that my feedback to the GP and her experience of us as a communicating couple, in contrast to the lack of communication within her own family, will have had some positive therapeutic effect.

Kamaljit

When a patient raises the question of confidentiality in relation to the feedback that is given to the GPs at the very beginning of the first assessment interview, this will usually be meaningful. Kamaljit, who was in his middle twenties, was referred by his GP because he was experiencing difficulties in his relationship with his partner. He began the first session by immediately seeking clarification about the extent to which the sessions would be confidential, and what would be shared with the doctors in the surgery. I gave him my usual summary of these boundaries, emphasizing that if there were matters that he wished to remain confidential to me then this would be respected. He then explained to me that there were cultural issues, which made the question of confidentiality particularly important to him. Both Kamaljit and the doctors belonged to a small Sikh community. His parents knew the doctors and he was worried that if the doctors knew some of the contents of what he would be divulging to me in the counselling sessions, that this could be conveyed back to his parents. He clearly did not want this to happen. I accepted this explanation but it was only later in the session that its full significance emerged, for he was to reveal that he had been frequently sexually abused by a relative who lived with his family during his childhood, and that he had never felt able to talk about this with his parents or any of his older siblings, for fear of the consequences that this would have upon the extended family. In sharing this with me, he clearly needed to experience the safety of firmly held boundaries, particularly in respect of confidentiality. He needed to feel that he had control over with whom this information was shared, as he emerged cautiously out of his isolated position. It is unlikely that he would have been able to engage in the counselling process at all, or to establish a working alliance with me, without such a framework having been established from the outset.

The establishment of a predictable and clearly articulated boundary in relation to confidentiality can therefore be seen as an essential pre-requisite to the establishment of a secure base from which this patient could begin his narrative. Deviations from the frame in this case needed to be kept to the utmost minimum.

Helga

The complexity of the boundary of confidentiality and the need for a flexible frame emerged with another client, Helga. She was referred by her GP, because of difficulties that she was experiencing in negotiating with her former husband concerning his access to their children. She was divorced and had three children, two daughters and a son. It was evident that her former husband's access to her children was unsettling them, and there were frequent conflicts and arguments over the timing of the access and over the ways in which limits and boundaries were being maintained with the children.

As with Kamaljit, Helga began the first session by questioning me closely about the extent of confidentiality in the counselling sessions, and I gave her my usual summary. At the beginning of the third session Helga arrived with her eight-year-old daughter, and arranged for one of the receptionists, whom she knew quite well, to look after her daughter whilst she had her counselling session with me. She then explained that she and her husband had been to a mediation service, in order to try to resolve the conflicts that were arising concerning her husband's access to their children. During the session at the mediation service her husband had made allegations that Helga's brother had sexually abused their daughter in some way. The allegations were rather vague, but enough for the mediation service to decide that they could not in the circum-stances continue with the process of mediation. Helga herself did not think that the allegation was true, but nonetheless I faced a dilemma as to whether or not I had an ethical responsibility to discuss the question of the possible sexual abuse of her daughter with her doctor, particularly as Helga had expressed anxiety about the issue of confidentiality from the outset, and clearly had wanted the boundaries of confidentiality to be carefully and firmly maintained. I decided that there was no need to rush into any hasty action, and that I would give myself time to reflect upon the issue and consider it in supervision. This I did, so that in a subsequent session I told her that, having considered the matter carefully, I thought it was important that I had some discussion with her doctor about the allegation that her husband had made, so that her doctor was adequately informed in case the matter needed to be dealt with further in any way. Helga readily agreed to this and seemed relieved both that she had discussed this matter with me and that I had taken it seriously, without over-reacting to it. Later I was able to speak to her doctor, and it became evident that in the meantime Helga had spoken to him about the allegation of sexual abuse. It was clear that in her doctor's judgement Helga was a caring mother and that, in his view, Helga's former husband had been generally making life difficult for her, and that he was using the allegation of her brother's sexual abuse of her daughter as a lever in the conflict over the access to the children. This coincided with my own assessment of the situation, and, significantly, Helga was able to make very good use of the remaining sessions, never failing to attend an appointment. Moreover she was able to find a way of negotiating her husband's access to her children in a more amicable and satisfying way, and one that reduced the strain for all concerned. In this case, the flexibility with which I approached the boundaries of the counselling relationship and the dialogue with her doctor proved both containing of the patient's anxieties and therapeutic in its effect.

In this case it had appeared at first that the maintenance of the frame, and the keeping of deviations to the frame to a minimum, would, as in Kamaljit's case be an essential prerequisite for the process of exploration. In the event, however, it was a carefully considered loosening of the boundaries, and a dialogue with the GP, reflecting my concern for the safety of my client's daughter, and representing a parental couple communicating seriously and thoughtfully about such an issue, that proved to be both containing and therapeutic.

Mary

I have so far given a number of examples where it was important either to firmly maintain the boundaries of confidentiality, or to be flexible, depending upon the situation and context of each particular client. I intend now to give one further example, where the dance of firmness and flexibility around the boundaries of the counselling relationship varied at different points during the work with the same client. In certain ways I needed to maintain the boundaries very firmly, whilst in others I needed to be quite flexible. Mary was a patient who made extensive demands upon the time, energy and patience of the doctors in the practice. She had long standing problems of depression and anxiety, and an unusual physical condition known as Sjorden's syndrome, which was a variable condition resulting in periods of physical exhaustion and tiredness. It also had psychological effects, and in the past she had been assessed by a psychiatrist who diagnosed her depression as being secondary to Sjorden's syndrome and recommended counselling. She was in her late forties, divorced with three grown-up children, two girls and a boy, who made substantial demands upon her time and energy because of their own difficulties. Her youngest daughter, who was at college, still lived with her, and was experiencing some difficulty in sepa-rating from Mary and in establishing her own independent life. Mary had developed a dependency upon anti-depressants, and took steroids in order to deal with the Sjorden's syndrome. In the paper which I referred to earlier in the chapter (Jones et al. 1994) it was argued that the 'double transference', that is the transference to the GP as well as to the counsellor becomes particularly significant in the work with patients who express their conflicts psychosomatically. Bearing this in mind, I spent some time with the GP learning about Sjorden's syndrome, how it was affecting this particular patient, and what the longer term prognosis for her was expected to be. This discussion was important, for it formed the basis of the collaborative work that was later to follow.

In the counselling sessions themselves Mary's discourse ranged from a discussion of her present difficulties, particularly as she experienced them in relation to her children, to an exploration of a very deprived and disturbing childhood. Her father had died when she was very young, but his death had been largely denied and very rarely referred to or talked about by either her mother or her step-father. When they had also died, when Mary was an adult, she found that she could not face this reality, so that her bereavement became distorted and her mourning very incomplete. It was these losses that became the focus of my work with her, but it was also evident that the boundaries of relationships had been very poorly maintained as she grew up and I speculated about the possibility that she might have been sexually abused. She had certainly been deprived of much physical expression of warmth or care.

From the outset, she challenged the boundaries of the counselling relationship, offering me notes in which were written her despairing thoughts about herself and the counselling relationship, and repeatedly seeking reassurance about whether or not I thought she was 'mad'. I listened carefully to what she told me, empathized with her anxiety and made links between her childhood experiences and her present worries, including her fears about her mental health. I maintained a firm frame and thereby contained much of her initial anxiety, as we established a working alliance. However, as the sessions progressed, and she explored her losses a little more deeply, she experienced a flare-up of her Sjorden's syndrome. It was evident from what she told me that she was making substantial demands upon her GP and taking up a considerable amount of his time in expressing her anxieties to him about her mental health, and in calling him out unnecessarily to attend to a physical ailment of her daughter as well as for her own Sjorden's syndrome. She then described how at the end of the last consultation with him she had returned repeatedly after leaving his room to seek further reassurance as to her mental health.

At this point I became concerned about the additional pressure and burden that this was placing upon her GP, as well as the possibility that this could adversely affect my collaborative relationship with him, evoking a split in our collaborative work that would mirror the splits in Mary's inner world. I chose at this point to raise with Mary the possibility that I would have some discussion with her doctor about her difficulties and anxieties, sharing with him some of my thoughts about them, to enable him to have a fuller understanding of what was troubling her. Mary agreed to this quite readily, and seemed relieved at my suggestion. I then spoke to her GP who in fact had a good appreciation of her difficulties. I suggested to him that he respond quite firmly to Mary's anxieties by tactfully encouraging her to share them with me, rather than with him or any of the other doctors in the practice. I also explained that I thought that her heightened anxieties and demand upon his services could continue for a while, during the work of the counselling sessions, and that this could be a direct consequence of the work of the counselling itself. I added that the counselling sessions with Mary had limited aims, but my hope was that she would begin to see her problems as having a greater psychological component, thereby reducing the extent to which her anxieties became channelled generally into concerns about her physical health, which had been her characteristic way of expressing them. The longer term aim was to lessen her overall demands upon the doctors.

The GP responded well to my suggestion and comments, and we engaged in a fruitful dialogue which strengthened our collaborative relationship in our work with this client.

Interestingly, at the end of the counselling session which followed my discussion with the doctor, Mary left the counselling room, only to return a few minutes later to ask me whether I thought she was 'cracking up', just as she had described she had done with the doctor. I gently but firmly told her that I appreciated that she was still worried about her mental health but we could discuss this further when I saw her again the next week. This mixture of firmness coupled with flexibility, particularly in relation to the discussion that I had with her GP, had the effect of substantially containing Mary's anxieties. She completed the full course of counselling and developed some important insights into her difficulties, enabling her to face and support her youngest daughter in her development towards greater independence and separation, and to explore ways of enriching her own life.

In this case the client herself put a considerable amount of pressure upon the boundaries of the counselling relationship, and in view of what I knew of her childhood experiences of poorly maintained boundaries, it was clear that I needed to be particularly firm in maintaining these boundaries, to contain her safely, just as one would protect a toddler from exploring in dangerous places. When however she began to place considerable pressure upon the referring GP as well, I was faced with a dilemma. A collaborative discussion with the GP, which seemed necessary, could have been experienced as a weakening of the boundaries of the counselling relationship and a lessening of the secure base. In the event, however, a carefully considered discussion with the GP, which involved a minimal disclosure of the contents of the client's narrative and which focused upon working together collaboratively proved to be containing. Its therapeutic effect can also be considered to have arisen from the client's transferential experience of a parental couple in a creative, caring and thoughtful dialogue about her physical and psychological well-being; one that recognized the importance of boundaries in relationships, and of differences in roles. Within organizations and working relationships boundaries can become barriers to communication through processes of splitting, projection and other primitive defences (Hinshelwood 1987). The collaborative discussion with the GP can also be seen to have reduced the likelihood of these processes operating within our working relationship and to have ensured that we remained focused upon the reality of our task.

Conclusion

The frame of the classical counselling relationship provides a basis from which the counsellor can reflect upon issues concerning the maintenance of boundaries when working in a primary care setting. It remains an important point of orientation from which the counsellor can consider the meaning of any variations in the nature of the frame. The metaphor of a dance, when applied to the frame of the counselling relationship in this context, is a useful one inasmuch as it conveys the need for the counsellor to provide a safe holding frame, but one that allows sufficient freedom of movement and flexibility to meet the particular needs of the work in this setting. The case examples that I have described illustrate some of the principles that can inform decisions that the counsellor may take in relation to these boundaries. Firstly, the counsellor needs to be alert to the communications from the client, both conscious and unconscious, that indicate that confidentiality or other boundary issues have particular meaning or significance. In this respect the counsellor needs to keep in mind the complex nature of the boundaries in this setting, how the client may experience them, and what anxieties or phantasies they may evoke. For some clients, clearly drawn and firmly maintained boundaries may be of paramount importance if the work is to take place effectively. Secondly, the counsellor needs to keep in mind their responsibilities to the agency (or the doctors in the case of fundholding practices) and the limits to the principle of client autonomy and the privilege of confidentiality that arise where the safety of the client or others, particularly children, is seriously in question. This can in itself be a holding experience for a client. Thirdly, the counsellor needs to balance the need for confidentiality with the need to maintain a sound working relationship with colleagues, and in some circumstances to consider the therapeutic value to the client of experiencing the counsellor and colleague, whether GP or other health care professional, as a parental couple who are able both to communicate with each other and to maintain appropriate boundaries.

REFERENCES

M. Balint (1964) *The Doctor, His Patient and the Illness*, London: Churchill Livingstone.

J. Bowlby (1988) *A Secure Base*, London: Routledge.

C. Bollas and D. Sundelson (1995) *The New Informants*, London: Karnac Books.

E. S. Bordin (1979) 'The Generalisabillity of the Psychoanalytic Concept of the Working Alliance'. *Psychotherapy: Theory, Research and Practice*, 16.

P. East (1995) *Counselling in Medical Settings*. London: Open University Press.

A. Gray (1994) *An Introduction to the Therapeutic Frame*, London: Routledge.

R. D. Hinshelwood (1987) *What Happens in Groups*, London: Free Association Books.

L. Hoag (1992) 'Psychotherapy in General Practice Surgery: Considerations of the Frame'. *British Journal of Psychotherapy* 8(4).

J. Holmes (1994) 'Attachment Theory – A Secure Theoretical Base for Counselling?' *Psychodynamic Counselling* 1(1).

H. Jones, A. Murphy, G. Neaman, R. Tollemache and D. Vasserman (1994) 'Psychotherapy and Counselling in a GP Practice: Making Use of the Setting'. *British Journal of Psychotherapy* 10(4).

J. Lees (1997) 'An Approach to Counselling in GP Surgeries'. *Psychodynamic Counselling* 3(1).

E. Noonan (1983) *Counselling Young People*. London: Routledge.

D. W. Winnicott (1960) 'The Theory of the Parent–Infant Relationship', in *The Maturational Processes and the Facilitating Environment*. London: Hogarth.

4 Counselling within a time limit in general practice

Annalee Curran

Introduction

As primary care realizes that patients' emotional well-being and mental health are as important as their physical health, it has become clear that there is a huge need in this area. As reported in Corney and Jenkins (1993), it can be estimated that one third of people attending a GP surgery at any given time have some psychological difficulty, whether or not it is this with which they are presenting. Life out there is tough: tough in the sense of the stress and anxiety caused by difficult living conditions and tough because of the often painful experience and history so many people carry with them.

Many general practices have recognized the importance and relevance of counselling in primary care and have set up a service for their patients; in doing so they have come to see how widespread are emotional distress and psychological problems. The demand inevitably stretches the counselling service available in a practice and raises issues about time limits and rationing.

There is a grave danger here as these issues are discussed. The present day focus on resources – or rather *limited* resources – has led to a climate in which the concept of 'less-rather-than-more' is almost sacred; where the cry is 'How little can we get away with?' rather than 'What does this individual actually need?' Our understanding of individual people's needs has become increasingly two-dimensional, measured solely in terms of input and outcome and pursued in a framework of consumerism and quick 'fix-its' and glossy charters. A third dimension, I believe, is being gravely overlooked: the dimension which recognizes and values the individual as a whole being, embarked on a rich journey of self-discovery and fulfilment; which recognizes that this is a difficult journey with many pitfalls, but which strives to offer help in terms of reaching the person where they are, respecting the complex wealth and wisdom of their conscious and unconscious experience and empowering them to find meaning.

And so, the danger when it comes to providing counselling in primary care, is that a two-dimensional concern for numbers – numbers of patients, numbers of sessions, numbers of pounds – will dictate what kind of service is offered to patients. We should distrust arrangements where the offer is determined by the holder of the purse strings, rather than by the counsellor within the context of the particular interaction with a patient and of the unique culture of that particular GP practice. Inevitably, each GP practice will need to make decisions about how a service can be made available to its patients. The very ethos of general practice is that of embracing all its patients and entitling them all to the services available. To make this at all viable, there has to be respect for time and the challenge is for each counsellor, in conjunction with the GP practice, to find the right sensitive balance between need and resource.

The GP setting

The GP surgery represents the hurly-burly of real life on the pavement. People go 'down the doctor's' for their illnesses and aches and pains; for their worries and crises; for cure and for reassurance; in their distress and confusion and joy and grief. It is often the first port of call for them, where they can bring their raw, unsorted feelings, both physical and emotional, and the care needs to have a *primary* quality which can respond to the patient holistically as a person, not as a diagnosis coming through the door. The patient needs to be seen as a person in the context of their family and community and culture and in the context of the on-going relationship they have with the practice. In an inner-city practice particularly, there will be a large proportion of patients whose life is centred on that particular area and in their particular socio-economic class. I am struck by the number of people I have seen over the years who have never 'crossed the water' (meaning the River Thames), even though they live no more than two miles from it. And for many of these people contact with middle-class people is often confined to the school and the GP practice and often instills a feeling of inadequacy and passive acceptance of authority. It is vital that this relationship – between the patient and the practice – can be as free as possible of any inhibiting factor, that the patient does not feel that a gulf exists that can never be crossed between themselves and the health professionals. The way in which we work in this setting needs to encourage and enhance feelings of equality and empowerment rather than intimidation and passivity.

There is obviously a great deal of movement in an inner-city population so that some patients stay with the practice for only a short time, but the general practice ethos is one of 'being there' for patients in a continuing way, as they negotiate different crises and life events through the years.

I am lucky to work with GPs who believe that, above all, the patient/ person in general practice needs to tell their story (whether that is the story of in-grown toenails, or of panic attacks, or of childhood sexual abuse or of their time in the war); and the story needs to be heard. The writer Primo Levi (1987) relates a dream he had while in a concentration camp: he dreams that he is back home amongst his family and friends and is trying to tell them of all that is happening in the camp. But they don't seem to hear or to take any notice, so that he wakes feeling devastated and forlorn. He then tells his friend in the camp about the dream and the friend says that he too has had that dream; and they find that many people around them are having similar dreams of not being heard.

This must not happen in general practice. It is often the first time that the story is ever spoken and the patient may only have a glimmer of an idea that there could be a problem behind the story. So, general practice needs to listen 'widely': to have a wide canvas of possibility as it listens. A primary care team which is working effectively together will be able to make this possible. First, they will have a shared understanding of the philosophy which underpins general practice: that the aim is not only to cure the symptom, but to hear the person. Second, the multi-disciplinary nature of the team will bring a wide and diverse repertoire to the shared work of 'listening widely'. This process will be all the richer if the individual professionals involved are themselves open-minded and open-hearted so that they can generously embrace the perspectives of their colleagues and generously give their own view of things; this attitude in the individual professionals will obviously benefit the patients greatly too, so that they feel that whatever they bring to the surgery can be heard, accommodated and worked with. For a primary care team to be able to achieve this there needs to be a lot of opportunity for discussion, sharing of ideas and indeed just getting to know each other. Although time is always a scarce commodity, the GP surgeries where time is set aside for this kind of interchange do seem to notice the value of it. A practice counsellor can have a very useful role in facilitating this sharing of views and understandings and can often be the person who highlights the less obvious dynamics operating in the lives of patients (and in the life of the team).

General practice also needs to be attuned to the emotional content of whatever the patient brings. A stomach ache may be only a stomach ache, or it may be the visible tip of an iceberg which is calling out for notice to be taken of what is in the emotional depths. So primary care is *primarily* about listening and about giving the person the experience of being heard. It is also about sorting and naming and focusing and helping people find understanding and meaning.

How can a counsellor in a GP practice help to achieve this? I think our aim, as counsellors, is not to operate a kind of World War I triage in order to get people 'back to the trenches' as soon as possible. Nor is it only to make them cope better, remove their symptoms or to reduce the number of consultations they have with the GP. Rather, I would like to think that we can help people find meaning in their distress, symptoms, unhappiness or depression so that they can get a better understanding of why they are the way they are, where the distress has come from and how it might lead them to find more fulfilling ways of being. This could be seen as a tall order within the context of counselling in general practice and the constraints of time-limited work. But I have a firm belief that it *is* possible to work at considerable depth in a short time and that short-term does not have to mean short-changed. It is my background in Cognitive Analytic Therapy which has particularly enabled me to find ways of working which can be short and deep. I think it would be useful to explore some thoughts about time limit generally before going on to describe Cognitive Analytic Therapy and my use of it.

Time limit

It is a harsh fact that it would be impossible to offer a meaningful counselling service in a GP practice if patients were seen in an ongoing, open-ended, unlimited way. Perhaps up to twenty people, at the very most, could be taken on, but it could be months or years before there would be space for any more. The reality of general practice is that there is a constant trickle of peope who are in distress or who could benefit from counselling.

   The challenge is to be able to make time-limited offers which can foster a working alliance in which the patient can explore deeper levels than only those of the presenting problems. Some approaches to time-limited work call for the focus to be on very specific and therefore often limited problems and goals. So often, though, what a patient brings initially is merely the tip of the iceberg which serves primarily to draw attention to the fact that there is something painful and important beneath the surface. Many of the symptoms which present typically in general practice, such as sleeping difficulties, panic attacks, phobias or mood swings are like flashing beacons warning that all is not well in the whole person. Of course, these presenting problems are very distressing in themselves and it would be wrong to ignore them. Sometimes, it seems valuable to remain with these and to offer some behavioural and/or cognitive strategies to help the patient overcome them. However, I have seldom – I feel I can say never – come across a person where the presenting problem was all there was to the story. So I would always look for the deeper significance of the symptoms, even if all that was gained was a more symbolic framework in which the symptom can be seen as speaking metaphorically for the psyche in some way: 'the knotted gut'; 'a pain in the neck'; 'fear of falling into chaos'; 'having to keep awake and vigilant' etc.

Margaret was a 53-year-old woman who came to see the GP because of stomach pain. He recognized that she might be be suffering from Irritable Bowel Syndrome, but because he was listening to her in a 'broad canvas' way, he explored a little further and made the connection for her that the symptoms had started more or less at the time of the second anniversary of her father's death, whom she had cared for during a long terminal illness. It seems that the GP really touched on something important for Margaret. She had not seen the connection before and was able to say how much she still grieved for her father. The GP felt there was more work she needed to do around this and referred her for counselling. Over a period of eight sessions, Margaret was able to see that she had not grieved enough for her father. But what also emerged was that she was harbouring anger towards him. She found it very difficult to admit this and felt extremely guilty. It came to light in the sessions as a result of monitoring her physical symptoms which she'd presented as one of the issues she wanted to deal with. It was again, through 'listening widely' to what she said about these symptoms, when they occurred, how she was feeling at the time, that we could discover their connection to anger, initially experienced in relation to current people in her life. In hearing her story, though, it was possible to suggest that she might actually be feeling anger towards her father who had always favoured her younger sister. The work could then focus on her entitlement to this anger and she wrote an 'imaginary letter' to him to have her say. She found this very painful especially reading it aloud in the session. But we were then able to look at her long-standing low self-esteem, where this had come from, and why it had been maintained. Margaret could recognize that caring for her father in his illness had been the only role of any worth she'd ever had and now he had robbed her of that by dying. The counselling ended with Margaret beginning to ask herself what she really wanted from life and she was planning to do a training course offered to older people by a supermarket chain. The physical symptoms still troubled her from time to time, but the remedies suggested by her GP were helping and she didn't feel it interfered with her life.

This, like so many cases in general practice, shows how the initial presenting problem is by no means the full problem. It is the quality of listening, however, by all the people involved with the patient, which allows the deeper levels to be reached. Working with a time limit therefore does not imply going into quick 'fix-it' mode; nor does it imply withholding or keeping a distance. It can be an offer given with a generosity of spirit and one which concentrates on the quality of the work rather than the quantity.

There are ways in which a time-limited approach can be seen as beneficial in itself, not just a virtue arising out of necessity. Given the quality of rawness and confusion which often characterizes the material people bring to the surgery, a time-limited contract can offer a clarity and a safe structure in which the patient can begin to sort the confusion and make sense of things. It can also bring into focus issues like ending and loss (the ending of the therapeutic work being explicit from the beginning) and more generally, it can 'heat up the emotional water' so that difficult issues and feelings can come to the surface more quickly.

When I first started working in this practice, I generally worked in a more open-ended way. I recall one patient, a woman of 28 who was struggling with difficult feelings from her childhood when her parents separated and she felt she had to 'choose' between them. This was linked to current difficulties around sexual involvement with two men whom she felt she couldn't choose between. After eighteen months of open-ended weekly sessions, we decided to work within a time-limited framework of twelve sessions of Cognitive Analytic Therapy. It was very striking that once we had the time limit in place and ending was explicit, with all its potential echoes of loss, the work we did became much more powerful and the patient was able to experience some frightening and quite primitive feelings in the room with me. One could argue that this would have happened anyway, but I did experience a real sense of a 'gear-change' when a time limit was established.

I recognize that there can be disadvantages to working in this way. It is not possible to use the transference and countertransference in six sessions in the same way as one could in a longer, psychodynamic framework. I don't think, however, that transference and countertransference considerations need to be jettisoned entirely; there are ways in which these interpretations can be used effectively, particularly within the context of the Cognitive

Analytic Therapy model. Within the GP surgery it can be important for a counsellor to be aware of transference and countertransference at work in the broader context of the setting; the patient's interactions with GPs and nurses and receptionists, as well as with other health workers will already have given rise to transference and countertransference reactions. Sometimes too there is a clear group countertransference towards a patient which can enlighten the work the counsellor is undertaking and can help the other professionals to understand their own reactions.

Sometimes, when the therapeutic work needs to be mainly about witnessing the emergence and strengthening of a fragile sense of self, open-ended, long-term work may be called for. Yet, from my experience, even this can be accommodated within the time-limited world of general practice, by having a series of time-limited packages, or by offering a series of reinforcing follow-up sessions after the initial concentrated, finite piece of work.

Tracey had been known to the GP surgery all her life, first as a baby with eczema and then at 14 when the family experienced the tragic death of her young brother who was knocked down and killed by a delivery van driven by an uncle. Two years later, Tracey became pregnant and had an abortion. Her GP referred her for counselling. She attended only one session and being unable to engage with her feelings about this did not come to the second planned session or reply to my letter. A few years later, a new GP in the practice started working with Tracey because of bulimia which was developing. I was not directly involved as the counsellor, but provided some supervision for the GP who eventually referred Tracey to an eating disorders clinic at the local hospital. As Tracey approached her twenty-second birthday, she came to another GP in the practice, having been beaten up by her boyfriend. She wanted to see the counsellor and was disappointed that she had to wait a few weeks. However, when I did see her she was far more able to be in touch with her feelings than six years previously and agreed to eight sessions of counselling. This allowed her to see how vulnerable and unentitled she felt beneath the brash, superficially gregarious exterior she had developed and also to admit to crippling guilt both about her brother's death whom she felt she should have saved and about the abortion. She did important work on this and on beginning to feel her true self-worth. But she could easily slip back into being 'open and tough Tracey' as she called it and would become disparaging of the gains she had made. It felt that her sense of self was still very fragile and although I could have been tempted to extend the counselling indefinitely, we planned to meet once every two months as a way of my being witness to this emerging sense of herself as a worthwhile person in her own right.

This idea fits in with the general practice ethos, where the GP and the other workers are there for the patient throughout their life, where important life events and the emotional ups and downs of life generally can be brought, logged, heard and understood and where the patient can take stock of their own overall personal growth and development. So, while the clarity of a discreet time-limited contract is important and very valuable, this can, where appropriate, take in the more extended GP ethos, by offering intermittent counselling, in the form of a series of clear packages of counselling or of one-off opportunities to take stock along the way.

David's case is an example of intermittent counselling. He was a 32-year-old classical musician who referred himself to counselling because he was experiencing a lot of stress related to his work. He was suffering from insomnia and found himself falling into procrastination, which was affecting his practising and therefore his career. He hoped counselling could offer him stress management. It was clear that David was caught in a Narcissistic need to perform and do well which seemed to have its origins in his experience of a very critical and violently abusive father and a sweet, but ineffectual mother, who was a music teacher and whom David adored. Apart from telling me the bare facts, David was very reluctant to go into his past so all we could do at that stage, during the four sessions we had planned, was to name his vulnerable, abused past on a diagram and show how his striving had arisen from that and how procrastination was a sort of passive resistance to his own inner critical, abusive voice. He seemed to be able to make some cognitive use of this understanding and found a relaxation tape useful, but was not prepared to go any deeper. We did name 'unbearable, painful feelings' on the diagram and when we ended our planned counselling sessions, I reiterated that he might find that he would need to return to that some day.

Eighteen months later, David's father died and he became quite severely depressed. The GP referred him to me and he agreed to another fixed plan of eight sessions. He used this as a time to grieve for his father, but could not get in touch with any anger. However, the diagram still made sense to him and we added the depression to it as one of the ways he blanked off deep and painful feelings. Again, at the end of this time, I pointed out that there were still important unbearable feelings he hadn't fully dealt with.

A year later, David contacted me again. He now felt he was ready to look more deeply into his feelings. Things had reached a very difficult state for him: he was obsessively having to clean and tune his violin and was developing restrictive rituals which prevented playing. We planned ten sessions of Cognitive Analytic Therapy during which time he was able to use drawings very powerfully to address the pain and rage he felt and began to break the compulsive behaviour by monitoring it and finding other ways of dealing with the feeling. He also found he did not need to be a professional violinist, but could play for pleasure and decided to do a course in desk-top publishing and work for a friend in that field.

These intermittent counselling experiences seemed to allow David to go at his own pace while still keeping within the basic remit of time-limited work. The fact of the underlying pain being named explicitly all the way through kept it on the agenda, even when he was unable to work with it, and allowed him to return to it when he was ready.

I have a number of patients whom I see only once every four to twelve weeks (having seen them for a more concentrated time to start with), for whom this provides a chance to take stock and reflect on how the process is going for them. Examples of this are a woman of 87 who was very depressed and took an overdose some seven years ago, but is now on an even keel which needs occasional reinforcement; an alcoholic man, now dry for the past six years, who is finding his way on a very profound personal journey which arose from the AA Twelve Steps; and a 'clean' heroin addict who has reconnected with his young child and is struggling to create a normal family life for her.

Time limit in general practice counselling can be very valuable, not only as a response to demand, but perhaps more significantly as a way of setting boundaries within which a safe place can be created so that the patient and counsellor can take the risk of working at considerable depth and can focus on the areas where there is the possibility of meaningful change. This presents a challenge to the counsellor to find creative ways of working and always to keep in focus a clarity of what one is doing with a particular patient and why.

Supervision is very important in this respect. Because there are a considerable number of patients 'on board' at any given time, I find it invaluable that my supervisor helps me maintain an overview and challenges my decisions about how I plan to work with a patient, enabling me to be clear about what the work is hoping to achieve.

Cognitive Analytic Therapy

I think I have shown that I believe it is possible to work in depth within some sort of time limit which is likely to be necessary in general practice. I have come to this conclusion particularly because of the understanding and focus provided by Cognitive Analytic Therapy (CAT), a model in which I have worked and been involved for the past twelve years. CAT has provided me with a way of looking which helps to focus on the fundamental dynamics at work within a person. In attempting to share some of my thoughts about this, I will not be giving a detailed description of the model, but rather will try to give an overview of the main theoretical and clinical features, particularly as they apply to my work in a GP practice. (A fuller explanation can be found in Ryle, 1990, 1995).

Cognitive Analytic Therapy is an integrative model of short-term, time-limited therapy which has evolved over the past fifteen years or so around Dr Anthony Ryle and those working with him. It grew out of his acute awareness of the extent of the need for therapeutic help and a commitment to trying to provide this within the NHS. He was influenced by the work of, amongst others, Kelly (1955) and his personal construct theory and use of repertory grids, by the cognitive work of Beck (1976) and by the time-limited psychodynamic work of James Mann (1973, Mann and Goldman, 1982) and Malan (1963). Ryle's recognition of typical patterns in which patients seem to be caught and of the fact that the therapist could share these with the patient and recruit the patient's ability to recognize and then revise these patterns, formed the basis of the beginnings of this model.

CAT basically aims to understand people's distress in terms of the repeated patterns in which they appear to be stuck and which developed in an attempt to defend themselves against the core pain, or what James Mann would call the 'chronically endured pain', probably stemming from childhood experience. The model has developed to incorporate an Object Relations dimension, so that early internalized relationships, described as reciprocal roles, are identified and named with the patient (usually in a diagram) to understand more fully why the defensive, repeated patterns are being maintained in spite of their inevitable repeated unsatisfactory outcome.

For instance, a person with very low self-esteem may have had early experiences which resulted in the internalization of reciprocal roles of being *critical/denigrating* to being *criticized/put down/worthless*. A hypothetical scenario could be that of a child who was always put down by a critical parent or older sibling or where expectations on the child were so high and unrealistic (probably because of the parent's own needs) that whatever the child did was not good enough. So this child would have internalized the critical, denigrating object, thus continuing in adult life to put themselves down and undermine whatever they tried to achieve. So a pattern might develop of *trying to succeed in something* → *feel I'm never good enough* → *expect criticism from self and others* → *therefore end up feeling worthless again*. This becomes a self-perpetuating repeated pattern as the 'chronically endured pain' of feeling denigrated and worthless is continually driving the person to try to succeed, or could also perhaps be defended against by them becoming critical and denigratory of others, in a way that might lead to rejection and thus reinforce the worthlessness again.

Traditionally CAT works in a framework of sixteen weekly sessions. More recent work with people suffering from Borderline Personality Disorder has led to twenty-four-session therapies with a series of monthly follow-ups and has been found to be an effective intervention, as described in *Cognitive Analytic Therapy and Borderline Personality Disorder* (Ryle, 1997). I find that within the GP practice I generally have to reduce the number of sessions to between ten and twelve in order to make it viable within the time constraints.

The first four sessions provide time for gathering material: the history, the current problems etc. and for early identification of the repeated patterns which may be operating. Because CAT is seen as being active and collaborative in nature, these early sessions would involve the patient doing homework tasks such as self-monitoring of their symptoms, writing or drawing some kind of life-line or chronology, sometimes writing 'positive' and 'negative' descriptions of themselves in the voice of a caring close friend and a critical outsider respectively and above all, starting to recognize the repeated patterns of belief, thought and action which I have already mentioned. The patient is given a list of typical patterns at the end of the first session to help them begin thinking in this way and to begin identifying what their own unhelpful patterns seem to be. And in the sessions this process continues alongside the usual ways in which a therapeutic relationship is allowed to develop; however, the therapist will share hunches and hypotheses more readily with the patient than in more psychodynamic or person-centred ways of working. The beginnings of transference and countertransference will be named explicitly in terms of the repeated patterns and reciprocal roles of the patient, as they are identified and jointly named.

At about the fourth session, the therapist shares a Reformulation with the patient. This is a key feature of CAT and takes the form of a piece written by the therapist (in the form of a letter to the patient or as a hypothetical 'as if' statement written in the first person on the patient's behalf) and a jointly created diagram. The written Reformulation attempts to name the core pain which the patient has probably borne all their lives, to describe how this came about and to enumerate the resulting reciprocal roles and repeated patterns of belief, thought and action, also suggesting what the way forward might be in order to begin effecting change. It is written in draft form and shared with the patient in a way that can invite collaborative fine-tuning and modification so that it feels to the patient like an accurate enough description of themselves. Often it is a very moving moment when the Reformulation is first read, as patients often feel properly heard for the first time in their lives.

The diagram, which generally grows out of shared visual descriptions of the patterns etc. from the earliest sessions, may be more or less finalized with the patient in the weeks following the written Reformulation, or may have been found to be useful and therefore in place earlier than this. With more disturbed patients who perhaps have sudden shifts from one mood state to another or where there is a powerful cut-off defence against the real painful feelings, early use of the diagram can be invaluable as it contains, on a single sheet of paper, descriptions of all aspects of the person's difficulties, even those which still feel too frightening to face.

Both the written and diagrammatic parts of the Reformulation are greatly enhanced by using the patient's own words and phrases and descriptions as far as possible. Working with images can provide a rich source of shorthand symbols which contain not only a description, but an emotional feeling and which then become an important part of the unique shared language used by a particular therapist and patient throughout the therapy.

The remainder of the therapy after Reformulation offers an opportunity for further recognition of the patterns in operation both out in the world and in the therapeutic relationship and also an opportunity for revision of these patterns, discovering ways of breaking the cycles and of challenging the negative internalized voices of the reciprocal roles. Work around this will often include revisiting past painful experiences, especially losses; helping the patient access unacknowledged and blocked off feelings; finding ways of expressing anger safely; hearing the voice of the hurt inner child; taking some risk in visiting the dark, hidden, unknown parts within themselves; and above all, to begin recruiting the more healthy, adult part of themselves which usually begins to emerge as the old patterns are challenged. Individual therapists will bring to this part of the work any other skills they have such as Gestalt, art therapy, dream work, CBT, Transpersonal Psychology, working with sub-personalities and guided fantasies etc.

The ending of therapy is always kept explicitly on the agenda, but as the last session approaches, it becomes more of a focus, especially in naming how ending and the loss of the therapist may feel and 'predicting' how the patient may defend against the ending in a number of ways: by a 'flight into health'; by dismissing or unravelling any gains; by denigrating the therapist; or trying to avoid ending altogether by missing the last session. However, these possible reactions should already have been voiced in the Reformulation as they are likely to be manifestations of the reciprocal roles and old defensive patterns. Addressing them directly can often prevent them actually happening, so that the ending can be seen as a corrective emotional experience where the patient can be encouraged perhaps to feel appropriate sadness without feeling abandoned and rejected yet again in their lives. The Goodbye Letters which the patient and therapist each write and which are usually read out and exchanged at the last session, provide a valuable way of summarizing what has happened and how change can be maintained. They can also name disappointments and what has not been achieved and indicate what further work might be done. The exchanging of the Goodbye Letters testifies to the attempt throughout CAT to have a degree of equality between patient and therapist, as far as this is possible in the therapeutic relationship, and, together with the other material, provides the patient with portable tools which they can continue to use after the therapy ends. Generally, a follow-up session is arranged after three months to review how the patient has managed to be 'their own therapist' and to see if further work is needed. This could take the form of a few more follow-up sessions, or a further series of four to six sessions as a 'top-up'; sometimes a further sixteen sessions may be called for or the patient may themselves choose to continue the work in a group or long-term therapy, or by following a specific avenue such as art therapy, psychodrama etc.

CAT offers a way of working with patients which is containing while also being flexible. In spite of its apparent proscriptiveness, it is not the therapeutic equivalent of painting-by-numbers; rather, the structure provides a scaffolding within which each interaction between a patient and a therapist is a unique experience and it creates a space in which there can be profound personal experience. The scaffolding is not a cage. It is a frame on which things can grow.

My use of CAT in GP practice

With up to eight referrals a month and sometimes more, it would be impossible to offer everyone a complete sixteen session CAT as described above. Even reducing the sessions to ten or twelve as I do, does not make it feasible. Nonetheless, CAT provides a 'way of looking' with all my patients which enables me quite quickly to see the patient's distress in terms of core pain, internalized reciprocal roles and repeated defensive patterns. It also provides tools which I find invaluable in order to share such understandings with the patient and to work collaboratively.

The CAT model, in the context of counselling in general practice, is flexible enough to be adapted to suit the particular conditions of the setting. The idea of naming explicitly what is going on for the patient and how their distress is maintained, and sharing this directly with the patient, often in the form of a diagram, can be very helpful even in a single, one-off session. CAT also offers 'tools' which can be used by the GPs and other health professionals in their consultations with the patient. I have run mini-workshops for my colleagues to teach them some of these relatively easy and quick skills for monitoring and naming things explicitly.

It is this CAT framework which creates a safe place in which I believe it is possible to work in a way that is short and deep. It allows me to take the risk of naming my hunches regarding the core pain early on with the patient and, because of its collaborative nature, allows the patient to challenge my hunches, so that we can try another angle to find ways of naming things meaningfully for the patient. There are many different ways in which I do this. It may be no more than drawing a family tree which highlights significant aspects of the patient's life and the role they may feel they have always had to play. I could use a simple diagram, scribbled with the patient during a session, or a more extensive one I might draft out between sessions or together we could draw up a list of several problematic repeated patterns and appropriate ways of breaking the cycles. Then too, having established a rough idea of the patient's situation, we could explore deeper levels by means of some work with the imagination: spot imaging, Gestalt exercises with objects or an empty chair, asking the patient to write a 'fantasy letter' (i.e. one which will never be sent, to someone living or dead or even to an aspect of the self, such as the hurt inner child or the controlling inner bully), inviting the patient to do drawing, painting or collage in order to explore important aspects of their life or to get in touch with difficult feelings. Sometimes I will use patients' dreams or do a short guided fantasy with them. But however we choose to work, the overall purpose is to help the patient understand their pain and distress in terms of the deeper, underlying dynamics and to empower them to find ways of responding to their core pain that are more self-valuing and affirming than the defensive, negative ways in which they have done so in the past.

What makes it possible to work in a GP's surgery in this way? First, I believe that recognition and respect from the GPs for the way in which a counsellor works is imperative. Second, the patient needs to feel safe both in terms of the physical space in which they relate to the counsellor and in terms of the emotional safety which appropriate boundaries and reassurance about confidentiality can provide. And third, the counselling work needs to be respected in practical ways: there needs to be a pleasant, set aside, appropriate space in which patients can be seen by the counsellor free from interruption. Procedures for referral and feedback need to be clear and understood by all and the counsellor's commitment to confidentiality needs to be honoured.

CAT, therefore, whether used as a complete therapy, or as a way of informing more general counselling work, fits in well to the primary care context. It can provide the clear, safe space in which patients feel able to tell their story and, by encouraging explicit responses from the counsellor, it offers the patient the very real experience of being heard. The flexibility of CAT allows for the counselling work to adapt to the needs of the patient which may require that attention is given to the specific medical situation in which the patient finds themself. The context of the GP setting is intrinsic to the work, for the patients' benefit (for example, by helping them see their response to illness in a broader context, or by empowering them to develop the most helpful ways of relating to the medical professionals) and for the benefit of the practice, by providing a way of understanding patients' emotional distress and of enhancing the collaboration between counsellor and the other primary care workers. For instance, I have found basic CAT explanations very helpful for the receptionists at the surgery in understanding and dealing with the very demanding and unpredictable behaviour of a patient who suffers from severe Borderline Personality Disorder.

Fundamentally, I believe that working as a counsellor in a GP surgery means that one is inevitably bound into that context and that this requires a concern for the constraints of time and for the overall setting in which the patient is being seen.

Conclusion

Fundamentally, I believe that working as a counsellor in a GP surgery means that one is inevitably bound into that context and that this requires a concern for the constraints of time and for the overall setting in which the patient is being seen.

Time-limited counselling interventions in a general practice setting need not be superficial, but can have a degree of sophistication that enables the patient and counsellor to reach deep levels of meaning, even in a short time. For me, the understandings and tools of Cognitive Analytic Therapy are invaluable in trying to achieve this.

There is a challenge facing those who do counselling in primary care to find creative and meaningful ways of working while still respecting the issues of resources and time. And there needs to be generous sharing of this amongst counsellors so that a climate can be created in which the whole person of the patient can be respected and in which the counsellor's art can be allowed to flourish.

REFERENCES

Beck, A.T. (1976) *Cognitive Therapy and the Emotional Disorders*, New York: International Universities Press.

Corney, Roslyn and Jenkins, Rachel (1993) *Counselling in General Practice*, London: Routledge.

Kelly, G.A. (1955) *The Psychology of Personal Constructs*, New York: Norton.

Levi, Primo (1987) *If This Is A Man – The Truce*, London: Abacus

Malan, D.H. (1963) *A Study of Brief Psychotherapy*, London: Tavistock.

Mann, J. (1973) *Time-limited Psychotherapy*, Cambridge, MA: Harvard University Press.

Mann, J. and Goldman, R. (1982) *A Casebook in Time-limited Psychotherapy*, New York: McGraw-Hill.

Ryle, Anthony (1990) *Cognitive-Analytic Therapy: Active Participation In Change*, Chichester: Wiley.

Ryle, Anthony (ed.) (1995) *Cognitive Analytic Therapy – Developments In Theory and Practice*, Chichester: Wiley.

Ryle, Anthony (1997) *Cognitive Analytic Therapy and Borderline Personality Disorder*, Chichester: Wiley.

Wilde McCormick, Elizabeth (1996) *Change For The Better*, London: Cassell.

5 A holistic approach to working in general practice

Jonathan Whines

In this chapter I wish to discuss a holistic approach to counselling in general practice. My concept of holism is informed by my practice as a Gestalt Psychotherapist. Initially I would like to consider what this approach offers from a philosophical perspective.

Introduction

Gestalt therapy has its philosophical roots in both existential and phenomenological thinking. It also draws upon notions of holism and Field Theory. The existential concepts which continue to inform Gestalt include the philosophical notions of freedom, responsibility, authenticity and anxiety. People are seen as meaning-making beings who strive constantly to create meaning for themselves in an environment where meanings change.

Juxtaposed against this existential austerity is an equally powerful belief in the inter-connectedness of all life, in terms of figure and ground and of the intrinsic holism of the individual. These latter notions are taken, in part, from the work of the South African Jan Smuts (Smuts 1926). Facilitating the client in the awareness of the authentic truth of his whole being remains central to Gestalt practice. The emphasis of the therapeutic work is placed upon the lived experience of the therapist and the client in the here-and-now.

My own practice, and much of contemporary Gestalt counselling, has moved away from its origins in confrontation and challenge towards a more dialogic stance (Hycner 1987). This approach emphasises a dialogue in which the therapist explores what Hycner (1985:26) terms the client's 'relational stance'. In this approach 'theory is only the initial movement but no substitute for the encounter' (Hycner 1985:27). Thus the client is encouraged to be aware of his contact with the therapist. Central questions in this approach become 'How are you meeting me and how does this meeting reflect upon the issues you bring?'

This means that the client's process of contact and meaning-making becomes a primary focus within the therapeutic session. It is in this close attention to the meaning-making and processing of the client beyond the specific content of what the client brings, that Gestalt therapy is possibly distinctive. Whilst other approaches may track the client's process, interpret the client or establish the client's goals, the Gestalt counsellor engages both with the client's way of meeting and with the client's meaning-making processes: i.e. 'How do you make this a good or bad experience?'. In this way the client is encouraged to explore how, in the present relationship, he re-plays the unfinished Gestalts or patterns of the past.

Central to this approach is the belief that if the individual as a child is formed in relation then new awareness must also occur through relationship. Even more radically, Gestalt therapists believe that the self *is* contact. Thus the self is not some static 'personality' or structure but rather a process which arises through contact with the Other. Whilst clients will frequently present with a 'symptom', the issue that will frequently produce deep and sustained change is addressing how they make or interrupt contact with their own process or with the counsellor. At the same time the symptom clearly needs to be addressed in its own right, as I shall discuss later.

The general practice setting: the medical model

Importing the above model into a medical setting is clearly not going to occur without some difficulty. Clients will inevitably arrive with a set of preconceptions about the nature of counselling. Frequently these preconceptions will be based upon their previous experience of professional health workers whose practice will fit into a predominantly medical model.

The medical model is characterized by a number of features. There is usually considerable emphasis placed upon the symptom and its relief, without reference to a wider, more holistic, picture. The body is seen as a sophisticated machine with little reference made to the social and emotional field. As Gerunds and Kampmann state, discussing the medical model:

> The first assumption is that a human being can be exhaustively described as a highly complex machine. The second assumption, logically connected to the first one, is that this type of machine – like all machines – is susceptible to dysfunction caused by inbuilt irregularities or by external damaging factors. The third assumption is that this machine is unable to reconstitute itself actively or even consciously, is

unable to define dysfunction or to re-establish its way of functioning. All 'repair' work has to be done by an external agent while the human being remains passive and subject to the disease and suffering.

(Gerunds and Kampmann 1996:84)

If we contrast the medical model suggested above with Tom Greening's five basic postulates of humanistic psychology, within which Gestalt broadly stands, we can see that the two models exist in stark contrast:

1   Human beings, as human, supersede the sum of their parts. They cannot be reduced to components.
2   Human beings have their existence in a uniquely human context, as well as in a cosmic ecology.
3   Human beings are aware and are aware of being aware i.e. they are conscious. Human consciousness always includes an awareness of oneself in the context of other people.
4   Human beings have some choice and, with that, responsibility.
5   Human beings are intentional, aim at goals, are aware that they cause future events, and seek meaning, value and creativity.

(Gerunds and Kampmann 1996:3)

Whilst the medical model has clearly been demonstrated to be highly effective in its application to disease, the danger is that the patient can be reduced to a cluster of 'components'. Further, the presenting symptom is not explored within the holistic environment of the patient's own innate self-healing capacity but is treated in isolation. Reducing the patient to a physical symptom divorced from the emotional context is the *reductio ad absurdum* of this approach.

As Perls notes: 'We believe that the mental–physical or mind–body split is a totally artificial one, and that to concentrate on either term in this false dichotomy is to preserve neurosis not to cure it' (Perls 1976:53).

At the same time clients may collude in this sense of their own fragmentation and passivity as they look to the doctor to 'cure' not just symptoms but aspects of their life for which they are unwilling to take responsibility.

There are clearly tensions which exist in the dialectic between the medical model and the holistic model. Yet with sensitivity these tensions can generate a very creative outcome. The presence of a counsellor within a general practice can allow the doctor to focus more clearly upon the medical and physical ailments of their patients in the knowledge that they have support available for patients who are emotionally distressed. Equally, the very distinctiveness of the relationship with the counsellor, who has far greater time than the doctor and can explore in detail the wider field, makes the impact of the meeting and the potential for healing all the greater. The holistic approach will certainly offer a challenge both to the client's sense of passivity and fragmentation. As Perls states:

> We are as we are today – fractionalised people – people who are split up into bits and pieces. It's no use to analyse these bits and pieces and cut them up still more. What we want to do in Gestalt therapy is to integrate all the dispersed and disowned parts of the self and make the person whole again.
>
> (1976:181)

The general practice setting: the client's preconceptions

The attitude of the client, determined in part by previous encounters with the health service, may manifest in a number of ways which distinguish them from counselling in other non-medical settings:

- The client will sometimes be surprised at the interest taken in their wider life. They may initially see this interest as 'not relevant'. There is often an expectation that the counsellor will focus exclusively upon symptoms. Symptomatic relief is initially seen as more important to the client than a wider holistic exploration which incorporates the figure of the symptom within the wider field of their life and their history. However, taking a detailed history of the client's life is invaluable in order to understand the client's predominant interruptions to contact. Central to this is an appreciation of the nature of the relationship between the primary carers and the client as a child. Whilst Gestalt tends to focus strongly on the client in the present, a firm understanding of their past will enable the counsellor to understand rapidly how current behaviour is a repetition of unfinished patterns. Helping the client identify these patterns throughout their life can in itself produce significant new awareness.
- The typical six-session model used in many surgeries can induce a sense of urgency in the client which can be experienced as positive or negative. How the counsellor handles this and especially the framing of what is achievable within six sessions is crucial. For example, a client with a desperate history of neglect may wish to 'get totally sorted' in six sessions, whereas what is achievable may be creating a sense of trust or that the client simply feels heard. The counsellor needs to be realistic and honest about what is achievable. Equally, a well motivated client may use the six sessions to work through a full and highly specific agenda of issues.

- Counselling within a medical setting is currently a free service for the user. For the client this may mean that there is literally less investment in engaging in the counselling process than if they were to attend privately. The client preconception can therefore swing both ways: the relationship can thus be valued both more and also less precisely because it is free. It is certainly true that many counsellors report anec-dotally that clients within a medical setting appear less committed than those who pay.

- The client's attitude towards the counsellor and the counselling process can be considerably influenced by the nature of the referral. The GP's own orientation towards counselling can clearly help to establish the client's expectations. The client who arrives saying 'The doctor said you'd sort me out' clearly has a long way to go as does the doctor in his understanding of the process of counselling! Where there is a GP-led referral the development of the working alliance can be more difficult. If the patient feels coerced into attending then it clearly takes careful and subtle work even to begin.

- The whole medical setting is likely to engender heightened trans-ferential issues, as the counsellor is initially invested with the power and authority of the Primary Care setting. Clients in this setting may be more likely to seek 'advice' and be more compliant with the requests of the counsellor. Clearly the counsellor in this situation needs to be 'transparent' with the client and explain that his role is one of facilitation.

- There is often a preconception by the client that even though the session is fifty minutes they should be quick and/or that they are 'wasting the counsellor's time'. Patients in Primary Care are used to five-minute interviews so that fifty minutes is often perceived as a luxury.

The general practice setting as a context for counselling

The medical setting can clearly affect both the counsellor's view of them-selves and of their client. The counsellor needs to be fully aware of these issues and the impact they may have upon the work:

- The counsellor may be aware of 'kudos' relating to working within the medical establishment. This may or may not confer upon the counsellor a slightly different sense of value or importance compared to working in other settings. The counsellor will frequently use the GP's own room and have access to all the same administrative back-up. This may engender a greater sense of personal authority within the counsellor. This can clearly be either useful or detrimental in the establishment of a working alliance with the client i.e. the client may assume a greater level of competence in the counsellor because he is seen in this setting. Equally, if the patient has had bad experiences in the practice it may take time to generate trust and the beginnings of a working alliance.

- The counsellor will usually have access to detailed medical notes encompassing the whole of the client's life. Reading these notes may immediately affect the counsellor's response to the client if, for example, they have a history of violence, crime, abuse etc. In addition, access to these notes may enhance the counsellor's sense of omnipotence and power in viewing the client.
- The client will usually already have a history in the surgery prior to referral. Comments from doctors or receptionists may also establish preconceptions: 'Oh, Mrs Jones, you'll just love working with her'.
- Finally the counsellor brings with them their major preconception: the theoretical model with which they work. The belief that any single theory or methodology is sufficient when working in general practice is likely to be quickly challenged by the diversity of patients' needs. Counsellors in this setting need to be adept at creative adaption. Holistic, in this sense, means a willingness to draw upon a wide range of approaches to meet their client's needs. Whilst one client may respond beautifully to a goal-oriented cognitive approach the next client may require a careful regression back to a specific piece of unfinished business which prevents them moving forward.

A holistic methodology for general practice counselling

Clearly the counsellor needs a methodology out of which to operate, although such principles need to be constantly available for deconstruction or re-appraisal. Central to my own practice in general practice currently are the ideas of:

- Assessment and time-conscious counselling: phenomenological exploration
- Field theory
- Dialogic relationship
- Contact functioning and body process
- Creative experimentation

Assessment and time-conscious counselling

Some counsellors struggle with the concept of assessment, as it appears to be part of the medical model where the counsellor is seen as constructing themselves as an 'expert'. However, it seems that it is impossible *not* to assess. As we meet our new client so we are inevitably generating an inner dialogue about how we perceive them. It would therefore seem more useful to place our assessment within a model which is respectful of the individual whilst clearly acknowledging the danger of labelling. My own approach to assessment is based upon the principles of phenomenological exploration which contrast significantly with a traditional psychological assessment. Whilst the latter may involve a diagnosis which results in the application of a category or label such as found in DSM IV, the holistic approach involves the minute exploration of the client's view of themselves. Thus the client's uniqueness is respected whilst not precluding the use of data such as that found in texts like DSM IV to help support and understand the client's distress. The phenomenological methodology involves three elements. These are, epoche or bracketing, description and horizontalism:

- *Bracketing* requires that we meet our client's experience as Bion (1959) says 'without memory and without desire'. Thus we endeavour to experience our client without interpretation or association. This is not to say that we may not have personal reactions, but that we temporarily set these aside in order to meet our client where they are.
- *Description* again requires that rather than interpreting our client we allow the client to explore their own phenomenology and that the counsellor simply describes this evolving process. As Perls states: 'Since contact always occurs on the surface, it is the surface the therapist must see. But make no mistake about it that surface is much broader and more significant than the average therapist will admit' (Perls 1973:75). He further suggests that we have to 'shift the concern of psychiatry from the fetish of the unknown, the adoration of the "unconscious", to the problem of the phenomenology of awareness' (Perls, Hefferline and Goodman 1973:53).
- *Horizontalism* requires that all aspects of the client's experience are given equal priority. The counsellor's power of selection is temporarily suspended so that the totality of the client's experience is simply held. This process of equalization allows the true figure of the client's concern to emerge.

From this paradoxical perspective of 'detached engagement' the counsellor can proceed to observe more specific aspects of the assessment via phenomenological exploration:

- **Contact functions**: How does the client move? The quality of their voice; the process of their eye contact; how easily they can hear what is said to them.
- **Contact boundary**: How does the client meet me? How do they hold or break contact? When do they engage and when do they move away?
- **Cycle of experience**: How does the client start, continue and finish a train of thought or an activity both within the session and in his life? How does he contact or interrupt the meeting of his needs? What prevents the meeting of these needs? What unfinished business or fixed Gestalts impinge upon the meeting?
- **Self and environmental support**: How does the client support themselves internally? How do they support themselves physically within the session? How well do they breathe? Can they take support from the counsellor? Are they very needy or over independent?
- **The field**: How is the environment impacting upon this client? To what degree are there aspects of the client's life which are out of their control?
- **Counsellor's response**: How do I feel about this client? Do they remind me of anyone? Are there issues of countertransference?
- **The client's goal**: What does the client wish to achieve? If they could wave a magic wand how would they wish to change their life? What needs to happen for them to move from their present state to achieve their goal? The client's stated goal, frequently the expiation of symptoms, sits within a complex nexus of their history, their environment and their relational stance. It is only in the subtle exploration of all these elements that the client can begin to move forward. An accurate assessment can therefore enable the counsellor to become very precise in co-defining the area which most needs attention. Where this occurs the client's progress can be extremely rapid.

The counsellor in general practice is constantly faced with choices. The first choice occurs in assessment; is this client available for counselling? Jenifer Elton Wilson describes three types of client:

- Clients 'in crisis' – who are not seeking psychological change.
- Clients who are 'visiting' – they are testing out whether counselling is for them.
- Clients 'willing to engage' – they are willing to take personal responsibility for their psychological change and commit to a specified number of sessions.

Clearly the three different categories of clients require different responses and levels of commitment from the counsellor. Clients in the first two categories may require a 'holding' arrangement whilst their needs are clarified. Clients in the third category may require an initial commitment which, subject to review, may lead to longer-term work or to termination of the commitment. As Elton Wilson describes: 'At each stage, the client is invited into a clearly stated two-way commitment with an established focus related to the type of relationship operating between client and therapist (Elton Wilson 1996:2).

Having clarified that the client is available to commit to the counselling process, the counsellor in time-conscious work is immediately faced with further choices. For example, a client presents because she is experiencing panic attacks. The counsellor needs to establish the degree to which they work with (1) the wider field within which the symptom exists or (2) the management of the panic. The client will frequently be very focused upon (2) the removal of the symptoms; i.e. shortness of breath, palpitations, or the feeling that they may die. Yet the counsellor's experience will suggest that exploration of (1) the wider field may yield a more sustained outcome. At the same time the symptoms are disabling and if the counsellor is working in a phenomenological fashion he must respect his client's pressing need. However, therapies that work in a purely solution-focused way, which responds only to the client's stated need may miss the more causal layers of contact functioning and field theory whilst therapies which are purely phenomenological may lose the drive and 'edge' generated by more goal-orientated approaches. Effective counselling clearly needs to engage with both the field from which the symptom has arisen and its management within the present.

Time-conscious counselling will therefore almost always involve some degree of negotiation with the client as to what is attainable and possible within a finite number of sessions. This is where it is most important that the counsellor works within a dialogic methodology which both respects the client's needs and also the counsellor's commitment to an authentic dialogue.

Field theory

Field theory, as Lewin (1952) suggests, is not so much a theory as 'a way of thinking'. This approach requires that 'the overall picture or total situation is appreciated as a whole'. There needs to be a recognition of 'the organised, interconnected, interdependent, interactive nature of complex human phenomena'. As Parlett comments: 'With a field theory outlook, we abandon looking for single causes. . . . Within a field there is a constantly changing distribution of forces affecting things in the field. Events are determined by the nature of the field as a whole' (Parlett 1992:2).

Assessment thus allows the counsellor to generate what I conceive of as a 'landscape' of the client's life, or field, in which the symptom is initially the focus. The client cannot be understood in isolation but only as an interactive whole within the field. It is only by holding the client's field and the meaning with which they endow this, along with their presenting issue, that the counsellor can allow the true figure of the client's need to emerge. By understanding this wider environment the symptom can become significantly re-configured.

The dialogic relationship

Whereas the medical model is necessarily characterized by a fundamental imbalance of power and knowledge, the practitioner engaging in a dialogic relationship constantly strives to explore what occurs 'between' the two participants. The therapeutic relationship is therefore used as a microcosm within which to explore the client's wider world. Every point of contact within the session is a reflection of the client's history and as such can be respectfully explored to develop awareness. The dialogic relationship is characterized by three main elements which are seen as necessary qualities for achieving what Martin Buber (1984) calls an 'I–Thou' dialogue where two people encounter one another openly and non-defensively:

- **Presence**: Whilst other forms of counselling may emphasize the centrality of the client or adopt a stance of neutrality, Gestalt counselling is strongly committed to authenticity. This means that the counsellor is willing to meet the client honestly rather than simply adopting a caring role. By modelling authenticity the client is encouraged to both be honest and discover their own authenticity.
- **Inclusion**: Working with here-and-now awareness the counsellor endeavours to enter the experience of the client and then confirm that they have understood what they have apprehended. At the same time it is important that the counsellor retains a sense of self and does not become immersed in the client's feelings.
- **Genuine communication**: Being both present and inclusive, the counsellor offers the client authentic responses. The counsellor is 'not just a mirror or an interpreter' (Sills, Fish and Lapworth 1995:112). Thus he offers authentic reactions whether of irritation or pleasure whilst holding respect for the whole being of the client.

Contact functioning and body process

At the heart of any holistic practice must lie a willingness to explore not only mental/emotional processes but what Kepner (1993) calls 'body process'. Central to this idea is that the body has its own truth, yet because of our absorption in 'the middle zone' (Sill, Fish and Lapworth 1995:27) or the realm of fantasy and projection, this wisdom is frequently avoided. In body process the client is encouraged to develop awareness of what their body is telling them. This will often involve the client re-educating how they breathe and re-establishing a new relationship with their body as a purveyor of valuable information.

Gestalt counselling sees health as a return by the client to organismic integrity (Perls, Hefferline and Goodman 1973), that is to the fundamental truths of his biologic body and being. Central to this understanding of the self is the belief that human beings strive for health, balance and growth. During early childhood the individual does its best to adapt to its environment. However, this will frequently involve the blocking of needs as they will inevitably not all be met. This in turn results in the individual interrupting contact both with themselves and their needs and with other people. These processes of blocking and interruption to contact are often carried into adult life and will affect all relationships, including the therapeutic one. Thus the client's development is intrinsically connected with his identification of these blocks and their subsequent deconstruction.

Using this notion of contact and interruptions to contact, the counsellor may observe both how the client makes contact with himself and how he makes contact with the counsellor. Thus some clients will frequently have a very low level of awareness about themselves. They will be unable to tell you what they like or what they feel sometimes even about the most simple aspects of their life. They will typically use alienated language when referring to themselves, 'one feels depressed', 'it feels bad'. Another client will find it very difficult to stay in the here-and-now of their pain. They will do anything they can to avoid the actuality of who they are. They will frequently speak quickly or in a rather elliptical fashion. Yet another client will have absorbed rules or parental edicts from the past and be acting on them without awareness. 'I really should work harder and be a better person.' 'I really should do the homework that my counsellor sets me in a perfect fashion.'

These interruptions to contact should not be conceived as pathological but rather as creative adaptions to a former inhospitable emotional terrain. They should also not be seen as inevitable fixtures but rather as current, and hopefully, transient solutions. If in their childhood it was not acceptable to feel emotions then to emotionally desensitize would have been an entirely appropriate solution. Thus there may be times when it is important to interrupt contact. What is crucial is that the blocking or interruption to contact occurs in full awareness.

Creative experimentation

Whilst an awareness of interruptions to contact is a central aspect of Gestalt counselling the use of creative experimentation enables this understanding to be more fully developed. The use of such experimentation as role play, dance, artwork and any other naturally occurring forms of creative process are central to my therapeutic work. Experimentation is crucial to a holistic practice for it enables the client to begin to loosen and free the energy which is blocked and atrophied within their being and which is constellated within the 'symptom'. Whilst it is very seductive to 'talk about' one's dis-ease, it is altogether more challenging yet potentially liberating to experiment with new ways of being or behaving. As Zinker suggests, within the ongoing dance between challenge and support, experimentation is a crucial form of exploration:

> In the creative process, the therapist enables the patient to join him in an adventure in which the pair constantly play all parts of this conflict drama. The therapist helps the client to be the experimenter, the teacher, the active modifier, while maintaining an attitude of understanding and respect for his client's existing stance. It is in this process of rhythmic sharing and active exploration of the client's inner life that his original personal structure begins to change.
>
> (Zinker 1978:22)

As the client experiments with new ways of behaving and discovers that this is acceptable, so the old patterns can recede and the client is enabled to move forward.

Case history: Sally

The client

This client was an attractive 24-year-old woman. She had received a degree level education. She was articulate and reasonably insightful about herself. She held a management position in a local company where she was very happy. She described her childhood as happy and her parents as loving.

Presenting symptoms

The client initially attended because she was experiencing massive panic attacks which she found very debilitating. The most recent one had occurred whilst she was on holiday abroad. As she was hoping to work abroad in the future she was very anxious at any recurrence of the feelings. She had been referred by her GP.

Client's goals

- For the panic attacks to stop
- To understand the specific cause of her panic

The client was clearly very symptom focused and believed that there was one single cause rather than a nexus of causes existing within the wider field of her life.

Initial time-conscious contract

Whilst I understood that the client wanted her symptoms to abate I explained that we would need to explore the wider context in which this was happening. She was initially quite resistant to this idea and seemed unwilling to take any responsibility for the fact that she was generating her panic. However, as we worked through the first session she grudgingly agreed to explore what might be driving her feelings of panic. We agreed to meet for a further five sessions.

Initial client phenomenology

Everything about this client was very fast including her verbal delivery and her processing of responses from me. It was as though she was constantly trying to guess what I was going to say. In addition she would veer rapidly from stating that she was OK to collapsing into despair regarding her panic attacks. At the beginning she constantly returned to the issue of her panic yet when I focused her experientially upon the panic she would work very hard to move away from any sense of personal responsibility. Initially Sally would literally look at me for answers to her problems as if I was a doctor who was going to dispense advice. She clearly saw me as an authority figure.

Managing the symptom

Whilst it is important to explore the wider field of the client's life, the management of symptoms are nonetheless also imperative to any holistic approach to counselling. In the early sessions I therefore pointed out to Sally the pace at which she was both presenting herself and leading her life. I also remarked upon how little she fully breathed and spent time on showing her a method of breathing more fully. Her heightened awareness of her body and her breathing made an immediate impact and her symptoms started to reduce.

Childhood emotional blueprint

Sally brought a number of beliefs from her childhood which were causing her to establish an internal environment in which panic was likely to occur. Whilst her upbringing had been essentially loving, there was a considerable emphasis upon achievement. Sally felt that she should consistently be a high achiever and therefore set herself impossibly high goals. In addition it was not acceptable in her family to show emotional distress. It was expected that she would 'cope'. She therefore worked and played very hard but was unable to reveal any feelings of stress regarding this demanding pace.

Contact styles

Sally was clearly interrupting her contact with herself and with me by a variety of blocks including her fast pace, fast talking, her goal-orientated way of thinking and the fact that for her it was not acceptable to display 'negative' feelings. These were all aspects of her contacting style. In the early sessions Sally was quite wary of sharing her emotions. At one point she asked about my qualifications as a counsellor. It felt as though in her perfectionism she demanded that she must have the best qualified counsellor. Similarly, as her trust of me developed so I pointed out that she was trying to be the perfect client by always completing all her 'homework' in a very exacting and at times punitive fashion. Finally, whilst she was comfortable to intellectually speculate about her panic she found it difficult to slow down and sit with herself and the real possibility that in the silence she might panic. This was in part because Sally's history had led her to expect criticism if she was not busy 'doing'.

Sally imagined that I would easily become bored with her and criticise her apparent lack of 'progress'.

Developments: the wider field

As Sally began to practise slowing down, breathing more fully and being generally kinder to herself so she became more trusting of me. On the second session she commented that she felt 'met' by me and was glad that I'd been 'honest' about her need to explore beyond the symptoms. As her trust developed she recalled a very intense relationship which had occurred in the early months of her time at university. She had met a man who whilst initially kind had become violently possessive. Sally described her upbringing as very protected and that she felt she had no resources with which to stand up to such emotional intensity. On several occasions the man hit her and once threatened to kill her. As she had only been at university a short time she felt very isolated and unable to tell anyone. One day after she had been speaking with another man her boyfriend grabbed her around the throat: she suddenly remembered that this was the first time she had experienced a panic attack. After five months she finally managed to leave him.

Creative experimentation

Having described this experience I suggested that she imagine bringing the man into the counselling session and expressing how she felt about his behaviour. This creative experimentation allowed Sally to complete something which was clearly unfinished in the relationship. By encouraging her to work 'in the present' with the man who had caused her so much pain she ceased to 'talk about' but rather, experienced, a sense of emotional completion. Sally did this with considerable energy and returned the following session feeling a lot better. However she felt that ever since the strangling incident she had been waiting for an apology. Again, it seemed that his behaviour did not fit into the emotional blueprint of her upbringing, he 'should' have apologized. As she gradually and painfully accepted that he never could apologize so she withdrew her energy from him and let go of her attachment.

The panic which she had previously described as a 'bulldozer', 'a powerhouse out of control', became invested with a totally different meaning. Rather than seeing this as an alien energy which overtook her

Sally saw it as all the dammed up anger about the abuse she had received, which she had turned against herself. Ever since this relationship she had continued the punishment which the man had begun. The painful lesson which she had learnt was that in her childhood she had not been taught to defend herself, which had left her open to attack and abuse.

With this dissociated energy re-connected Sally rapidly regained her equilibrium. She became more confident and acceptant that she might occasionally panic but that if she did she would both know why it was happening and how to manage herself. As her symptoms became re-configured within the light of her history and her understanding of the interruptions to contact so Sally was enabled to move forward. At her final counselling session she had not experienced a panic attack for several months and had gained promotion into a new job. It was her intention to work abroad the following year.

Sally initially had a very punitive view of any emotions which she considered 'negative'. Yet by modelling acceptance and conveying empathy she began to cease being so critical both of others (including me) and of herself. Similarly by modelling my authentic reactions to her she began to give herself permission to be more congruent. It was only when this had occurred that she was able to relate the most difficult part of her history and produce a satisfactory resolution.

There is clearly an inherent tension existing between an open-ended phenomenological approach which slowly allows the client's needs to emerge and placing this within a typical six-session time-conscious framework. Yet this tension can frequently be highly creative. Whilst Gestalt has historically been orientated towards longer-term work it adapts very successfully into a time-conscious framework which is comprised of mini-contracts. The client can be met with all the respect and confirmation which characterizes longer term work whilst being periodically re-focused by such solution-orientated questions as: 'What do you wish to achieve here'? 'If this was the last session what would you have hoped to have achieved'? Initially focusing on the client's history enables the counsellor to move fluidly between the contact styles of the past and how this is repeated in the present within both the session and the client's current life.

Conclusion

A counselling practice which adheres to holistic principles within a time-conscious frame clearly requires considerable skill and sophistication on the part of the counsellor as all the various elements within the therapeutic field are held. As the client and counsellor arrive for their first meeting it becomes apparent that they frequently bring with them two distinct agendas. The client is likely to be symptom-focused and to see the counsellor as an authority figure who will provide answers. By contrast, the counsellor is likely to be concerned with a wider, more holistic picture of the client and with the solutions which emanate from this context. He will probably view himself as a co-worker rather than an authority figure. In addition the client will often perceive their current symptoms or sickness as something about which they feel shame. Again in contrast the counsellor will frequently see symptoms as a message from the wider system of the self. For the counsellor symptoms may be seen as metaphors which the client has not currently de-coded accurately. The deciphering of the symptom-metaphor is frequently a crucial aspect of the healing process.

Clients will often describe their symptoms or particular distress early in the session. It therefore becomes crucial to take a detailed history of the client's life so that the symptoms may be seen within the wider landscape of their life. The symptoms or issue which the client brings is initially figural for them. Yet as the client becomes increasingly aware of his contact functioning and is encouraged to experiment with new ways of being and doing so the symptoms as with Sally, almost invariably become invested with a different and healthier meaning.

If we again contrast these ideas to that of the medical model it is apparent that counsellors offering a holistic approach are creating a very distinct and special environment in which their clients can re-discover themselves. With the increasing adoption of counselling within medical settings it seems crucial that the principles and practice of holism are not replaced by mere goal-orientated, technique based solutions, i.e., that the medical model does not simply absorb the techniques of counselling whilst rejecting its fundamental ethos. At the same time counsellors need to remain open to a creative dialogue which uses the best from both the medical and the holistic models. This may in turn mean that counsellors become more rigorous about outcomes and evidenced-based practice, without losing the fundamental principle that if healing is to occur it does so through the authentic meeting of counsellor and client within a transparent dialogue.

REFERENCES

The American Psychiatric Association (1996) *Diagnostic and Statistical Manual of Mental Disorders*, DSM IV, The American Psychiatric Association, Washington.

Bion, W.R. (1959) *Experiences in Groups*, Basic Books, New York.

Buber, M. (1984) *I and Thou*, (2nd ed), T. and T. Clark, Edinburgh.

Elton Wilson, J. (1996) *Time-Conscious Psychological Therapy*, Routledge, London.

Gerunds, H. and Kampmann, B. (1996) 'The medical model and the Gestalt approach', *British Gestalt Journal* 5 (2): 84.

Hycner, R.H. (1985) 'Dialogical Gestalt therapy: an initial proposal', *The Gestalt Journal* 8 (1): 23.

Hycner, R.H. (1987) 'An Interview with Irving and Miriam Polster' *The Gestalt Journal* 10 (2): 29.

Kepner, J. (1993) *Body Process*, Jossey-Bass, San Francisco.

Lewin, K. (1952) *Field Theory in Social Science*, Tavistock, London.

Parlett, M. (1992) Transcript of Plenary Lecture at the European Gestalt Conference, Paris.

Perls, F., Hefferline, R. and Goodman, P. (1973) *Gestalt Therapy: Excitement and Growth in the Human Personality*, Penguin Books, London. [Originally published by Julian Books, New York 1951.]

Perls, F. (1976) *The Gestalt Approach and Eye Witness to Therapy*, Bantam Books, New York. [First published 1973.]

Sills, C., Fish, S. and Lapworth, P. (1995) *Gestalt Counselling*, Winslow Press, Bicester.

Smuts, J. (1926) *Holism and Evolution*, Cape Town: N and S Press.

Zinker, J. (1978) *Creative Process in Gestalt Therapy*, Vintage Books, New York.

6 The matrix at work: a post-Jungian approach to general practice counselling

Anna Bravesmith

Introduction

I have been thinking about what is central to psychodynamic work in general practice and what makes it so challenging to the medical conceptual framework that predominates there, along with the administrative/financial conceptual framework. For me the central issue is the symbolic quality of the counsellor's work and the great extension of symbolic thinking that can begin to happen as a result, in patients and other general practice staff. This chapter presents a psychodynamic perspective within the Jungian/Kleinian tradition. Some of the ideas presented were developed in consultation with my colleagues in the London Implementation Zone-funded GP counselling project based at Thorpe Coombe Hospital. The main themes are the place of the analytic attitude in primary care; the defences used against anxiety and the fear of thinking about paradox; and the notion of counselling as part of a matrix rather than a dyad and the analysis of unconscious processes in making referrals. The idea that GPs refer parts of themselves represented in the patient is explored with disguised clinical examples.

The analytic attitude

The basis of the work is what Fordham and others have called 'the analytic attitude', which consists of an attitude of mind that is impartial and 'seeks to elucidate the patient's conflicts with a view to helping him to resolve them' (Fordham 1995: 146). Furthermore, the counsellor, or psychotherapist's, technique is to provide conditions under which the patient can express himself freely, and in which complex data can be unpacked in each encounter and reduced to its simplest components. The attitude is the same as that which is used in analysis and Fordham went on to make the controversial statement 'Once the analytical attitude is grasped, it becomes apparent that interview frequency is not the essence of analysis. It can take place in a single interview, or in meeting once a week, once a month or even occasionally' (Fordham 1995 : 147). How can we reconcile this idea with the reality of short-term work that often extends for only eight or twelve face-to-face sessions? I hope to be able to illustrate with clinical examples how I personally have begun to integrate an 'analytic attitude' with the conditions of short-term work. I do not know if analysis can take place 'in a single interview' as Fordham claimed – certainly what is achieved cannot be compared to what can be achieved in a rigorous, frequent, long-term analysis where things go well. Nevertheless perhaps a qualitative sample of analysis is available to patients who would not embark on analysis. I think of this as resembling a slice of layer cake that is deep and includes all the textures and flavours of the whole cake, despite being limited in substantiality.

Focus and the analytic attitude

One of my patients in the GP surgery setting said to me that he did not know how I could help him, but he knew how I could fail, and that would be if I tried to focus on his positive feelings. I indicated my impartiality about whether he felt positive or negative and encouraged him to make use of the counselling sessions as he wished. He was then able to talk about the despair and violence inside him, and explore in the transference how much he feared being overwhelmed by these, as it emerged that he thought it was I who was afraid to hear about his fantasies. This patient brought in the concept of 'focus', as he was an experienced counselling patient who had received brief counselling from a number of professionals. The necessity of having a mutually agreed focus is a subject I will now explore since it has an important bearing on my subject.

The young man who objected to a focus on 'positive thinking', which he had encountered with a previous counsellor, illustrates how it may be that the choice of focus undermines the analytic attitude. The focus is necessary because of the brevity of time available, and also serves a function in the process of forming a working alliance with the patient because of its mutuality. It also offers a sense of security for patients who are usually new-comers to psychodynamic work, and may even be unfamiliar with talking about themselves in any way. However some patients need a focus less than others, or can usefully re-define the focus after some work has been done. The challenge lies in using a focus that does not incorporate partiality, stipulate, even by implication, the removal of symptoms, or tie the work to a concrete mode or a mode that excludes unconscious material. Therefore a focus in psychodynamic work would usually involve seeking to explore, understand, elaborate or find meaning in some conflict of the patient, rather than having a concrete aim like getting back to work, stopping rows with a partner or giving up an internet addiction.

The patient who could not finish his third MA

An example that comes to mind in my own experience is that of a man approaching thirty who arranged to be referred to me by the GP because he could not finish his MA dissertation. He asked me to focus on this in the first meeting as an aim and I commented that to do so would pre-suppose that he *should* finish his dissertation, and pre-empt all exploration of the meaning behind his reluctance and its place in the organization of his life. It emerged that this was his third Masters Degree, and in talking he mentioned that he had met a Chinese girl, become interested in Chinese culture and went to China to study it. I said 'So it was not because you fell in love with the Chinese girl?' He was then able to discuss the difficulty he had in loving, or falling in love, and to indicate the extensive use of intellectual defences against relatedness in his personality. He was on the brink of becoming aware of these defences, as he was now getting more involved with his girlfriend with enormous difficulty and self-punishing manoeuvres. The dissertation revealed itself as sterile and he could no longer effect a feeling of having intercourse with his own ideas through it. The girlfriend nevertheless was seen by him as a destructive influence that he should discard in order to further his studies. A crisis was reached when she became pregnant with his child during the period in which he had counselling. Amidst terrible anxiety, this forced him to explore his ambivalence and allow emotional feeling its place in him, a human being who was frightened but not feelingless. I referred this patient for long-term psychotherapy after completion of his work with me, as he made leaps into developing tolerance of his own ambivalence. He extended his capacity to think on a symbolic level and thus began to be able 'not to know', even to contemplate paradox. I cannot say whether he was 'cured' or 'got better' but he developed.

Paradox and the fear of thought disorder

The doctors I have worked with often ask me if a patient is 'getting better' and I give them rather qualified answers, for example, saying that the resolution of one problem has now given way to the emergence of another. This leads me on to describe what I see as an important contributory factor in the medical resistance to symbolic processes. The phenomenon is described by Meltzer in a paper called 'Conflicts of desire and paradoxes of thought' where he says: 'That is to say, what conflict of love and hate (ambivalence) is for emotional disorders, paradox is for the thought disorders' (Meltzer 1987: 559).

It saves us from despair to know or feel that we know, and the contemplation of paradox can be too great a burden and requires arguably, a great deal of maturity. I say 'arguably' because there can also be a type of avoidance in deliberate confusion of the truth, which is not mature. This, it seems to me, is where incompatible pieces of knowledge are agglomerated perversely, and is different from paradox where there is an understanding that pieces of experience only seem incompatible but in reality fit together or are two aspects of the same thing. In the pressurized, stressful environment of GP practice, workers often want quick solutions to problems that are seen as 'right'. Psychodynamic work often yields meaning that is uncertain or changes the initial problem, and symbolic thinking poses the task of looking in different ways at the same thing. Therefore resistance to analytic practice in medical practitioners is something like the fear of thought disorder – the disorganization of certainty in thought. What we hope actually happens, however, is only temporary and contained disorganization – a process more like what Fordham (1995) called de-integration and reintegration. This is where the psyche comes into relation with an aspect of the environment to which it must react by unpacking more of its developmental potential, achieving, optimally, a new level of integration, subsequent to a period of loss of completeness.

The matrix and the counsellor

As I move on to describe some of my clinical work I would also like to balance my analysis of the resistance in some doctors by saying that an analyst, analytic psychotherapist or psychodynamic counsellor coming from private practice or long term NHS psychotherapy will also deintegrate and reintegrate in primary care. I found myself, after nine years of long-term analytic psychotherapy in private practice, having to make major adaptations which I wrote about in 'The Shadow in short-term counselling: an exploration of resistance in the counsellor using a Jungian perspective' (Bravesmith 1996). What I realized at first was that I had central fantasies based on the idea of being in an archetypal coupling with the patient. The fantasied couplings were those of marriage partner or parent/infant, parent/child. These dyadic relationships all require altruism and devotion over very long periods and I had to reorganize my ideas, to understand, or fantasise new fantasies, about brief work. At the time of writing the article in 1996 I was beset with feelings that I might be symbolically more like a casual lover than a spouse, or more like a part-time or abandoning parent than a 'good-enough mother'. Thinking over a period of time about this I have re-organized my concepts and fantasies to feel myself to be more a part of a matrix than a dyad. That is to say that in brief work in the GP surgery, I am relating to the patient as both myself and as a representative and part of the matrix which consists of the group of workers in the surgery. The matrix continues to be available to the patient after our brief work is finished and I think the patient internalizes the matrix, and the setting too, as a good object. I should also add that in the context of my work patients are able to re-present for counselling and there has been a 'revolving door' system. This greatly reduces the fears I had about making and breaking attachments with patients.

The workaholic twin

A patient I worked with in a busy GP surgery in East London was suffering, as a result of his senior post as a head teacher, stress that was so extreme that he feared he would 'break down'. He took time off work and was referred for counselling where he arrived, close to tears, gaunt and almost unable to speak. When he did so it was in a very faint, almost inaudible voice. The aetiology of his condition emerged clearly from his life story. To put it simply and succinctly he had always overworked and dedicated himself to vocational activities. This was due to exaggerated needs to make reparation which emanated from the circumstances of his birth. He was the surviving twin while his brother died soon after birth. Childhood was 'good enough' and he was gifted in certain respects, being bright and able to understand others, with a faith in life and people. However, first as a priest and then as a senior teacher, he described to me how he always pushed himself 'one step further' in his work, taking risks to help others and damaging his physical health by over-conscientiousness. He was in his fifties.

This patient's libidinal/sexual needs had not been grossly repressed and he had left the Catholic priesthood in his late twenties as a result of falling in love and wishing to marry. This major, and positively resolved, crisis resulted in a good marriage and two children. It had not, however, represented a sufficient development away from his depressive guilt feelings and their need to be transformed into excessive acts of reparation. The patient had a spiritual quality that I find difficult to describe; it could not be reduced to a psychological formula such as I have put forward, but co-existed with the pathology. We both acknowledged this spiritual quality whilst working to understand the psychological roots of his situation. If I try to define his spiritual quality I can only say that he felt blessed and that in his personality there was patience and gentleness not exclusively arising out of masochism. The work we needed to do in the counselling required care and subtlety inasmuch as his integrity and pathology were so close together. They could be seen as two parts of a paradox, though the paradox he truly needed to grasp was that his integrity now lacked vitality due to his insufficient ruthlessness, selfishness and sensual greed/libidinal satisfactions.

The focus of short-term counselling was his capacity for making boundaries that would protect his vitality. He had eight sessions which stimulated an exploration of his current difficulties, birth and childhood, religious experience and relationship to himself. His relationship to me involved shifting transferences. Initially I was his environment mother co-operating with the GP to give him permission to stay away from work, and containing his anxiety. At a later time I represented his split off ruthlessness which was to be resisted and viewed negatively. During the terminating sessions I was the non-surviving twin who he needed to leave but could not allow to die. My survival beyond his departure was evidenced when he returned later for his review session, and he had predicted this because we could interpret his final phase of transference. These fears could then be ego-related. The original birth/death experience cannot be apprehended, in my view, in terms of pre-representational fear or loss since it was presumably the only experience available at first. After birth, in babyhood and childhood, however, the event became represented in the patient's mind through mother's mourning, perhaps a dimly registered sense of only being one where there had been two, and gradual transition from 'unthought known' to 'thought known' (Bollas 1987). I imagine the transference encapsulated something of the secondary representation of the event more than the primary experience. Nevertheless, very early developmental material was being accessed.

Dream and transference in the workaholic twin

Alongside the emergence of transferences in the counselling which were in themselves symbolic processes, and which we could interpret, the patient also produced a striking symbolic image in a dream. It was reported in a 'throw-away' manner, as he did not at first realise that he meant something by dreaming it. In this case my containing involved Bion's (1970) notion of Alpha-function, and I had to be the equivalent of a thinking mother who could connect and process seemingly fragmented bits of mental content. My importance shifted from the initial phase where I had been needed to provide a more or less concrete/physical holding space where he was given respite from professional work. I was now processing and feeding back to the patient elements with which he could construct meaning. The material was presented with an un-prejudiced attitude by the patient, who was open to exploration and had the capacity for surprise which indicates, I believe, a readiness to contain interpretation. He was surprised at his own material once he understood its symbolic significance and the surprise could be seen as a by-product of de-integration. I will describe what happened.

The patient had been telling me in one session about his hobby, which was making picture frames out of wood. Father's Day came and his teenage son gave him a small saw suitable for cutting up the wooden pieces for the frames. He was touched; it seemed just what he wanted. The following week he dreamed of this saw and of making a frame. He had taken the concrete event into his dream symbolism and he now needed to unravel through his associations what it represented. He felt the action of cutting was important and showed me by moving his arm back and forth how satisfying this was. The frame he said made clear what was to be inside and what was to remain outside. It was composed of straight lines meeting in angles with sharp corners. The sharp corners showed its uncompromisability. The straight wood was inflexible and impermeable but also home-made, not imposed. He realized that he had made for himself a clear boundary between his inside and outside worlds, the ruthless lines and corners protecting his inner world. This dream concerned his deep unconscious realization that he had been allowing the exploitation of his self (through overwork) and his emerging consciousness of the need to make potent, paternal (Father's Day) cutting actions and constructions. Could he also have been representing some deeply unconscious awareness of his pre-birth situation, where he shared his mother's womb with a twin whom he was never able to differentiate from developmentally, in the natural course of time? This line of interpretation would mean that a frame of his own partly represented a womb of his own.

The work with this patient extended long enough for him to regain much of his vitality and significantly increase his capacity for metaphorical thinking and symbolic process. His 'frame dream' we interpreted together as central to his focus in short-term counselling, i.e. his capacity for making boundaries. He was able to think about the practical immediate implications in terms of a more aggressive defence of his working conditions professionally. He was able to think about his inner world as differentiated from the outside, and the possibility of not acting on some reparative urges where they seemed to be exaggerated. Keeping certain urges inside the frame of self would be as important as keeping impingements out. The hypothesis I had about his legacy as a womb-sharing twin remained only a hypothesis in my own mind. In the context of short-term work it seemed wise to leave this area more or less unexplored as it would have been likely to open up fantasies that we did not have time to address. As I described, there was interpretation of the transference in the final termination sessions, when I realized he was feeling concerned about my survival, in terms of the twin's death, or rather the later representation of it in his mind. This was essential, rather than optional, in my view because otherwise he would have finished with an uncontained anxiety.

Bridging with the GP's treatment of the workaholic twin

I would like to compare and contrast the clinical description given above with the GP's work with the same patient and describe to what extent he and I were able to communicate and influence each other. Bion wrote: 'as psychoanalysis has grown so it has been seen to differ from physical medicine until the gap between them has passed from the obvious to the unbridgeable' (Bion 1970: 6). Working with an 'analytic attitude' in a GP practice centrally consists of extending the capacities for symbolic process in patients, doctors, other medical staff and, to some lesser extent, administrative and financial workers. I shall elaborate further on the impact of the counsellor on the essentially concrete ways of thinking used by these categories of primary-care workers and their back-up staff. Using Bion's (1970) model of 'container and contained' one can think of the psychodynamic counsellor as being the carrier of a 'Messianic idea' into the group that is the staff of the GP surgery. What is the nature of this idea? It is the idea that symbolic process, the exploration and interpretation of fantasies, images and relationships through metaphorical thinking is central to health and produces changes uniquely. Whereas a medical model uses concrete measures to promote health, such as medication, surgery, or physiotherapy, a psychodynamic approach is abstract, non-sensuous.

Whereas financial managers use concrete formulae to define and determine expenditure and achievement, and administrative workers produce letters, appointments and records, counsellors working with the analytic attitude trade in understanding. The resulting culture clashes can be creative or destructive depending on the fluctuating capacities of all factions to form partnerships that work. In my view it is usually easier to encourage the capacity for symbolic processes in patients than in other practice staff, unless they have a leaning towards its value. I think this is because transference relationships cannot be interpreted with staff members unless there is a group specifically designed, and contained by an organizational consultant other than the counsellor, for this purpose. It is also because of the marginalized position of most counsellors, who are part time and low in the medical or management hierarchy.

Bridging with unconscious aspects of the referrer

I will return to a brief discussion of how my work with the patient I have described bridged with the GP's work with the same person. In my experience a doctor's referral of a patient usually represents a referral of part of himself/herself to the psychodynamic counsellor. This notion co-exists with the doctor's conscious, and optimally appropriate, assessment of the patient for counselling and needs to remain unconscious to preserve the professionalism of the doctor/counsellor relationship. Only in dysfunctional teamwork does it become a problem and otherwise is an interesting channel for communication flowing in both directions. The counsellor's analytic attitude which is neutral and alert to unconscious material can be helpful to the doctor, who has the opportunity to see its use in relation to the patient who represents a troubling part of himself to a greater or lesser extent. In the case of the GP who referred the patient I have described some of this is relevant. He was an older male doctor who was rumoured to have planned to retire several times, according to other workers and patients in the practice. He had not actually retired apparently because of his dedication and good reputation with patients. During informal conversation he confided in me that he often felt too tired to be sufficiently confrontational with difficult patients. He had a particularly warm, supportive and appreciative attitude towards me – concerned that I should survive in the practice (where there was a fair amount of hostility towards psychological thought and any financial expenditure). It is clear that the over-tired, compulsively reparative quality of the patient also belonged to the doctor. Can one conjecture that there may have been some parallel aetological factors? It would have been intrusive to verbalize the connections and there might have been many others. What did emerge as the doctor became more relaxed with me, was sorrow at his wife's disability. I conjecture that this contributed to the strength of his need to repair others in a broadly similar way to the patient's survival of the twin.

Concrete and symbolic modes

It is clear that the GP had plenty of personal experience which enabled him to identify with the plight of the patient. When the patient had first come to him he was decisive about his need for some months' leave of absence from work, and also prescribed sleeping pills and recommended counselling. He used his authority as a doctor to influence the course of events in the patient's external world by providing a brief medical report to his employers and a medical certificate. He prescribed medication and referral to another more specialized colleague – myself. These actions were all appropriate and necessary but ultimately insufficient unless balanced with work in the symbolic mode which could find meaning in the situation. The two modes of operating could be put in diagrammatic form thus:

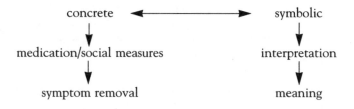

Critics of those working in a symbolic mode that centrally respects and acknowledges the existence of fantasy and states of being that cannot be sensuously apprehended, like guilt and anxiety, often argue that in this mode veracity is hard to establish and that achievements are hard to measure. Proof is taken to be a concrete entity and symptom removal the only measurement of success. On the other hand critics of the concrete mode view it as developmentally primitive and belonging to a childish level of functioning – Piaget's (1954) level of concrete operations, or something akin to Klein's (1988) paranoid schizoid position with anxiety being evacuated through action.

In the case of the patient I have been discussing there was little conflict between the two modes. There could have been if the GP had prescribed heavy tranquillizers or limited the patient's respite from paid work so that he had had to comply with an early return, necessitating 'getting better' quickly. What happened was that in discussion the GP and I were in broad agreement about the patient. However, there was a gap between our understandings that was only partly bridged. The doctor wanted to know what had happened in the counselling and what lay behind the situation the patient had presented. It was our policy to discuss material with each other and regard the boundary of confidentiality as being triadic rather than dyadic i.e. patient–counsellor–GP rather than patient–counsellor. Accordingly I explained some of the patient's story to the doctor concerning his history of compulsive dedication arising out of guilt and loss, which, I commented, was very deep-seated and difficult to make fully conscious. When I linked this to the effects of his being a twin who had survived while the other twin died, the doctor felt this was preposterous. He pointed out that the patient would not be able to remember this event. I conceded on this point but added that he was brought up in a family that would have remembered it; mother and father would have been in mourning/depressed, the event would have been constantly present and fantasized if not remembered. The fantasy life of the patient was centrally and irrevocably influenced and this then influenced his life in every other way. This was one of the first times I requested the doctor to think about fantasy and he became better and better at it with later patients that we shared.

Making fantasy relevant

Thinking about the strong aversion to fantasy as a subject for discussion and consideration I have come to some possible explanations. It is necessary to explore fantasies as far as possible, within the context and within the patient's capacities, in order to find the present and past meaning of his/her experiences and to open the possibility of constructing new meanings. However, the misconceptions revealed in fantasy are strong and vital and threaten to seduce or overwhelm the individual who enters into the fantasy world in order to understand it. Money-Kyrle (1968) wrote that analysis has come to be about analysing misconception and I think this occurs in short-term therapeutic work in a condensed form, as well as in 'analysis', when the counsellor has an analytic attitude. Without this openness to unconscious material harbouring misconception, the fantasy level appears irrelevant and useless to the healer and, more than this, to be threatening to sanity. We must 'keep our feet on the ground', laugh at or distance ourselves from fantasies in order to avoid being overwhelmed. In the case under discussion the misconception may have been that being alive could only continue as long as the patient worked reparatively to ward off death and to make up for 'murdering' his twin. The doctor's feeling that this was preposterous contained enough surprise for me to know that he had listened to my communication. With some other GPs this ability to listen and register a response was completely lacking or took much longer to occur. I shall give clinical examples to illustrate more of this.

The clinical example already given had a result which was satisfying to the GP, in that the patient's behaviour became better adapted to his external world and there was some shift in his internal world. The patient returned to his job after several months better equipped to live productively. The part of the GP which had been presented through the patient unconsciously had been unusually transparent. In other cases parts which were more deeply unconscious were presented, and there were also cases where I could discern no link. Results that require GPs to struggle with their own values and practise aspects of the 'analytic attitude' themselves, necessitate the counsellor spending some energy on establishing the meaning for the patient as a comprehensible entity for the GP. Thus, for example, the younger man mentioned earlier who came to counselling 'because' he could not complete his MA dissertation decided to give up the MA, and I needed to discuss this with his GP. This was not in order to justify an outcome, or rob a GP of an emotional response to it, but rather to extend understanding and the impartiality of the analytic attitude into the GP's repertoire. As I discovered that my role as counsellor involved working deeply embedded in the matrix of workers in the surgery, I also found that a strict division of labour was unrealistic.

Agape in the matrix of primary care

The attitude which Jungians, following Lambert (1981), call Agape was a necessary ingredient in the matrix as well as in myself as an individual. Agape, in brief, means an attitude of altruism, dedication and impartiality with the development of a capacity to manage one's own envy, rage, moralism and self-interest. It represents an ideal which is not fully attained.

In my experience Agape in the matrix needs to be developed with consciousness rather than relied upon as a function of the 'natural' personalities that make up the group. For example, soon after I had become established in one practice the receptionists triumphantly excluded a particular patient from counselling because she had missed two appointments consecutively. There were three receptionists who all felt angry and wished to punish the patient. The response of anger was absolutely understandable and contained a communication from the patient about her own anger. However, the receptionists wanted to operate a form of talion law (retaliation) which was unacceptable. We had, on logistical grounds, to make a limit on cancelled or missed appointments but decided against a fixed rule. Only when the receptionists understood the anxiety patients feel about counselling appointments could they change their attitude. It was also important that I understood their frustrations and offered to share, where possible, the difficult telephone work with this patient. This meant bearing torrents of bitter complaints about her life, whilst at the same time tolerating her cancellations and re-arrangements of appointments over the telephone. In some respects this could be harder than actually working face-to-face with the patient, and the receptionists were naturally at first responding with primitive affects.

Financial decisions and symbolic process

The tolerance of great anger in the surgery matrix requires workers of all kinds to develop symbolic process, the capacity for interpretation and struggle for meaning. Even financial managers remaining in predominantly concrete mode disadvantage the patients. The reduction of psychic development and/or healing to only two dimensions – success or failure – with a condition that what is construed as 'success' is the criteria for financial investment inevitably restricts vision to very narrow confines. There is of course a need for practicality, but financial culture can often attack psychological culture. For example in my own work I could cite two examples out of many where my method and approach met with attacks from financial ways of seeing. One was where a finance worker brought influence to bear within the matrix, through the doctors primarily, to deem it undesirable (uneconomic) to keep a counselling session 'empty' in the midst of an agreed course of sessions if the patient did not arrive in person. Another patient, it was argued, could be slotted in at the last moment in such a case. The symbolic importance of the counsellor waiting, reflecting on the emptiness and receiving the patient's unconscious communication was outside the finance worker's repertoire of ideas. Another instance is the insistence that patients be reminded by telephone on the day a few hours before their appointment. This is aimed at ensuring that physical attendance occurs and effectiveness can be measured by whether or not patients arrive in person. I found that the destructive experience of intrusion/control generated by 'reminder' phone calls could be apprehended after discussion with the finance manager. I was able to explain how a missed session often generated creative work between counsellor and patient and could be a re-enactment of the past, or a new achievement in ruthlessness, or of the capacity to feel guilt following the absence.

'Illness' as avoidance of coherent meaning

A clinical case where sadness rather than anger had to be tolerated by the matrix emerges strongly in this context. The patient was an older man who had been medicated for about a decade on anti-depressants. His GP sent him to me because in his view it would be beneficial for him to stop taking anti-depressants. The patient was deeply frightened about this and, after meeting him, I felt there was no possibility of replacing medication with counselling. He had a deep underlying depression, although he was mostly able to work and had a responsible job as a draughtsman. The patient had a positive attachment to his doctor and initially came for counselling both to please him and because he respected his advice. When I communicated an impartial attitude regarding anti-depressants he relaxed visibly and was able to realize he could have counselling and medication. He was of the Islamic faith and, although he said he felt he was not strict in practising his religion, his belief actually was deep and his self-image had to be based upon it. He attended for a two-part assessment and we agreed that he would attend six sessions at weekly intervals as soon as I had vacancies, which would be in two months' time. He cancelled a week beforehand and went abroad to work, failed to re-contact me on his return, but re-presented six months later. The essence of his counselling was of a confessional nature but he was at first unconscious of this motive for coming, and also he did not have a coherent story to confess. He had been partly convinced that he simply had an 'illness'. The patient suffered a meaningless depression which gained a meaning through our work. Eventually the meaning was understood by at least four people – himself, myself, his doctor and the psychiatrist to whom he was referred.

The patient who felt unforgiveable

This patient's 'illness' was a defence against thinking about himself and was largely due to his view of himself as unforgiveable. He had been sent away from the Punjab when India was partitioned as a teenager of nineteen years to stay with his older brother's family. There he met his ten-year-old niece, seduced her, fell in love with her and had a secret relationship with her for twenty-five years, during part of which they lived as partners in Europe. They were terrified of having deformed children and terrified of discovery. She eventually left him, married someone else and moved to a far away country. Her departure was a full twenty years ago. He became an alcoholic but hit rock bottom and joined Alcoholics Anonymous with successful results. He was, he told me, always shy and introverted and the youngest child of four in a family who had called him the 'baby'. He never contacted the woman he had loved and she had been the only person who 'knew' him. He had made more than one suicide attempt in the past, and had attended group therapy for two years in another city after these attempts. He suffered severely from shame, and we could not agree on a focus for our work – maybe because he was too depressed.

On re-presenting this patient was even more severely depressed than when I had first met him – or perhaps he allowed me to see it more. He appeared to have forgotten what he had told me, and to be expecting me to have forgotten it too and be casting about for solutions to his 'illness'. He could barely speak and sat slumped over. Although Bion (1970) tells us to be without 'memory and desire', I felt what was important was my ability to contain in memorable form what he felt was too shameful and unforgivable about his sacrilegious abuse of a child, a blood relative and from within the traditions of hospitality extended to him as a refugee. I felt he was deeply punitive to himself and that the quality of mutual love between him and his niece that had endured for many years, lent him grace. Who was I to judge? It was an unusual transference and when I discussed it with a senior analyst (also of Indian ethnic origin) he expressed the opinion that I had, in transference, become a godhead from whom forgiveness might come but could not be internalized. The silent depression yielded to some articulation when the patient understood that I had contained his life-story and could contemplate it. I asked him if forgiveness and reparation were part of his religion, as I did not know. He thought not, and asked me what reparation meant as a word and as an idea. I felt quite out of my depth and in a realm other than psychological, so perhaps the senior analyst was right about the transference. Inarticulately I tried to explain, and he became very concerned about whether reparation could occur towards some other person than the one he had damaged. I cannot say quite what this conversation meant, as he said he could only just feed and dress himself and no reparative actions could be relevant, but the idea woke him out of his passivity. He had told me that I was the sole recipient of the story of his abusive actions and that he wanted it at all costs kept confidential from his employers, but not his doctor.

Bridging with the GP's work with the patient who felt unforgiveable

I had to see the patient's doctor after our meeting as she was very anxious about another suicide attempt. I told her I agreed that the patient was at risk, and a psychiatrist did need to see him. The doctor then behaved oddly. I told her why the patient felt so guilty and depressed and she averted her face and clearly did not listen. The doctor is deeply religious and also Indian, but of a different faith. I felt she was unable to hear about it and this filled me with sadness and loneliness. However, weeks later I returned to ask her the outcome of the patient's visit to the psychiatrist. She showed me a confidential report which I was glad to see had been written by a psychiatrist known and respected by me. In this report it was clear that the patient had articulated his story to the psychiatrist and was in possession of the link that gave meaning to his mental state – simply he felt guilty about his actions and his depressive illness was the punishment he exacted from himself. The doctor was also able now to look at me, hand me the report and say the illness was due to guilt about the patient's niece. No electro-convulsive therapy had been prescribed, since the psychiatrist felt this would be experienced as part of the punishment and so it would collude with the patient's attitude. He now had different medication, greater containment and we all lived with continual anxiety about the suicide risk – but it looked less likely because deep human contact had occurred in the face of unutterable loneliness, secretiveness and shame. It is probable that the GP had to work in herself to overcome her feelings of moral outrage or disappointment in the patient with whom she had had a long-term professional relationship. Prior to these events she had respected her patient in a more conditional way that added to the need to keep the secret. Perhaps the part of the doctor that was referred through the patient was the harsh super-ego, religiously tinged. If this kind of work requires us to be open to changes in our own personality, as Lambert says in *Analysis, Repair and Individuation* (1981), what change occurred in me? I think it was that rigidity in my thinking and feeling was challenged by the compassion I felt for a person who could be categorized an 'abuser'.

Conclusion

I hope I have illustrated in this case how deeply challenging the understanding of the symbolic nature of an illness or state of mind can be, and that such an understanding brings changes in the matrix that is the general practice. It was a painful process in my final example, but is not always so charged. The psychodynamic counsellor using what could be called a dialect of psychoanalysis based on the analytic attitude, but with adaptations to work in a short time within a matrix that can reverberate with the effects of each piece of work, brings symbolic processes right into the heart of the GP surgery. Meaning and interpretation become central, where they were marginalized by the medical/financial culture and disguised by illness for the patient.

REFERENCES

Bion, Wilfred (1970) *Attention and Interpretation*, London: Karnac.

Bollas, Christopher (1987) *The Shadow of the Object*, London: Free Association Books.

Bravesmith, Anna (1996) 'The Shadow in short-term counselling: an exploration of resistance in the counsellor using a Jungian perspective', *Psychodynamic Counselling* 2(4): 533–5.

Fordham, Michael (1995) *Freud, Jung, Klein: 'The Fenceless Field'*, London: Routledge.

Klein, Melanie (1988) *Envy and Gratitude and other works 1946–1963*, London: Virago.

Lambert, Kenneth (1981) *Analysis, Repair and Individuation*, London: Academic Press.

Meltzer, Donald (1987) *Sincerity and Other Works*, London: Karnac.

Money-Kyrle, R.E. (1968) *Cognitive Development* in D. Meltzer and E. O'Shaugnessy (eds) *Collected Papers of Roger Money-Kyrle* (1978), Strathclyde, Perthshire: Clunie Press.

Obhelzer, A. and Roberts, V.Z. (1994) *The Unconscious at Work*, London: Routledge.

Piaget, J. (1954) *The Construction of Reality in the Child*, New York: Basic Books.

7 The generalized transference in general practice

David Mann

Introduction

This chapter looks at the transference manifestations in general practice. A generalized transference is highlighted whereby a patient may experience and relate to various members of the staff team in a similar way, e.g. doctor/nurse/psychotherapist equals mother. By the same token, the doctor, nurse and psychotherapist may experience the patient in much the same way. Such patients may be treated by the whole team. The concept of *the general practice as therapist* is developed, whereby the psychotherapist interprets for the whole practice.

I work with a psychoanalytic orientation. Though the concept of transference receives subtle and detailed elaboration in psychoanalytic literature, broadly it can be defined as a repeat or re-edition of the past or the individual's experience. Transference distorts perception. The adult will repeat patterns of relationships from his or her childhood. The transference will also include how aspects of infantile or childhood relationships have been digested (incorporated, internalized and become owned by a process of identification). These childhood patterns, feelings, behaviours and fantasies distort the adult's experience of the world when they are transfered on to new relationships (e.g. the patient talks to and treats the therapist as if he or she is the patient's mother or father). To the extent that the transference inhibits a mature relationship with the world it is pathological. The therapeutic process aims to reduce the influence of unresolved childhood experience by first seeing how the patient repeats the transference in the relationship with the therapist and then working to take the distortion out of the memory. As I often tell a new patient, we cannot change the past but we can change how it affects us.

When working in private practice it is usually the custom to think of the therapist as the main focus of the transference. Elsewhere (Mann, 1997a, 1999), I have discussed how it is usually possible to discern other significant relationships in the patient's life where the transference may be intense: to their boss at work, for example, or to close friends or sexual partners via the underlying eroticism of the unconscious. Other writers have also detected transferences outside the analytic setting: as early as 1936 Fairbairn describes the significance of the death of a king on patients in analysis; other notable candidates for transference include celebrities, politicians, the police or the NHS.

The development of the patient's transference when working in a psychiatric or general practice setting is usually not so clear-cut. In these settings it is often useful to think of the transference in more diffuse ways. The patient's transference experience is likely to be affected by the instituiton itself in a variety of ways. Two forms of transference in particular are noticeable: (1) the split transference and (2) what I wish to focus upon here, general transferences. The latter is the main object of this particular article (see below), but I will say a few words about the split transference.

Before proceeding further it might be useful to say something about the practice where I work. I work full time in a general practice in a fairly deprived area of South East London. The practice consists of five partners, trainee doctors, nurses, midwives and community support. It is busy, and sometimes frantic, with 10,000 patients on the practice list. I usually see patients for six sessions, though there is scope for some longer interventions if appropriate. On average I would expect to see twenty-five patients a week. I attend weekly meetings with all the practice staff and will arrange individual meetings with GPs if I need to talk about particular patients.

The split transference

Often there are a number of professionals involved in the treatment of each patient. In general practice patients may see the doctor for one aspect of their problem, the practice nurse for something else and the practice counsellor or therapist. There may also be others making a contribution: in the practice where I work a patient might be in contact with the practice midwife, health visitor or osteopath. A particular patient may, therefore, have a large emotional investment with a number of health professionals. This has been noted previously and has frequently been discussed in terms of the splitting this may induce in the staff and patient, e.g. Main (1957) and Correale (1994). Problems with splitting are now well understood: a patient may idealize one professional and denigrate another as a consequence of a paranoid-schizoid intolerance of ambivalence which requires that the good and the bad become detached from each other.

A brief example may illustrate. During my first meeting with Mr A he reported how desperate he felt at the prospect of his psychotically ill wife being prematurely discharged from a psychiatric hospital. He said he had implored the authorities to let her stay in until she was better and then gradually let her out for brief visits home before discharge. Mr A painted a grim picture of the remaining years of his life caring for his chronically sick wife with little support. Since I felt quite concerned by how suicidal he might be, after our meeting I spoke to the referring GP. The doctor gave a very different story: it was the hospital who wished to discharge Mrs A gradually and it was Mr A who had sabotaged the treatment by wanting to keep her at home for good after the first visit. The GP felt he was, in fact, partly responsible for driving his wife to psychosis. I thought he was not only driving his wife mad but me also by having totally convinced me and having drawn me into his version of reality. In this instance the patient had momentarily but successfully split me from the team: the 'good' concerned therapist from the 'bad' unconcerned doctors. In the case of Mr A I then thought a re-reading of a paper by Searles (1959) on 'The effort to drive the other person crazy' might be useful.

The patient may also find that any intrapsychic splits he or she experiences are reflected by splits within the treatment itself. In a previous publication (Mann et al., 1990), I described how the staff team in a psychiatric unit itself became split by the running of an incest survivors' group. In that instance, the split was between those working with this special group and those not included: rivalries and envious and narcissistic fantasies were generated on both sides. These splits were reflective of the pathology of the patient group.

In general practice, this split in treatment is often centred around the division between mind and body: the doctor or nurse treats the physical complaint whereas psychological interventions are referred to the practice therapist, counsellor, clinical psychologist or a psychiatrist. Such a split is, of course, more apparent in theory than in practice: physical illnesses have psychological consequences, psychological problems may have a relationship to physical illnesses. Furthermore, many patients visit their GP not for physical illnesses but because of psychological problems: depression, anxiety, relationship difficulties etc. Joyce McDougall (1982, 1989, 1995) has made several studies of physical illnesses from a psychoanalytical point of view and this has greatly influenced my own approach, since I regularly work with the physical symptoms as well as more obvious psychic material.

By its very nature, therefore, the general practice setting encourages splits in the transference. In some respects, this exists quite apart from the individual patient's own psychological defensive structures. However, it becomes apparent that general practice is likely to feed any tendencies the patient has to use splitting as a defence and will provide abundant opportunities to play upon, exaggerate or in some way amplify any of his or her tendencies to use splitting.

The generalized transference

I would suggest that the level of the patient's splitting often disguises other aspects of the transference. In my experience, it is not simply that a patient projects one aspect of him- or herself onto one person, and another aspect onto a different person. Sometimes what is transferred is very similar in all instances, but with variations in intensity. We may think of this as a variation on a theme. I would make an explicit parallel with music here. A composer may introduce a main theme followed by variations. The fourth or fifth variation may, if taken in isolation, seem a long way from the preliminary theme, but its effect upon the listener is due to the musical development and the relationship to previous variations, in particular to the original theme. What I am describing is that a patient, under the influence of the transference, may treat the doctor, nurse and therapist in exactly the same way. On these occasions the transference is not split in the usual paranoid-schizoid way that we commonly think of as splitting. Rather the patient replicates the same, or very similar, material with different persons. The transference is split not into good or bad, mother or father etc., but more like doctor/nurse/therapist = mother. That is to say, the transference remains the same, though the level of intensity may vary according to the kind of relationship or intensity of contact with doctor or therapist. We may think of this as the patient developing two or more parallel transferences. The generalized transference pervades the individual's life and resides behind the experience that everything in life, work, relationships, outside interests, therapy (even visits to the fishmonger), all feel the same. The individual is making a transference to their whole life experience. In this description the unconscious is not conceived as an intrapsychic phenomenon that focuses on a single target, e.g. exclusively to the therapist. The unconscious is conceived as intra- and inter-psychic and colours the experience of all objects. To a certain degree the generalized transference can be found in everybody. What I am describing here, though, is a particular group of patients where the generalized transference takes a more intense form. These patients tend to pose a challenge to the whole practice, but a challenge of a different nature from those patients who present problematic split transferences. The crux of this generalized transference is essentially that the psychotherapist, GP, nurse, etc. will experience the patient in much the same way because the patient's transference is to treat everybody as though they are one; his or her use of objects is non-discriminatory.

By the time the patient eventually sees a practice psychotherapist, the patient has already established a transference to the practice as a whole, especially the doctor. One of the tasks of the therapist is, then, to disentangle this transference as it is projected onto him or herself as distinct from the rest of the staff.

I think of this in terms of what I call the generalized transference. By this I mean a transference that is focused not on one but on several individuals: the whole general practice receives the transference that is commonly focused on only one person (the therapist) in private practice. The existence of this generalized transference has implications for psychotherapy in general practice.

What I wish to explore here is the idea of what I think of as *the general practice as therapist*, that is to say, the practice as a whole psychologically treats the patient. This does not mean that all the various members of the staff team are giving interpretations in a quasi-therapeutic free-for-all, but rather that various aspects of the patient's generalized transference are contained by the separate disciplines of the practice. Consequently, the patient receives a wider level of containment for his or her splits which are therefore understood as a generalized transference. Since these are integrated and focused on the practice as a whole, it is hoped they will be contained and integrated by the staff team (the *general practice as therapist*). The specific function of the psychotherapist is to speak on behalf of the *practice as therapist*, to address the generalized transference and to bring the splits together to enable a working through via interpretation. The therapist's function is to interpret this particular variation in the patient's parallel transference. In so doing the therapist is making the generalized transference more specific, like focusing on one face in a crowd, or, to continue the musical analogy, returning the patient back to the principal theme.

We may now consider that the therapist is the articulated container of the transference. By this I mean the patient's relationship to the doctor or nurse etc. may be strongly transferential, but in all probability it is only in the relationship with the therapist that the transference may be mentioned explicitly and explored for its deeper meanings. That is to say, the therapist will probably be the only member of the staff team who will have the function of interpreting the transference. Other members of the staff team will have their hypotheses about the patient but will in all probability not put these directly to the patient. The therapist may or may not be the recipient of the patient's most intense transferences. Nevertheless, he or she will be the voice for the whole practice in interpreting the transference the patient has made to the practice.

This has advantages and disadvantages over the therapist in private practice. The disadvantage is that the therapist's attempts to dissolve the transference (that is to say, lessen the effect of the infantile repetition in the patient's adult life) may be circumvented because the transference is less focused, less clear-cut in the therapeutic relationship. In other words, the transference can be diluted when projected onto too many figures. When diluted in such a manner, the transference onto one particular individual can sometimes become more ephemeral or vague, making its perception more difficult. I would stress, though, that this is not always the case.

The advantage of the generalized transference is that the therapist may be able to see quite graphically how the patient employs his or her transference in relation to different practice members. In addition, as I will shortly describe, since the therapist is part of a team, he or she will have access to the experience of others in relation to the work with specific patients.

Clinical examples

In the practice where I work, referrals for therapy are made mostly by the doctors, though occasionally other members of the team will also refer. Patients are seen for brief psychoanalytic psychotherapy in which the emphasis is placed on the importance of early experience in symptom formation (either physical or psychological symptoms), the influence of the unconscious and the manifestations of both in the transference. Though the work is time limited I make no compromise on psychoanalytic technique. I believe, and experience confirms, that the time limit on sessions will consciously and unconsciously compel the patient to bring the most pertinent issues during free association. The pertinent issues will be the characteristic forms of resistance but also the patient's experience of creative transformations; these represent the patient's regressive and progressive developmental conflicts, the destructive versus life forces, the repetition compulsion versus eros. In a manner of speaking, the patient's whole life history and story is embodied in his or her presenting symptom. I do not intend this to be a grandiose claim. Rather, what I mean is that the symptom includes not only the aetiology and history of the ailment but also any unconscious issues expressed somatically. In addition, the transference is visible via the patient's relationship to both his or her symptom (how they experience it) and how they expect others to relate to their symptoms (e.g. how they expect to be looked after, or, alternatively, do not expect help and so 'lick their own wounds').

Ms B was in her late forties. She was initially referred because of stress at work leading to an inability to sleep and eat, loss of concentration and depression. She reported not having dreams but sometimes waking up anxious and sweating. She described herself as a workaholic. It seemed she was in a very high-powered job but she felt the management never did anything to help her do her job better; on the contrary, they wanted to give her the sack. She stated that the whole cause of her problem was feeling undermined by the management and that this was the sole cause of her stress and current problems. In answer to my questions she said further that she was not very good at looking after herself: she never had time off sick and at best only picked at junk food. She felt she was always putting the needs of her employees first, though she was able to see that her compulsion to be busy was also serving her own ends. We agreed a time limited number of sessions.

From early on in the next session she established a rather fixed transference pattern. Her material was largely a repeat of her earlier complaints about her job. None of my comments seemed to have any appreciable effect on her monologue. Fairly soon she was reporting that the therapy, too, was not helping. She reported that the GP had prescribed anti-depressants but she had stopped taking them. She felt very stuck and that nobody cared about or understood her.

She said she felt at the end of the road but denied any suicidal intent. However, by the end of the fourth session I was sufficiently concerned by the deterioration in her mental state and the new depth of her depression to talk to her GP. I suggested to both Ms B and the doctor that we have a joint session, as the patient was clearly finding our different therapeutic attempts quite useless.

As I saw the situation, Ms B felt that nothing her employers did helped her predicament. This was also the case with her GP, who prescribed medication she decided not to take. The pattern was repeated in the psychotherapy, too, which seemed unhelpful to her, rendered useless by her inability to take in any nourishing interpretations. This also seemed consistent with her self-care: she was not good at looking after herself and ate badly. She was, essentially, an ineffective parent to her own needy parts, whilst also experiencing everybody else as a neglectful parent to those needy parts. I understood that her experience of her managers, her GP, her psychotherapist and her self-management was essentially the same; that we were variations on a theme of the generalized transference.

The joint meeting was certainly of benefit to the GP and myself, since we clarified experiences and perceptions of the patient and our treatment. This joint meeting allowed the practice as therapist to bring various themes into a unified whole. I interpreted this generalized transference to the patient. When I next saw her individually she reported that things had stabilized at work and that she herself was taking measures to improve matters. In my view, this shift was due to the fact that the various themes of the generalized transference had been gathered together and were then treated by the staff collectively as *the general practice as therapist*. This unification of the staff helped the patient integrate some of her inner splits. A result was achieved collectively that was out of reach when working in isolation. In the terms of Bion (1962), the practice as therapist acted as a container and, after reverie, returned the projections in a more manageable form.

Ms C presented a different scenario. She was depressed following the break-up with her boyfriend. This had been a very violent relationship that had left permanent physical damage but Ms C reported that she still loved him. Her previous marriage had also been violent; she later discovered that her husband had had an affair with her best friend and was a secret cross-dresser. She declared she had no idea why she was drawn to choosing the 'wrong sort of man'. She described having vivid dreams and reported one in which a knife was thrust into her throat. She could not see the attacker.

About her family life she said that her parents had moved a great deal when she was a child. Mother had died when Ms C was in her late teens. Her father had later disappeared from the face of the earth: he left no trace of departure nor was his body ever found. The police kept his file open for more than a decade largely because Ms C had maintained an interest in finding out what had happened. The loss of her father seemed to find an active re-edition while I was seeing her. She got back together with the ex-boyfriend one night but he then disappeared without trace for several days immediately afterwards, stimulating a severe crisis in Ms C.

In the therapy I had begun to notice that, though Ms C was eager for my comments and interpretations and, on the face of it, seemed to think about what I said, she was not using therapy in a creative play of free associations. Rather, interpretations were being rendered useless, ineffective, by her tossing them about until they broke, like a child being rough with a toy.

The sudden disappearance of her boyfriend had produced a panic and a severe relapse in her mental state. When he later returned into her life they had an explosive encounter. Fearing he was going to hit her, she dived head-first through a first floor window in order to escape. She was quite badly hurt with lacerations from the glass and the impact of the fall. After initial hospital treatment, she was seen by a general practice nurse to have her dressings changed. During the consultations with the nurse Ms C would bring a friend, an ex-nurse, with her own ideas about nursing procedures. When at the practice Ms C preferred to do her own dressings and apply antiseptics herself. This is quite unusual as patients usually allow the nurse to carry out these procedures.

In my view, the experience of the practice nurse was virtually identical to my own. The patient was voracious for a therapeutic intervention, be it medical or psychotherapeutic, but she did not want to use the relationship therapeutically. Instead, in an almost literal manner, she preferred to lick her own wounds in order to avoid any dependence on or need for others. This left both the nurse and myself feeling annoyed with her as she plainly was asking for help but was not taking the help available. I suspect that what she set up with the GP surgery was something similar to her relationship to her boyfriend, with its sado-masochistic undertones which resulted in a more destructive than fruitful or creative encounter. (A fuller discussion of transference perversions can be found in Mann (1997a) and (1997b).)

In retrospect, I have wondered if there was a strong influence of the father in the way she related to the surgery. Father had disappeared in mysterious circumstances, presumed dead but with no body as confirmation. This had, of course, made the grieving process very difficult for Ms C. She was caught in an intermediate state, father was neither dead nor alive, held in suspended animation. I think the GP surgery was experienced similarly. Inasmuch as the nurse and I received the generalized father transference, Ms C was unable to use the living relationship we offered her but neither was she able to ignore us or let us go. In that odd way we were there and not there, she wanted us present but effectively behaved as though we were not in the room. In other words, we see here another instance of parallel transference: the patient's way of being and relating to the world in general and to different members in the practice in particular was almost identical. Each encounter was made the same by the generalized transference, the patient's habitual ways of relating to the people in her life. Strikingly, it was only after I had interpreted this generalized transference that the patient seemed interested in using anything I said (in this instance, that after our brief intervention she might consider joining a support group for battered women) and was willing to allow somebody else a part in the healing process. Again we may say that the generalized transference was manifested towards the *practice as therapist* and only once her pathology had been understood in this organizational context was she able to take anything therapeutically on board.

Ms D presented a different kind of problem. She was a frequent attender to the doctor. Though she had a number of chronic physical problems that were not severe her major difficulties concerned the psychological stress created by her relationship with her mother. At the time of referral to me the doctor was seriously concerned that Ms D would either kill herself or her mother. Her father had died when she was an adolescent. She had never had a sexual relationship nor left home. Her mother was under the care of the local psychiatric service and was known to the surgery as being very cantankerous and difficult. Ms D herself was very pleasant but always seemed desperately needy for advice, encouragement, reassurance or sympathy for how much she had to contend with at home.

When I saw her I did not think she was a suicidal or homicidal risk. But like the doctor I found myself being drawn into her perception of things: it was difficult to stay objective. I found myself silently taking sides with the patient against her mother, and thinking something along the lines of 'Poor Ms D, having to put up with all that nonsense at home and she is so pleasant and nice!'

This went on for several sessions until I detected the seductive and collusive way she spoke, which felt as though she was trying to manipulate my thoughts. I then began to notice the sub-text in what Ms D said, much of it angry and provocative and indeed full of matricidal intent. She was not actively going to kill her mother: hers was an unconscious murderous desire that even she did not like to acknowledge, this gave it a phantastical aspect. It was this that the GP had detected first. I then began to direct my interpretations to this side of the patient's thoughts. Though Ms D was very shocked at my articulation of her ideas, it did make her aware of some of her part in winding mother up. Interestingly, when I next spoke to her GP some weeks later he reported that he was no longer worrying about her now she was talking to me. This was partly because he felt the burden had been shared and the patient was now focusing on me. But there was also another dynamic. Both he and I had found that getting caught up in Ms D's view of her predicament was quite irresistible. My more interpretative stance with the patient not only helped me break her hypnotic grip but in so doing enabled the doctor to extract himself from the patient's mesh. The generalized transference was how the patient had managed to get the GP and myself to view her side of events uncritically and without discernment. Once this cycle was broken we were both able to see Ms D more realistically and thereby offer a more viable intervention.

Discussion

The therapeutic issues generated by the idea of the generalized transference and the *practice as therapist* may be considered in terms of how we think about the therapeutic frame: how we consider operations of holding and containment, specifically of the transference.

Winnicott (1960) thought of holding and containment in terms of the mother's physical care for the infant: the infant experiences psychological containment through a physical process. In a therapeutic context, holding and containing are also thought of in terms of structural processes: the same setting, regularity of sessions and length of session, a set fee etc. These regular habits of the analytic situation act as the mother's arms. Various authors describe the importance of the setting on the therapeutic relationship. Bleger (1967) and Viderman (1974) draw attention to the need for a secure frame to enable the patient to develop the necessary trust in the therapeutic process.

Regarding psychotherapy in general practice, the idea of what constitutes the containing frame has generated some disagreement, see, for example, Hoag (1992) and Launer (1994). Launer, writing from a GP's viewpoint, proposes that a flexible frame is a necessity in general practice since the nature of general practice makes a secure frame almost impossible. He therefore outlines three levels of counselling that may take place. (1) 'Big-C counselling' describes the planned, structured approach generally used by the practice counsellor; (2) 'Little-c counselling' is that which 'probably occurs in most good GP consultations', denoting when the doctor uses counselling or a therapeutic mode in general consultations. (3) 'Middle-C counselling' refers to the GP wanting a wider perspective, e.g. a family view conducted in protected time at the end of surgery.

Hoag (1992), writing from a psychotherapist's view, argues for a much tighter frame. She cites Langs (1976a and 1976b) who states that the therapist aspires to an 'ideal frame' which requires absolute confidentiality and the need for a sound-proof room as well as regular times and setting. Hoag herself goes further and stresses the importance of the fee as part of the frame: the patient needs to know how the session is paid for in order to feel he or she can take the therapist's time. My own view is that I find the prescriptions of Langs and Hoag rather rigid, while matters concerning the therapist's fee seem to be more of a countertransference issue for the therapist than anything else.

However, this leads me to a point I would like to stress. The analytic frame may be necessary for the patient's psychological containment but the therapist also needs to feel psychologically held and contained by it. There are various reasons for this and I wish to highlight only a few pertinent issues here. The therapist needs to know he or she can tolerate the patient's unconscious phantastical assaults upon the therapist's own unconscious. Also, the therapist needs to feel secure enough to be able to say what needs to be said, in other words, he or she needs to know that the interpretations that liberate unconscious material can be said (or at least thought) without driving either the patient or the therapist mad. Depth interpretations can be spoken or thought without encountering internal resistances if the therapist feels secure with the patient. All this is facilitated by a secure analytic frame.

Returning to the issues raised by Hoag, I would re-interpret her material in the following light. The rigid ideal frame she describes serves as a containment for the therapist. If the therapist feels contained, the patient is then able to feel held by the therapeutic process. Put another way: the therapist's sense of security helps the patient to feel secure; an insecure therapist may lead to insecurities in the patient. Hoag goes so far as to cite Schafer (1983) who notes that lapses in the analytic attitude support the patient's expectation that the work is too dangerous to proceed. Again, I would not take such an apocalyptic view. Indeed, the patient sometimes needs all-too-human lapses in the therapist in order to disillusion his or her phantasies about the therapist's omnipotence. This phantasy can exist in either party. Hoag suggests that the therapist's breaching of the frame may be indicative of Oedipal conflicts. This is true, but the case cuts both ways: an over-emphasis on structure for the therapist/patient couple may be indicative of pre-Oedipal issues. I would further add that an over rigid, 'ideal frame' quite easily plays into the therapist's grandiose narcissism that it is the therapist who has the special knowledge and the special arrangements with the patient. This may frequently be a countertransference identification to idealized pre-Oedipal material with the patient. In my view, the therapist is best left to decide on the flexibility or rigidity of the frame depending on the particular patient's requirements: any insistence on one approach or another exclusively sounds rather like a countertransference fixation. In that sense, I am probably more in agreement with Launer because often the transference to the therapist needs to be considered in the context of the patient's transference to the practice as a whole.

In general practice it is sometimes easier to see how the frame may hold and contain the therapist rather more than the patient. Most usually patients do not know the rules and routines of psychoanalysis (fixed time, setting, fee etc.) before they begin therapy. However, they will quickly adapt to the therapist's expectations about the therapeutic frame once this has been established.

The frame is, therefore, the context in which psychotherapy occurs. Since the therapist does not operate in a vacuum, the context of the frame extends to the practice itself via the generalized transference. In that sense, the frame can be the *general practice as therapist*.

The therapeutic function of the institution, and not just the individual therapist, has been discussed by Bion (1961), Hinshelwood (1987) and Correale (1994). Correale draws attention to how the institution may transcend the capacities of the individual therapist, and states that the institution itself needs to act as a container for 'intense emotive forces'. I would elaborate this idea by saying that the generalized transference may help the patient deal with psychic material, especially of a destructive nature, that may be too intense to focus on one individual. Of course, de-intensifying such emotionally charged phantasies may also be necessary for the therapist's psychological containment, that is to say, the *general practice as therapist* acts as a container for both the psychotherapist and the patient. Correale thinks of the therapeutic function of the institution in terms of providing a safe container: 'Indeed, while the institution "contains", at the same time it absorbs, transforms and reclaims many explosive moments, activating many levels of experience and significance simultaneously' (p. 79). He thinks of this as 'a global institutional field of phenomena'. Bion (1961) also describes how groups induce a certain depersonalization which makes individual members permeable to the pressures of trans-personal emotive forces. I would wish to describe this in my own terms: the *practice as therapist* may 'absorb, transform and reclaim' the generalized transference. We may say that the *practice as therapist* becomes the good breast that offers emotional enrichment and nourishment. The institution receives the generalized transference and, by treating the patient as a whole, will ideally seek to reintegrate the split parallel transferences.

The notion of the *general practice as therapist* should not be seen as an alternative function of the individual therapist. While it is clear that the individual characteristics of the practice and the particular personality and therapeutic model of the therapist have their own unique contributions, what I am describing is perhaps more determined by the psychopathology of particular patients. With some patients who are easily contained (less prone to splitting or acting out) the therapist may indeed be the principle source of transference and containment; with other patients, however, this role would be taken by the therapist and the GP or even a wider network of practice staff. It is these patients who particularly activate the *practice as therapist*, as they do not engage just a single individual but a large part of the institution.

There is no consistency in the type of presenting problem that characterizes these patients' use of the generalized transference. However, we may note some similar features in the way these patients related to the general practice. Typically, they are able to raise a good deal of concern amongst the staff group. On the other hand, while good at making others anxious, they are equally good at stopping others from being able to help them, thus making any curative intervention, be it medical or psychotherapeutic, very difficult. Staff want to help but feel they cannot. Where patients split affects this usually leads some staff members to be idealized while others are denigrated. The idealizations can often find a resonance in any narcissistic aspects in the therapist's psychology, and the staff member may indeed feel they are special. The patients I am describing tend not to produce such diverse reactions in the staff. More commonly different members of the staff group feel the same way, usually inadequate. I would suspect that many of the so called 'heart-sink patients' fall into this group. In fact these qualities sound similar to the patients described by Main (1957), though those seen in general practice were much less disturbed. It is my impression, though, that a diluted generalized transference can be detected with most patients.

Since containment is a necessary process for the therapist as well as the patient, this raises the question of what are the containment requirements (or countertransference issues) for the *general practice as therapist*?

Main, in his classic paper 'The ailment' (1957), describes the debilitating effect on all the staff working with chronic patients who do not respond to treatment. In particular these patients aroused all manner of negative feelings in the staff team in their therapeutic efforts. Failure to show benefit from the treatment was unconsciously experienced as a crushing defeat for the therapist's omnipotence. Most of these negative feelings were ego-alien and, therefore, remained unconscious, where they began to exert affects on more than just the team's professionalism. They were also reflected in professional conflicts between staff and even filtered into the personal life of staff, creating a variety of health problems. Main went so far as to suggest that many of the worst features displayed by these difficult patients were best understood as 'characteristic not of them but rather of the hospital setting' (p. 133). In my opinion, such a view, which sees the disturbance entirely originating from the staff is too extreme. I would suggest that it is a more interactive process whereby the unconscious problems in the staff and patients alike mutually affect each other. (To clarify one point here: I do not mean the individual unconscious difficulties of a staff member; rather, I am emphasizing the unconscious dynamics in the staff group as a working unit; the unconscious assumptions of the institution itself.)

Institutions and practices vary in their ability to contain disturbance and phantastical assaults. We might draw an analogy with countertransference difficulties that are sometimes met in individual psychotherapeutic practice: dissociation, disavowal, repression, denial, and counter projective identifications. We may see how some of these can become acted out by institutions. The staff team may have its own internal difficulties that inhibit therapeutic function. Some patients are able to exploit splits in the team, even if the team are generally 'good enough'. The patient's pathology may focus on unconscious conflicts in the team. As a result, the team members may find themselves having internal differences about the patient without realizing that they are enacting splits in the patient's internal world. Indeed, Main (1957) describes how some patients are particularly sensitive to unspoken tensions unacknowledged by the staff; the patient's symptoms become worse as a result of an attempt to make the staff more reliable. The patient's distress can be dramatically reduced if staff can disclose and discuss their disagreements and reach a genuine consensus about how the patient could be handled in any particular matter. Clearly, then, one of the requirements of a 'good enough' *general practice as therapist* is for communication to exist between the team members, particularly, perhaps, between the GP and psychotherapist in order to avoid unconscious, patient-induced splits. What is required is a framed but flexible discourse.

In describing the generalized transference and the *general practice as therapist* am I trying to make a virtue out of a necessity? To an extent, yes, but if that is the case it is doing no more than following the psychoanalytic tradition. After all, upon discovering the transference, Freud thought it was a major obstacle to therapeutic work. It was only later that he realized this inevitable phenomenon provided the greatest opportunities for change. In that sense, if the transference does exist at an institutional level with parallel and split transferences, perhaps this, too, can be seized as a therapeutic opportunity rather than just a problem.

REFERENCES

Bion, W.R. (1961) *Experience in Groups*. London: Tavistock, 1970.

Bion, W.R. (1962) *Learning From Experience*. New York: Aronson, 1977.

Bleger, J. (1967) *Simbiosis y ambiguedad, estudio psicoanalitico*. Buenos Aires: Paidos.

Correale, A. (1994) The institutional field: an evolution of the container model. *British Journal of Psychotherapy*, 11 (1): 77–82.

Fairbairn, W.R.D. (1936) The effect of a king's death upon patients undergoing analysis. In *Psychoanalytic Studies of the Personality*, London: Routledge, 1986.

Hinshelwood, R.D. (1987) *What Happens in Groups*. London: Free Association Books.

Hoag, L. (1992) Psychotherapy in the general practice surgery: considerations of the frame. *British Journal of Psychotherapy*, 8 (4): 417– 29.

Langs, R. (1976a) *The Therapeutic Interaction*. New York: Jason Aronson.

Langs, R. (1976b) *The Technique of Psychoanalytic Psychotherapy*. New York: Jason Aronson.

Launer, J. (1994) Psychotherapy in the general practice surgery: working with and without a secure therapeutic frame. *British Journal of Psychotherapy*, 11 (1): 120–26.

Main, T. F. (1957) The ailment. *Medical Psychology*, 30 (3): 129–45.

Mann, D. (1997a) *Psychotherapy: An Erotic Relationship – Transference and Countertransference Passions*. London: Routledge.

Mann, D. (1997b) Masturbation and painting. In K. Killick and J. Schaverien (Editors) *Art, Psychotherapy and Psychosis*. London: Routledge.

Mann, D. (ed.) (1999) *Erotic Transference and Countertransference: Clinical Practice in Psychotherapy*. London: Routledge.

Mann, D., Sumner, J., Dalton, J. and Berry, D. (1990) Working with incest survivors. *Psychoanalytic Psychotherapy* 4 (3): 271–81.

McDougall, J. (1982) *Theatres of the Mind*. London: Free Association Books, 1986.

McDougall, J. (1989) *Theatres of the Body*. London: Free Association Books, 1991.

McDougall, J. (1995) *The Many Faces of Eros*. London: Free Association Books.

Schafer, R. (1983) *The Analytic Attitude*. London: Hogarth Press.

Searles, H. (1959) The effort to drive the other person crazy – an element in the aetiology and psychotherapy of schizophrenia. In *Collected Papers on Schizo-phrenia and Related Subjects*. London: Hogarth Press, 1965.

Viderman, S. (1974) Interpretation in analytic space. *International Review of Psycho-Analysis*, 1: 467–80.

Winnicott, D. W. (1960) The theory of the parent–infant relationship. In *The Maturational Processes and the Facilitating Environment*. London: Hogarth Press, 1987.

8 Counselling for patients with severe mental health problems in the general practice setting

Marilyn Miller-Pietroni

Introduction

This chapter describes counselling for patients with severe and long-term mental health problems in a general practice setting (Marylebone Health Centre in central London). Examples of recent work with four patients who have been diagnosed respectively as suffering from a serious sexual problem, dementia, bi-polar affective disorder and agoraphobia are described. The resource implications of such work are considered, as are the implications for communication and collaboration in the primary care and community mental health teams. The work takes place within a specific general practice setting where a differentiated approach to counselling has been evolved using five different service options.

It is suggested that a rationale for the continuance of work with patients with severe mental health problems is provided by the framework of values, the policy context, patient satisfaction and the counsellor's contribution to the primary care team. The evidence base on effectiveness is emerging slowly and needs now to be developed further in accordance with appropriate outcome criteria such as patient satisfaction, prescription changes and frequency of contact with GPs and other practitioners in the primary care team.

The setting, the culture and the counselling team

The counselling service to be described was first established in 1987. The work of the early years is described in a paper by Webber, Davies and P. Pietroni (1994) who identified GPs' referral patterns , with an emphasis on brief work with patients, mainly women, who were depressed or undergoing some kind of transition.

The counsellor was from the outset seen as part of what the health centre described as an 'extended range of clinical interventions' on offer to patients in a 'holistic approach' to inner-city care. In addition to the GP, practice nurse and counsellor, several part-time complementary therapists (osteopath, massage therapist, traditional chinese medicine practitioner and homeopath) also played a key part in the primary health care team (Pietroni and Pietroni 1996).

In 1996 the counselling service was re-organized to offer a range of five services; to give patients more say about which service they received; and to limit the counselling service to patients who demonstrated their motivation by completing a simple Counselling Application Form. A full description of the model can be found in a future publication and is summarized below (Miller-Pietroni and Vaspe forthcoming).

The team culture is a mixture of rigour and pragmatism, with each counsellor working in their own way within a shared policy about the use of resources, waiting-list management and the menu of services on offer. It is important for all the work but particularly that with severely disturbed patients that the team is supervised by a trained psychotherapist with a substantial mental health background and some years of experience in general practice counselling (Pietroni 1995). The team offer psycho-dynamic and cognitive approaches and receive fortnightly individual supervision. They meet once every six weeks for a case discussion and once every eight weeks to review the service and individual patients with the GPs.

A retrospective audit was carried out of patients seen and patterns of counselling practice over a two-year period. A critical analysis of that audit enabled the current structured menu of five counselling services to be generated. These five services were then made explicit to patients and GPs in a new Counselling Information Leaflet that asked patients to indicate their preferred service, if they felt able, at the point of applying for counselling. Patients are seen by a counsellor only after two forms are received: a Referral Form from the GP and an Application Form from the patient. The introduction of these changes successfully led to a reduc-tion in DNAs ('did not arrive') on first appointments from 30 per cent to nil in the next six-month audit.

Rationale underlying patient choice

The five services from which patients select at the health centre continue to operate today and are described below. It was hoped that the introduction of a more clearly defined set of services would provide patients and GPs with greater transparency and choice in line with the thinking around the NHS and Community Care Act (1990) and The Patient's Charter (1991). To organize the counselling services into a clear set of options also provides a foundation for further research.

To invite patients to indicate their preferred pattern (length, number and frequency of sessions) of counselling service at the point of their application is, however, unusual and was a considerable change in the balance of power between counsellor and patient from our previous pattern, where the counsellor decided how many sessions would be offered based on their clinical assessment. Currently, although the patient's rationale for their choice is explored with the counsellor in the first session, the patient begins by being more fully informed about the limits and scope of the service and having to think about their needs. If they want more help than is on offer at the health centre they are in a position to go elsewhere. To assist them, an information leaflet about the counselling service provides the numbers of other local counselling, psychotherapy and mental health services.

At its worst, patient choice about the health centre counselling service and other local services might be considered a gesture towards consumerism; at its best it is a genuinely empowering strategy that reduces professional mystification and helps the services to seem less remote and more accessible. Such information can also promote in the patient some reflection on the nature of the problem for which they are seeking help before they enter a consulting room and so contribute positively to the clinical assessment process.

The culture of general practice

The team of counsellors were attempting to find a way of providing counselling which, whilst rigorous in counselling terms, also respected and was appropriate to the rhythms of need and response in the general practice setting. At that time, there was insufficient data available on the clinical effectiveness of counselling in general practice and the research literature tended to present a rather thin picture of the setting, the work and the outcomes which did not do justice to the sheer complexity of our own experience. So we listened to the GPs. They were after all the experts about the nature of the setting, whilst we were competent in the practice of counselling and psychotherapy.

The GPs emphasized the heterogeneity of the setting, the delicate relationship between care and cure and the inherent limits of much clinical intervention. They recognized a natural history to the kinds of problems that presented in general practice. They would often state that the vast majority of problems are 'self-limiting' or improve in a limited time (about three months) whereas a small minority remain static or get worse whatever intervention is made. Only a very few *improve as a direct result of a specific intervention made by a practitioner*, they would state. They therefore emphasized the importance of containment and support and of being in partnership with the patient, trying to understand and respond appropriately to what is going wrong, rather than adopting a heroic model in which the professional intervention is centre stage and a cure culture predominates.

The care culture

This picture, accepted at Marylebone Health Centre as a goodenough description of the overall rhythm of care and cure in general practice, fitted well with counselling values and methods. It also had considerable implications for our approach to constructing a counselling service, particularly for patients with severe problems who are often listed in the literature as unsuitable for counselling. It seemed wise to expect and perhaps to accept that the overall outcomes of counselling would be likely to reflect the general practice outcome patterns, whatever clinical interventions we might make. Certainly it would be presumptuous to assume that we could do better. As a team, we therefore decided that counselling practice should contribute to the care culture as well as the cure culture in general practice and should be shaped accordingly within a carefully managed resource framework. Indeed, our retrospective audit showed that there were patients for whom this policy decision was critical to their access to the service.

The considerations that informed the five counselling services can be summarised as follows:

- to maximize the use of scarce resources in a setting with heterogeneous demands
- to improve access for the least privileged patients with chronic problems
- to increase transparency for patients and GPs about the limits and extent of the service
- to offer information and some choice over services to patients within these limits
- to respect the long-term care culture of general practice in the inner city
- to establish an information base for audit and future research.

The five services from which patients nominate a preference when completing their Counselling Application Form (alongside the GP's own referral), are now described.

The five counselling services

The A Service

This is the opportunity to see a counsellor for one or two sessions only to talk something over. It is nominated rarely and then only by patients who are in transition or face a crisis of some kind, such as recent bad news or around a key life decision. It is also selected by patients who are very defended and do not want to look at their problems in much depth but who recognize they need some immediate support and clarification to help them continue as before. Sometimes it will lead to the patient deciding to transfer to the B Service in order to have a further eight sessions

The B Service

This offers brief work of up to ten sessions for patients who want to take a short but serious look at a particular problem or life pattern. We extended the limit of this service from the original and more common six to ten sessions because experience showed that there was frequently a need to provide 'a few more sessions', both to reach a suitable stopping point and to accomplish work of some depth. Whilst the number of sessions remains few, the early indications are in line with the research of Sifneos (1979), Mann (1973) and Davanloo (1980) in the field of brief psychotherapy, namely, that with a clear focus and a motivated patient it is possible to achieve significant change in about ten to twelve sessions. After making the change from six to ten sessions, no further increase has seemed necessary. This number allows new work to start after a break and to continue to the next seasonal break (end of summer to Christmas, mid-January to the end of March or May to July). This may seem an odd point to make since obviously referrals do come at all times of the year but we always receive a bulge of referrals after Christmas (family problems or isolation), and around the holiday periods at Easter and summer when human distress seems to peak.

The C Service

This offers up to ten fortnightly sessions over approximately twenty weeks. This service is selected by patients with complex and less focused problems, who are ambivalent about change but recognize that they have entrenched difficulties 'that won't go away'. They want to be seen over a longer period of time but often cannot bear for the counselling to disturb their usual patterns. Some might say that they were unsuitable for counselling but our experience is that this longer and slower 'drip-drip' approach is selected sparingly by the patients and can in those selected instances be surprisingly effective. First, the patient and counsellor are working together over almost a six-month period usually including one holiday break. Since entrenched problems often include an element of perverse dependency, this structure can be used productively if the right relationship is struck between a focus on current life (C), past life(P) and transference (T) (Malan's TCP triangle (1979)). Next, this work contributes to the long-term support function of the overall general practice team. On a fortnightly basis, two patients can be seen alternately in a weekly one-hour counselling slot, thus sharing the hard core of the general practice load more with other practitioners. These fortnightly patients include those who present frequently to the GP with minor ailments. It is possible to demonstrate from a review of the notes that during the time such patients are seeing the counsellor they make fewer GP contacts, thus providing some temporary respite to the GPs and freeing their time for other patients.Whilst fortnightly counselling patients often revert to more frequent contact with the GPs when their counselling sessions are over, a small proportion decide to seek long-term counselling or psychotherapeutic help. Of these, a smaller proportion still (about one in ten) progress into open-ended talking treatment.

The D Service

This offers thirty or forty-five minute sessions (according to the counsellor's preference and the patient's need) every four to six weeks over a longer and ultimately open-ended period of time. Patients shift into this service after a referral discussion with the GPs or an assessment for one of the other services has identified the long-term need or when such a need has become apparent after brief work in Service B or C. We refer internally to the D Service as the Intermittent Service because of its open-ended pattern of regular but less frequent contact. When first introduced we described it as 'the psychiatric outpatients model' because the patients who needed this service often had serious mental health problems and the manageable pattern of contact (in terms of both resources and counter-transference burden) was similar to an old-style psychiatric out-patient clinic, with follow-ups every six weeks.

It is in the D Service that we are now able to provide skilled listening and continuous support for patients with serious long-term mental health problems. The three counsellors in the practice carry one or two patients in this category at any one time making a maximum of six each year. Given that each general practice of 10,000 patients can expect to have 1.5 per cent or 15 patients in this category, this is a significant contribution to a practice with approximately 6,000 patients. The examples of counselling work to be discussed in more detail in this chapter will, with the exception of the first patient, be drawn from this service.

The E Service

Finally, this provides an emergency slot of half an hour each week to see a patient referred during the same week. This slot is otherwise kept unfilled and is used about four times a year only for an emergency. GPs rarely if ever use it to bypass the normal referral system in which both GP and patient complete their forms and only if both are received is an appointment given. The emergency time has been used for counselling around a miscarriage, a termination of pregnancy, a bereavement and sudden unemployment. When the time is not used to see patients it is used for writing up notes, liaison, administration or audit.

Resources

Given that resources are always limited in general practice in relation to need and demand, it is vital that the maximum effective use is made of what is available. At Marylebone, we have only three times three and a half hours counselling time available each week, including administration and supervision. Each counsellor holds a one-hour slot for brief work (Service B). Then according to skill, experience and inclination, one counsellor sees a second brief case making a total of four in the B Service at any one time and about 18–20 per year overall. Two counsellors see two Service C fortnightly patients each in their second hour each week, making a total of four in this service at any one time and about nine per year overall. Each counsellor also sees one or two patients each in Service D, the long-term intermittent service, making about six per year ongoing. These are programmed over the year in the same hour as the A Service, new assessments for the B and C services, alternate week supervisions and two half-hour emergency slots which are kept free and are otherwise available for administration.

There is something of trying to squeeze a quart into a pint pot in these arrangements and like the GPs, we all tend to do a little extra in order to keep up with records, team liaison and managing the waiting list, but there is a lot of satisfaction in the fact that the tightly structured system which has emerged has solved a number of problems about 'difficult patients' and about patients with quite different counselling needs and has given us as a team a framework for future audit and evaluation. It seems to work for the range of patients seen as well as for the practice. We hope to carry out more systematic research on patient satisfaction and clinical outcomes in the future now that the overall system of services and resource management has been established.

Work with patients with severe mental health problems

In this section, some recent work will be described with patients who have serious mental health problems. With one exception (the first example described) they have all been seen in Service D, the intermittent service. The work of all three counsellors is represented here.

Patient one, Jack

The first patient, Jack, is a young policeman, thirty-five years of age, who was seen in the brief service (Service B) during the time when only six sessions were offered. He was referred because he was depressed and lacking in energy and had lost interest in his work. During the final session, in classic textbook fashion, he said, 'There is something I haven't told you . . .'. The counsellor had been puzzled by him because he had said very little of note and seemed emotionally blank. All attempts at interpretation or making more ordinary contact through questions were met with a brief reply followed by a bland gaze and there were long periods of silence if the counsellor stopped trying to communicate in this way. It looked as if the sessions were going to finish on a note of mystery until this classic comment in the last quarter of an hour. The patient went on to say that he was hiding something because as the counsellor had already commented many times 'it was difficult to discuss'. He then briefly explained that he regularly dressed up in women's clothes which he kept hidden in a locked compartment in his wardrobe, so that his long-term girl friend would not see them. He did not know why but he felt compelled to dress up and go out to a club where cross-dressing was tolerated, about once every few weeks.Then he would pack the clothes away carefully and continue with his normal life. He was terrified that one day his secret would come out and his life would be ruined.

The counsellor offered the patient a further two sessions at the end of the sixth session instead of ending, commenting on how difficult it had been to feel safe enough to unlock this part of his story with her. In the next session, he settled down to tell her more with visible relief. He had expected to be sent away at the end of the last session, he said. He was also very unclear about what he wanted and continued to maintain that his main problem was depression and lethargy and not being able to get very involved in life. The counsellor asked about his fantasies associated with the kinds of women's clothes he chose, which were very tactile; leather, silk, velvet and satin, and he was able to link these with exciting female characters in specific videos and films associated with his own adolescence. Such figures contrasted dramatically with his home life at that time, he explained. He had been a late and only child guarded closely by old-fashioned parents and then expected to look after his prematurely ageing mother after his father's early death. It was a home, as he experienced it, that offered no excitement or 'make-believe'. Some hope had also died with his father, although they had never been close.

The counsellor commented that perhaps there was some healthy but 'locked up' development in 'the wardrobe in his mind', and went on to suggest that 'all his sexual dreams and desires seemed to be mixed up with his nightmares of being found out as a developing sexual and physical being'. It was as if none of those dreams were to see the light of day for fear of being recognized as part of the sexual male that he was. He flushed at these comments and then said he couldn't remember the first time he had dressed up, he thought it had all begun by buying odd garments of clothing or pieces of material that he liked to touch. This led on to an exploration of his masturbation fantasies, which were about being admired by men and women for being an exotic, alluring and magic creature. Here the counsellor could hear and commented on the residual echoes of the little boy who wanted to be admired by both his mother and father as a magical child, who was fully and physically alive, exciting to touch and to look at and whose sexuality was recognized and appreciated.

The patient went on to explain that he now lives alone and his girl-friend stays at weekends but he keeps her at a distance.The counsellor worked in the transference about his distancing of her and his fear that their dialogue would be ruined by the stuff he kept hidden in the wardrobe of his mind. She suggested that he dressed up when he wanted to check that he was still emotionally and physically alive. She offered him four further weekly sessions followed by monthly holding sessions over a few months in the intermittent service. This extended period of about eight months allowed a referral to be prepared, with the patient's agreement, to a psychotherapy clinic that specialized in treating patients with sexual problems. The intermittent service sessions also gave a chance for further work on the material that the patient was now bringing openly. During this time the patient acted out in an integrative but potentially destructive way. He had an affair with a very sexy young woman whom he met on the tube, which lasted several weeks. He also did a short introductory training in massage therapy which allowed him to enjoy touching and being touched in a controlled but caring way. Here too, he fell for a young woman and survived her preference for someone else in the group. These developments were rather worrying and indicated that it would have been very easy for this patient to have had a manic breakdown with considerable risks to his social position if he had not been held just enough in the monthly sessions.

   This example shows how the Intermittent Service can work alongside the Brief Service to provide a holding environment for a patient with what he identified as a serious problem while the referral process is carefully negotiated and counselling work continues. Had there not been a highly suitable psychotherapy service elsewhere which could offer this patient skilled long-term help, he could have continued in the intermittent service at the Health Centre, working within the resource framework available. He could not have been given open-ended or long-term weekly treatment at the Health Centre. He had no money to pay for private treatment and was clear that he did want to talk to someone on an ongoing basis. The referral was successful and the patient is now in long-term psychotherapy. Periodic reports indicate that he is doing well.

Patient two, Benjamin

The second patient, Benjamin, is a solicitor of 68 years of age who was diagnosed as suffering from pre-senile dementia five years ago but who seems to have reached a plateau after an initial deterioration. He and his wife divorced earlier when he was still well, following extra-marital affairs on both sides, but they are still good friends. They have one son and one daughter who live outside London and keep in contact about once a week by telephone and once a month by visits. Benjamin also has several sisters who live in London and care about his welfare. For the time being, he lives alone at home but on his regular visits to the GP he seems depressed and comments on how he misses intelligent company and finds it difficult to have lost the benefits of his position as the eldest in the family who was always expected 'to know best' . He is in otherwise good health and still leads an active life, travelling and keeping up his attendance at concerts, the tickets and transport for which are organized for him by other family members. He has a housekeeper to help him to follow his daily programme.

He was referred to the counselling service after the GP noticed that he was not only dementing, but also depressed and was complaining of loneliness. The GP recognized that Benjamin's emotional life had not been eradicated by the dementia and after seeing him several times, he discussed the situation at the bi-monthly GP/counsellor meeting. This meeting reviews current cases, referrals and the waiting list and any problem areas. This potential referral was brought for discussion because it fell outside the normal range of referrals. Somewhat diffidently, the GP concerned asked whether such a referral might be considered. Since the counsellors had a commitment to working across a spectrum of need and had just established the intermittent service to provide targeted long-term care, the patient was assessed and offered regular sessions every six weeks. He has now been attending for the last two and a half years. In the sessions, he shares his recent experiences with the counsellor, grumbles in a normal way about his family and friends and describes the latest concert he has attended. He also talks about his isolation and mourns his lost youth and vigour. He is seen about once a year by the specialist neurological team that originally diagnosed his condition.

He is by no means fully demented and certainly experiences mental pain and conflict like other people. He misses his former family position and often feels like a little boy yearning to have his protecting mother back again. Sometimes he says he does not know why he comes to see the counsellor or the GP as there is nothing the matter with him, but he always keeps both regular appointments. Occasionally, one of his sisters will visit the practice to discuss the latest dilemma facing the family in managing his gradual deterioration. Joint sessions with her and the patient have been held with the counsellor and seem to have contained and even resolved passing problems between them. The family are relieved that the practice can offer care 'in the round' and have been assured that work will go on in this way indefinitely. They have been told that general practice continues for life and that his counsellor is likely to remain in the practice for the foreseeable future, where all information is readily available and can be easily co-ordinated. This work is a good example of the continuing care function of the Intermittent Service at Marylebone.

Patient three, Miriana

A third patient, Miriana, is a single woman in her forties, a European refugee who has been suffering all her life with what is termed by the psychiatrist bi-polar affective disorder. She was referred by a woman GP, who felt that she had been doing well and was ready to reduce her high dosage of drugs so that she could take up more of her former life as an artist. At that time she carried a diagnosis of schizophrenia which has since been reviewed. This case is described in detail elsewhere (Miller-Pietroni and Vaspe forthcoming) and is summarized here simply to show that such a disturbed patient can use a continuing limited contact of the kind offered in the Intermittent Service. Over a five-year period, this patient has been seen for only eight hours per year, slightly less than once a month excluding holiday periods. Her medication has been reduced over this period to a low maintenance dose, and she has been able to work for several exhibitions and to sustain an intimate relationship until a recent relapse. She was bringing to the sessions the kinds of relationship problems that many patients bring and was able to celebrate her 'normal life problems' which had taken the place of her 'illness problems'. As she put it one day, 'Just because I am sick does not mean that I do not have ordinary problems that I need to talk about, if you see what I mean.'

Three years ago, as part of her developing rehabilitation, she was referred to the Community Mental Health Team (CMHT) to provide her with a care programme with a regular psychiatric review system, in addition to the services from the health centre. The CMHT were aware that she was seeing a counsellor once a month at the practice but decided nevertheless to offer her a psychotherapy assessment. Not surprisingly, she was resistant to a change of worker and the offer was finally withdrawn (by telephone) because it was felt she had become too disturbed again and would not be able to use psychotherapy. At the same time her partner of several years moved away. For the first time in five years, she broke her appointments with the GP and practice counsellor and stopped taking her medication. Shortly afterwards she was re-admitted to hospital after some extreme behaviour which she herself described as 'very sick, very ill' and her drugs were changed and increased again.

A recent care programme review meeting at the social services department was attended by the whole team involved in her care, including the practice counsellor, GP, care manager, community psychiatric nurse, flexicare worker and consultant psychiatrist. It was recognized that Miriana's living circumstances had now deteriorated, as she had been evicted from her room and had become homeless and parted from her possessions; also that she had undergone terrible trauma through the return of her mental illness following a period of increased stress. The patient was present at this meeting and eloquently spoke about what it had been like and was still like to go through 'this hell'.

The support system of regular monthly appointments with the counsellor and with the GP for her drugs has now been reinstated even though she has now been placed in temporary accommodation outside the practice area. The health centre recognizes that patients with a long-term illness of this kind are likely, at times of crisis, to be mobile but that they need a long-term secure base to which they can return. In retrospect, it was regrettable that the delicate continuing care framework was disturbed but the proposed changes were perhaps mistakenly felt to be 'in the patient's best interest'. It has to be recognized also that a serious mental illness of this kind has its own internal rhythms, which are not always predictable.

The issue for the practice counsellor is whether or not to consider it appropriate to bear the disturbing complexity of being part of an inter-agency network of this kind, including the implied long-term responsibility for inter-agency liaison. Many counsellors would feel that to attend mental health review meetings is stepping out of role or breaking confidentiality. At Marylebone, we would argue that if you are going to work with very disturbed patients, the natural history of their disturbance is often life-long and it is necessary to recognize that one is likely to be working in a network and to seek the patient's permission for doing so actively. Certainly in this instance, we have had cause to consider whether it would have been sufficient three years ago to continue to limit the patient's care to the GP, practice nurse and counsellor rather than to extend it to the wider network of the specialist mental health team, just as that team has had cause to wonder what the practice team was doing at certain points in time. These doubts are inevitable on both sides and are not necessarily cleared up by direct communication. They are also exacerbated by the patient's tendency to split the agencies and individuals with powerful idealizing and denigrating feelings. The discomfort of living with doubt and regret, as well as recognizing and continuing to work with the results of one's real or imagined errors, is an important part of any counselling, nowhere more so than in general practice.

Patient four, Orianthe

The final example of work was undertaken with Orianthe, a 26-year-old Mediterranean woman who was unable to leave her bedsitter home unless she was accompanied by a friend. This friend accompanied her to her early sessions at the practice. The patient had managed to obtain work as an editor that she could do from home but had had to leave her job in publishing because of her phobia. She was seen by the practice counsellor who takes more of a cognitive behavioural approach to her work, in recognition of its positive outcomes with patients with such problems.

The patient was asked in the sessions by her counsellor to compile a journal of her week and from this was given a series of increasingly difficult challenges to her phobic pattern along with active encouragement, advice and support. From time to time there would also be side tasks, such as writing an imaginary letter to her mother to explain how she felt about her now and what she wished her mother could have done for her in the past but had been unable to do. Every step forward was actively noted by the counsellor and used as the foundation for constructing a further challenge. One day the patient brought a nightmare to the session and was very depressed. She had dreamt of revisiting her family home which was haunted by ghosts that threatened her but which she was just able to elude. She said the stairs and floor were carpeted with leaves.

In supervision, the counsellor discussed the possible meaning of the dream. She had become worried because the patient had become very depressed although she had improved symptomatically and was now able to come to the practice on her own and to go shopping locally twice a week. She had also held a small tea party for some friends from work and had set herself further targets of visiting an art gallery and going to see a favourite film. The supervisor suggested that the dream reflected a drawing together into one story of the counselling work which had already been undertaken: revisiting ghosts from the family past and going back to take her 'leave' from the family again differently, more sadly and less tempestuously. Now the family ghosts were more under her control, at just enough distance not to overwhelm her but within her conscious awareness and not dissociated, so that she did not need to become as phobic about 'leaving' her own home and all that it represented. This may or may not have been the right interpretation but it helped the counsellor to see the depression as a positive sign linked to deeper meanings. This was a good example of the complementarity of a psychodynamically oriented supervision with a cognitive behavioural counsellor.

This patient also was seen first in the brief service for ten sessions and then transferred to the intermittent service where she has been seen so far for four sessions. It seems likely that she will be able to stop counselling at some point in the coming year.

Containment by the individual, the team and the network: 'transformations and safety nets'

In the examples of work outlined above, our shared conceptual framework for work with such distressed and disturbed patients is that of containment; not always in the highly technical sense as described by Bion (1959) but in the everyday senses that we came to define at Marylebone in our monthly, multi-professional academic meetings. Following a team discussion on work with difficult patients it was discovered that there were very different meanings in use for the term 'containment'. These different meanings were not precisely linked to the different professional groups of GPs, practice nurses, complementary therapists and counsellors.

One meaning was close to that defined by Bion in the psycho-analytic literature and which we came as a team to call '*transformational*'. Here a patient pushes (projects) their sometimes inchoate and disturbing fears, feelings and phantasies into another who digests and detoxifies them and then organizes and articulates them back to the patient in the form of a reflection or interpretation (Hinshelwood 1989). This transformational form of containment can be seen in the individual relationship between patient and counsellor in the first and last patients (Jack and Orianthe) described above. The transformation is confirmed by behavioural change and a change in mental state and is closer to the curing end of the care–cure relationship in general practice.

A second meaning was called the 'safety net' form of containment and was more commonly used by the GPs. The second and third patients described above (Benjamin and Miriana) fall into this category. The second patient was provided with a safety net that comprised the counsellor, GP and the specialist hospital. It is working well so far, in terms of monitoring, keeping communication channels open and providing support. It can be seen as an anticipatory structure that supports GP, relatives and patient in the present and is ready for future change. The third patient was meant to be provided with a safety net by the primary care team in the practice which included the counsellor and by the wider network of the Community Mental Health Team. It is hard to know whether the over-complex inter-agency work was at fault here or whether what was being witnessed and shared was the natural history of one of the severe mental illnesses. Either way, this patient had a relatively normal life on low drug dosages for several years before her recent relapse and all concerned, including the patient, attribute that to teamwork in the practice and particularly to the monthly counselling sessions over several years.

A third meaning for containment used in the practice is that of suppression, or putting the lid on: 'we have to contain this: there is nothing we can do and we just have to recognize that and do nothing except set limits on use'. It is not exemplified in this chapter and is not often relevant to the counselling service because such patients are generally not referred or, if they are, do not arrive. However, on the front line of general practice it is a last-resort approach with difficult patients who are frequent users of the emergency and day services but who are unable to make much use of any help that is offered to them.

For the most part, and contrary to some common stereotypes, this group does not usually include patients with serious mental health problems of the type described in this chapter.

Acknowledgements

The work described in this chapter in certain areas reflects the thinking and effort of all the staff at Marylebone Health Centre, particularly, during the period under consideration: Dr Sheelagh Finlay, Dr Tania Eber, Dr Sue Morrison and Dr Patrick Pietroni and members of the Marylebone Health Centre's academic meetings. Most of all, it reflects the hard work, creativity and tenacity of my colleagues in the counselling team: Alison Vaspe and Romayne Jesty and the foundation provided by our predecessor, Vivien Webber. I am also indebted to Gerald Caplan, David Malan and Peter Bruggen who for me were formative influences at the Tavistock Clinic and Hill End Adolescent Unit. Responsibility for this text however, including any errors, is my own.

REFERENCES

Armstrong, E. (1997) *The Primary Mental Health Care Toolkit* London: Royal College of General Practitioners.

Bion, W.R. (1959) 'Attacks on linking' *International Journal of Psychoanalysis*, 30: 308–15 [republished in W.R. Bion, *Second Thoughts* London: Heinemann, pp. 93–109].

Caplan, G. (1964) *Principles of Preventive Psychiatry* London: Tavistock Publications.

Davanloo, H. (1980) *Short-Term Dynamic Psychotherapy* New York: Jason Aronson.

Department of Health (1990) *National Health Service and Community Care Act* London: HMSO.

Department of Health (1991) *The Patient's Charter* London: HMSO.

Hinshelwood, R. (1989) *A Dictionary of Kleinian Thought* London: Free Association Books.

Malan, D. (1979) *Individual Psychotherapy and the Science of Psychodynamics* London: Butterworths.

Mann, J. (1973) *Time-limited Psychotherapy* Cambridge, MA: Harvard University Press.

Miller-Pietroni, M. and Vaspe, A. (forthcoming) *Inside Counselling in General Practice: Community Mental Health in the Inner City* Edinburgh: Churchill Livingstone.

Pietroni, M. (1995) 'Inner-city general practice: the experience of one day's counselling' *Psychodynamic Counselling* 1, 3: 449–460.

Pietroni, C. and Pietroni, P. eds (1996) *Innovation in Community Care and Primary Health: The Marylebone Experiment* Edinburgh: Churchill Livingstone.

Rain, L. (1997) *Counselling in Primary Care: A Guide to Good Practice* Leeds: Mind Counselling in Primary Care Project.

Sheldon, M. (1992) *Counselling in General Practice* London: Royal College of General Practitioners.

Sibbald, B., Addington-Hall, J., Brenneman, D. and Freeling, P. (1993) 'Counselling in English and Welsh General Practices: their nature and distribution' *British Medical Journal* 306: 29–33.

Sifneos, P. (1979) *Short Term Dynamic Psychotherapy* New York: Plenum Press.

Webber,V., Davies, P., and Pietroni, P. (1994) 'Counselling in an inner city general practice: an analysis of its use and uptake' *British Journal of General Practice* 44: 175–178.

9 Working with different models: adapting to the context

John Launer

Introduction

When counsellors and psychotherapists work in primary care, problems commonly arise because of the different working styles and belief systems held by different professionals (Corney and Jenkins 1993). For example, one concern to counsellors and therapists is that they may have difficulty in organizing a 'secure frame' for seeing their own patients, with strict time boundaries, use of the same room on every occasion, and so forth. There may also be worries about confidentiality. Anyone trained in the counselling or psychotherapeutic ethos may find themselves caught in a dilemma: trying to be acceptable and useful to the medical hierarchy, while attempting to stick to the rules they believe to be necessary for therapeutic work (Hoag 1992).

While some of these problems may arise in practices where the doctors have little or no knowledge of therapeutic working styles and beliefs, they may be just as acute (or even more so) where the doctors have some level of psychological sophistication. It is reasonably common these days for GPs to have some basic training in counselling. They may even have some background in one of the psychotherapies, or in family therapy (Elder 1990, Launer and Lindsey 1997). Some will be members of discussion groups influenced by the psychoanalytic approach of Michael Balint (Balint 1957, Elder and Samuel 1987). Others may have had personal therapy which they have found helpful in their own professional development and practice and will therefore be sympathetic to psychodynamic ideas. There are also GPs who define themselves as having a special interest in mental health because of previous experience within hospital psychiatry. Most younger GPs will have been trained within vocational schemes where, to a lesser or greater degree, there has been an emphasis on listening skills and attention to psychological issues.

Where psychological work is offered both by GPs and by a trained specialist within the same practice, particular conflicts and rivalries may arise, in addition to the ones usually identified. Trained therapists may see the doctors' approaches as being too brief, superficial, eclectic or directive. They may have doubts about whether GPs are actually qualified to do such work (Rowland, Irving and Maynard 1989). They may be alarmed by doctors' readiness to share confidential information with their teams. They may also be troubled by hearing of cases where doctors have to cross boundaries between their various roles as counsellor, physician, surgeon, obstetrician and perhaps even family friend.

Conversely, even doctors familiar with counselling approaches may become impatient with therapists and counsellors within the busy work setting. The counsellor's traditional approach to the length and frequency of sessions, or to punctuality, confidentiality and professional anonymity may seem unrealistic to them in a general practice context. GPs and their staff may regard a therapist's refusal to deviate from such rules in the surgery as inflexible (McDaniel, Hepworth and Doherty 1992).

In this chapter, I give an account of a model which has evolved in the practice where I work as a GP and has helped us to negotiate these issues and achieve satisfactory working arrangements. We believe it has helped us to address issues of differing consulting practices and also of the variety of ways of conceptualizing and treating mental distress. Following previous writers, I use the words counsellor and therapist interchangeably in this chapter, since it relates to both kinds of professional within the context of primary medical care. This usage also takes account of the fact that a minority of those who describe themselves as counsellors in general practice are in fact qualified psychotherapists (Nickless et al. 1990)

The setting

Our practice is a five-partner training practice in an urban health centre. We are an entirely NHS practice, and we have a typical 'inner-city' demography, with considerable numbers of patients who are unemployed, lone parents, immigrants, refugees or non-English speakers. We also have a tradition of taking on partners and team members with an interest in the psychological, social and political issues relating to their patients' lives. The practice works with a team of employed and attached professionals. This includes GP trainees, practice nurses, health visitors, a community midwife, district nurses, a specialist nurse for the terminally ill, and a community psychiatric nurse. The team holds regular weekly meetings, and in addition a small number of consultations or home visits will be carried out jointly by more than one team member.

Most of the doctors, and some other members of the practice team, have had personal psychotherapy and many have attended training courses of varying lengths in counselling, psychosexual medicine or other therapeutic work. One of the partners (myself) is a trained family therapist. In 1989 a nurse practitioner, undergoing training in Rogerian client-centred counselling, also joined the practice; she subsequently completed her Diploma in Counselling. When she joined the practice, it was agreed that she should take on some counselling patients for part of her working week.

Soon after she joined the team, it became apparent that there was lack of clarity among us about what was meant by 'counselling'. The nurse counsellor used the words to refer to the structured approach she was familiar with using. This generally consisted of brief, focused work for six to twelve weekly sessions of fifty minutes each. She offered clients an agreed contract regarding consultation times, frequency, and the number of consultations. She had also negotiated with a small number of clients to see them for more extended work.

However, the doctors and some other team members used the words 'counselling', or 'therapy', to describe a variety of psychological work they did with patients, especially at times of family crisis. This might be opportunistic, arising spontaneously during consultations or home visits, or it might take place in a series of prearranged consultations. Because of the nature of the GP–patient relationship, psychological therapy offered by the doctors was more usually 'open-ended', taking place in consultations of undefined length, and organized *ad hoc* from session to session. Sometimes it would include problem-solving approaches more akin to the traditional medical consultation, but at other times it would involve the use of ideas and techniques from psychodynamic or family systems therapy.

In preliminary discussions around this area, both sides expressed some of the mutual reservations about each others' practices described in the introductory paragraphs. It was only with time that we saw the new situation as a welcome opportunity to clarify, and to develop, our team's approach to counselling.

The three-level model

As our discussions proceeded, we found ourselves using the expression 'big-C counselling' to describe the kind of planned, structured approach generally used by the nurse counsellor. Although the phrase was first used in a semi-humorous fashion, we soon found that it served a purpose by defining an activity for which we all agreed there should be a place. We agreed that 'big-C counselling' should offer, as closely as circumstances allowed, the secure frame, as taught within counselling training institutions. The counsellor or therapist should have facilities to provide sessions at punctual times, at regular intervals and for fixed lengths. Patients should make direct contact with the counsellor to discuss arrangements for counselling. (This usually, but not necessarily, follows a recommendation by the doctor.) The counsellor would not see more than one member of any family as a client. She would keep private notes, but nothing would be entered into the medical record except that a consultation had taken place. Information would not be shared with other members of the practice team unless issues arose of a statutory or medico-legal nature, or if the practitioner felt personally at risk. Supervision would be by trained specialists outside the practice, paid for by the practice.

Once we had established agreement that there was a place for such work, it seemed natural to use the phrase 'little-c counselling' to denote the kind of work which arose in everyday consultations by GPs. We now use this term to denote the times when GPs enter counselling or therapeutic modes of working during routine consultations. 'Little-c' counselling probably occurs in most good GP consultations, even in practices where doctors may lack specialized mental health training. Patients legitimately expect their GPs to understand their symptoms, and their attendances, as communications which have meanings broader than biomedical ones. Yet at the same time, most attenders will not want or need a structured type of therapy and might be put off by the doctor taking an overtly psychotherapeutic approach to the consultation. Although the doctor may be conscious of using 'little-c counselling', the patient may (and probably should) see this simply in terms of the doctor being an attentive listener.

Since such work forms part of everyday general practice, we felt no need to try to apply the same rules which were necessary for 'big-C' counselling. The ordinary GP context does not, of course, allow for anything resembling the 'secure frame' in terms of punctuality, regularity or constant length of consultation. With regard to confidentiality, patients clearly understand that details are recorded in the notes in most GP consultations and expect this to happen. Nevertheless, our discussions about 'little-c counselling' did lead us to become more aware of confidentiality as an issue. As a result, we decided to include in our practice leaflet a statement making it clear to patients that we sometimes share information within the team for mutual professional support and education unless otherwise requested. The practice leaflet also explains that patients may ask us not to enter information in the notes. There are times in consultations when patients clearly indicate to us that they would like to have a discussion about note-taking before disclosing material, and we are trying to be sensitive to this.

In addition, we introduced a confidentiality code for the primary health care team meetings which specifies, among other things, that patients will generally be told their cases are being discussed, and that team members who know the patient socially will leave during such a discussion. (This may happen, for example, if a community nurse happens to live locally. We do not accept staff as patients.)

As a result of our discussions, we also found it helpful to characterize an intermediate approach as 'middle-C counselling'. We use this term to denote the kind of work offered when a GP wants a wider perspective, or a family view, of a particular problem raised during a routine consultation. Such work usually involves arranging one or two sessions with an individual or family, set aside in protected time (usually at the end of a surgery when there will be no interruptions). Where this type of 'middle-C' work is concerned, we have agreed that GPs should use their discretion regarding note-keeping, sharing information with other team members, and seeking supervision. Sensitive information may be recorded separately outside the medical notes and shared only with one or two colleagues chosen for their special skills. These areas may need to be negotiated with the patients and should be made explicit. However, if topics are covered which would arise anyway in daily general practice, these are treated within the general professional guidelines for doctors.

Included within our definition of 'middle-C' counselling is another kind of approach, much used by myself but also on occasions by other partners. This is to conduct joint consultations with a clinical psychologist attached to the practice, seeing individuals, couples or families for relatively brief numbers of sessions. This style of consultancy or shared case work may be especially helpful to GPs who wish to maintain overall responsibility for their case management but also want the benefit of a trained outsider (Andersen 1987, Deys, Dowling and Golding 1989).

Case studies

The following cases illustrate some of the ways in which, over prolonged periods of time, individuals or families who are registered with the practice have moved between different kinds of psychological work offered by a variety of agents inside and outside the practice, working in accordance with different theoretical models. I have altered some personal details sufficiently to disguise identities.

Case one

Mr B, now aged 44, is a solitary person of high intelligence who has never held down a job or formed a relationship. He lives with his ailing elderly parents who are concerned about what may happen to him. Many years ago he was referred to the local psychiatrist but defaulted from follow-up. (His formal psychiatric diagnosis is of a schizo-affective disorder.) He also consulted us frequently in the past about psycho-somatic symptoms, and has had several inconclusive referrals to physicians.

Over a period of about ten years our counselling contacts with him fell into four distinct phases. The first phase lasted many years and was focused around his physical symptoms. Consultations always included an element of 'little-c' counselling, with attempts by a number of GPs in the practice to draw out his wider concerns about his isolation. Sometimes we would offer arrangements for some more extended consultations ('middle-C') but he did not take these up and would often then move to another partner in the practice.

However, after very many years he finally accepted an offer of a referral to the counsellor in the practice and saw her for three sessions at which he disclosed the level of his despair about his lack of confidence and his inability to make contact with people. Following this he once again defaulted.

About a year later his mother began to visit one of the GPs to express her increasing concern about her son's future. Mr B was also attending around the same time, complaining about chest pains. In separate consultations, the GP suggested to both mother and son that the family might attend for a joint family therapy session with myself.

They agreed to this arrangement and I saw them together with the clinical psychologist attached to the practice. The two of us agreed to work as co-therapists, and offered the family continuing work in family therapy. We saw them at roughly monthly intervals for eighteen months, sometimes with both of us present as co-therapists but also on occasions with myself alone, as circumstances dictated. In technical terms, we worked mainly in a 'systemic' style, using questions to explore the relationship between different family members, and the mutual effects which each person's behaviour had on the others (Penn 1982). In common with most other kinds of counsellors and therapists, we did not offer judgements or set tasks.

In early sessions the son generally presented himself as 'weird', with ideas which at times seemed borderline psychotic and were hard to follow. His mother spoke, often ramblingly, of her own disappointment with him. However, we noticed that towards the end of each session their contributions became more intelligent and focused. Gradually, we found ways of questioning them which helped them to focus on their family history and relate it to current interactions, including the father's non-involvement. The father himself did not attend.

As sessions progressed, it was possible to move the focus away from the son's psychological disorder to the central themes of conflict for this family: loyalty and betrayal, confidence and shyness, intelligence and its absence, closeness and separation. After six months, consultations had become very much livelier, with direct and lucid exchanges between mother and son. The father began to attend too. The son was taking steps to find employment as a courier. His surgery attendances for somatic complaints had greatly reduced.

In the most recent phase of his contact with us, Mr B has come to request referral for psychotherapy. He has recently had an assessment by the local NHS consultant psychotherapist. He has been offered, and accepted, a placement in a long term therapeutic group working on group analytic principles.

Case two

The K family consists of four members: the parents and two daughters aged 16 and 21. Mr K is a security guard, now retired on medical grounds. Four years ago he experienced a raid involving the security van he was driving. Although he was not physically hurt, he was so shaken that he was unable to continue work. What at first seemed like a transient reaction to his experience deepened into a depression, with feelings of worthlessness and loss of confidence as a husband and father as well as an employee. His GP within the practice prescribed antidepressants and also referred him to the counsellor (for 'Big-C' counselling.) However, over a period of several months his mental state continued to deteriorate. Eventually, following some ambiguous remarks about suicide in his counselling sessions, followed by a brief disappearance for several hours, during which his family feared he had indeed taken his life, he agreed to accept admission to a psychiatric ward.

During his admission, which lasted three months, his elder daughter came to see me as a GP in order to complain of feelings of panic. She also disclosed concerns about her mother and sister. I arranged to see each of them in turn in ordinary surgery appointments ('little-c') and tried to establish who had been affected in different ways by Mr K's difficulties. It soon appeared to me that the whole of the nuclear family had become paralysed by the transformation of Mr K from an apparently robust individual into a psychiatric invalid. All of the women felt constrained from developing their own lives until the husband and father improved – something he showed no sign of doing. Indeed, it seemed likely that the women family members had become so fixed in the role of caring for him that he might be insufficiently challenged to return to a more independent role.

Because of my own family therapy training I had a bias towards wishing that the mother and two daughters would come to see me together for some family work, but they were not keen on this idea. Instead, the older daughter asked if she could attend with her sister alone and I agreed to see the two of them for some longer sessions, working with another psychologist who had recently started to work with the practice. I continued to see the mother in ordinary appointments every month or so.

The psychologist and I saw the two daughters at approximately two-monthly intervals over about a year. Both the timing and the length of the work was determined by their own wishes rather than prescribed by ourselves. During our sessions we used questions mainly to explore how the young women were caught between a desire to get on with their own lives on the one hand, and feelings of guilt and responsibility for their parents on the other hand. During the time we saw them, the elder daughter managed to graduate as well as leaving home to live with her boyfriend. The younger daughter increasingly chose to stay overnight with her sister in the new home, where she was made welcome. Meanwhile, Mrs K continued to see me in a normal GP context (continuing 'little-c' work), mainly to discuss how to strike the right balance between accepting her husband's psychiatric invalidity and encouraging him to take up some of his previous interests and hobbies. One of her own decisions was to pursue some studies in evening classes in order to relieve herself from her preoccupation with Mr K's mental illness.

A further year has now passed since Mr K's discharge from hospital, although he continues to see a community mental health nurse who is offering him some cognitive-behavioural therapy. The two daughters come to see me together about every three months in ordinary surgery time by their own choice; they like to report their progress to me, but clearly no longer wish to be identified as psychological patients. Their decision to stop the joint sessions with me and the psychologist coincided with their parents' agreement to come to see me for some long surgery appointments together ('middle-C'). Mr and Mrs K continue to come to these appointments monthly. We use them mainly to keep track of Mr K's achievements in setting and reaching targets for a return to normal life, and Mrs K's ability to find the right point for herself on a spectrum between protectiveness and independence.

Advantages of the model

Our model of a flexible approach to counselling was developed in a practice which already had a strong tradition of support and healthy criticism. Regular meetings of the practice team and of the wider primary health care team allowed us to develop a culture of mutual supervision and internal referral. We have also been fortunate in having strong links with training institutions such as the Tavistock Clinic. While recognizing that this environment is unusual and may differ from many of the practices in which many trained counsellors find themselves, I would suggest that our informal model of three levels of counselling has many advantages in the context of general practice, whatever individual practices may be like.

First, thinking in terms of different levels of counselling *describes reality rather than prescribing perfection*. Although there have been suggestions that GPs should avoid counselling altogether as they are under-qualified for it (Rowland, Irving and Maynard 1989), we believe that this avoidance is both unrealistic and unprofessional. Demand for psychological under-standing from GPs is universal (McLeod 1988). Failure to meet it can itself be wasteful and time-consuming, in terms of repeated 'screen' consultations about apparently trivial somatic problems. It also means that interactions between the GP and patient remain stereotyped and limited. For us, therefore, the problem is not whether to meet that demand, but how. Like many GPs, we believe that the attempt to find answers to that question is central to our work (Balint et al. 1993).

A model which permits several levels of work can also *prevent fruitless discussions about the definition of counselling*, or about who 'owns' this. It is of course still possible for colleagues within the practice to challenge each other about taking on a case where someone does not have appropriate skills or cannot provide a suitable context for work. However, such challenges should concern ways of matching the right level of therapy with the patient or family, not whether GPs should be doing it at all.

In addition to this, a flexible model may help to *enhance our two disciplines' respect for each other*. A trained counsellor will learn about the variety and depth of human experience which GPs encounter every day, and which they have to deal with instantaneously, often simply on the basis of intuition and their use of self. Counsellors may discover that many patients, including some of the most seriously disturbed, will only accept counselling if it is given by the GP personally. Even if consultations seem ludicrously short in counsellors' eyes, the patients (and their doctors) may feel that this disadvantage is offset by the personal knowledge that the GP may have of the patient and the family, as well as by the accessibility of GP consultations and their lack of stigma. Conversely, GPs may learn that the hurly-burly of everyday surgeries is not always the setting in which people will disclose their innermost concerns, let alone work to change them. By having their own counselling role adequately valued, GPs may in fact acquire added respect for the 'secure frame' and for the kind of healing which can be done there and nowhere else.

One important benefit of a flexible approach is that it *recognizes that general practitioners may be keen to apply the benefits of their own personal growth* to their work, especially if they have had personal therapy or some relevant training. Being able to offer counselling at various levels, with a variety of mutual supervision, enables doctors to do this openly and safely, with less risk that they will pretend to their patients, or themselves, that they have greater expertise than they do.

Beyond these issues of professional respect between counsellors and GPs, there are some wider issues raised by our model. It *draws attention to the relationship of counsellors to the wider community of mental health professionals*. General practice counselling does not take place within a vacuum. It is part of a complex system of services in which many different disciplines play a role, including clinical psychologists, community mental health nurses and psychiatrists. Of necessity, GPs have to use the full range of resources available to them and maintain good professional relations with the various agencies. The counsellor who hopes or tries to work in isolation from other practitioners may alienate colleagues within the local health service, as well as depriving patients of a useful variety of treatment options.

If our flexible model allows for the existence of a wider professional community, it also *takes notice of the extended family life cycle*. As the two case studies above both demonstrate, some GP cases reverberate across years or decades, and affect two or more generations. Faced with many stories like these, most GPs have a healthy scepticism about the notion of an isolated 'episode' of mental illness in a single individual. They are likely to be even more sceptical about the chances that a course of 'treatment', whether drugs or counselling, will lay any problem permanently to rest. A counsellor who undervalues the long historical and family narrative lying behind any case (and often well known to the GP or to the practice collectively) will rightly risk accusations of naivety. Similarly, a counsellor who believes that the client, or client's family, is unlikely to need further interventions from other agencies in the future, is also in danger of a false sense of omnipotence. Implicit in our model, therefore, is a recognition that counselling is rarely if ever a cure for anything, nor is it expected to be. More often it just facilitates necessary changes at certain difficult moments in the life cycle.

Along with the historical and family perspectives, our model *draws attention to the variety of different approaches to conceptualization and treatment* in mental health. The counsellor who comes into general practice only through personal analytic therapy and the private consulting room may not find it easy to work collaboratively in an environment where psycho-pharmacology, cognitive-behavioural approaches and other models jostle with each other cheek by jowl. In our own approach, we explicitly acknow-ledge that there is not only *a range of intensity* available in psychological work but also *a range of working models* which referrers and clients may want to choose from.

Discussion

Our three-level model may in fact recognize something which always happens in general practice, namely that patients will effectively 'sculpt' their own experiences of counselling and therapy over long periods of time from the variety of approaches on offer. Like all GPs, we see many people who indicate to us that they want to remain within the mode of 'little-c' counselling, perhaps for years. They see 'Big-C' counselling, or even 'middle-C' counselling, as intrusive and intimidating. Over the very prolonged timescale of GP–patient relationships, the cumulative benefit of small episodes of 'little-c' counselling may be great. Perhaps also, as time passes, their safe experience of 'little-c' counselling will stimulate a curiosity to accept an offer for something more structured.

Conversely, there are patients who enter 'Big-C' counselling but cannot use it constructively. They need not experience this as a rejection by the practice. There are other ways they can make us useful for themselves. We try to work responsively, giving people the opportunity to move between levels of work at a timing which is right for them. We also try not to impose our own professional prejudices on patients with regard to the mode of counselling or therapy we think best for them. This is exemplified by the case of the daughters in the K family, who elected to be seen separately from their mother; all of the family appeared to benefit from this.

In terms of theory, there are two ways in which a flexible approach of this kind can be conceptualized. One is in terms of attachment theory (Bowlby 1969) which suggests that people continue to reproduce the attachment patterns of their early life, and will tend to do so in every situation. Thus, the way patients request different levels of involvement from their GP – or stimulate us to offer these – can be seen as important information about their patterns of attachment. Such information may come, for example, in the form of missed appointments and habitual wariness towards the doctor, or in frequent attendances accompanied by exaggerated warmth. Whether or not they are aware of attachment theory and its implications, many GPs will note such information intuitively, and some will be alert to its connections with the patient's family of origin and their patterns of relating. Within a fragmented and secularized modern society, GPs may also be aware that they and their practices (however they are used or misused) often represent an important secure base for many patients, who depend upon the GP to be there when family and other connections may be widely dispersed.

When GPs and counsellors respond to patients' attachment patterns, they can do so either sensitively or abusively. Abuse in this context might mean *trying to impose a single or inflexible style of treatment* which is incorrectly matched to the patient's wishes or capability. This kind of bossy and prescriptive response is sadly common among both doctors and counsellors, as well as other mental health professionals, but for many patients it only reproduces exactly what they have known in their early past: not being understood, heard or adequately mirrored. (It may also indicate an insensitivity to patients' different expectations according to social class and ethnicity.) Conversely, a sensitive response, whether it is done consciously or by instinct, involves *accepting the patient's style of attachment and trying to build on it* (Byng-Hall 1990). It therefore involves reassessing the patient's ability to accept challenge at each successive professional contact, and looking out for realistic opportunities to extend that ability. It is this kind of response which we hope our model encourages.

There is another way of conceptualizing the flexible model we offer, and that is in terms of systems theory. According to contemporary systemic understanding, general practice can be seen as a system where *everyone is participating in an attempt to assign forms of meaning to people's experiences* (Anderson and Goolishian 1988). Patients come into our systems bringing their own distress, and hoping that we will be able to help them assign new meanings to it which will make a difference to how they feel (Launer

1995). One common professional response to this hope is simply to offer standard medical or psychological formulations based on prior 'truths' which we and our own professional group have decided upon. However, if we have the courage and imagination to do so, we can also test out a variety of different models and approaches, in order to find the one which best seems to fit the patient's own perceived needs (Amundson 1997). This flexibility, I suggest, should apply not only to our cherished professional ideologies – psychoanalytic, behavioural, or whatever – but to the very rules of the consultation itself: whether it is long or short, single or repeated, for the individual or the family, and conducted by just the GP (or counsellor or psychologist) or by a combination of people.

Within the medical world, there is one other reason to commend a model which allows as much flexibility as possible. Flexibility between levels of engagement allows us to perform the essential task of mixing therapeutic work with medical practice. Neither patients nor GPs and nurses can protect themselves from the sudden physical crises that arise in our work – the severe acute illnesses, the unforeseen handicaps, violence, death. In the very week in which a counselling session has taken place, we may find ourselves having to carry out an intimate physical examination on the same patient on a home visit, or discussing a statutory order relating to them at a case conference. For the private counsellor these might be quite improper combinations, but for us they are the reality of our job descriptions. Our model allows us to carry out the work with good enough respect to both the medical and the counselling worlds.

To anyone trained for the private consulting room, general practice can initially seem like the work setting from hell. There may be very little apparent respect for the standards and discipline which counsellors and therapists believe are sacrosanct, and in its place there may seem to be a Babel of contradictory psychiatric and psychological models, and a bewildering range of mental health professionals. Yet the counsellor who can tolerate and adapt to this muddle and diversity may find within general practice a challenge, and an opportunity for fruitful work, which is available in no other work setting.

REFERENCES

Andersen, T. (1987) The GP and consulting psychiatrist as a team with 'stuck' families. *Family Systems Medicine* 5: 486–91.

Anderson, H. and Goolishian, H. (1988) Human systems as linguistic systems: evolving ideas about the implications for theory and practice. *Family Process* 27: 371–93.

Amundson, J. (1997) Why pragmatics is probably enough for now. *Family Process* 35: 473–86.

Balint, E., Courtenay, M., Elder, A., Hull, M. and Julian, P. (1993) *The Doctor, the Patient and the Group: Balint Revisited.* London: Routledge.

Balint, M. (1957) *The Doctor, His Patient and the Illness,* revised second edition. London: Pitman.

Bowlby, J. (1969) *Attachment and Loss,* vol. 1, *Attachment.* London: Hogarth Press and the Institute of Psycho-Analysis.

Byng-Hall, J. (1990) Attachment theory and family therapy: a clinical view. *Infant Mental Health Journal* 11: 228–36.

Corney, R., and Jenkins, R. (eds) (1993) *Counselling in General Practice.* London: Routledge.

Dlys, C., Dowling, E. and Golding, V. (1989) Clinical psychology: a consultative approach in general practice. *Journal of the Royal College of General Practitioners* 39: 342–4.

Elder, A. (1990) Psychotherapy in general practice. In Maxwell, H. (ed.) *An Outline of Psychotherapy for Trainee Psychiatrists, Medical Students and Practitioners,* second edition. London: Whurr.

Elder, A. and Samuel, O. (eds) (1987) *While I'm Here Doctor.* London: Tavistock.

Hoag, L. (1992) Psychotherapy in the GP surgery: considerations of the frame. *British Journal of Psychotherapy* 8: 417–29.

Launer, J. (1995) A social constructionist approach to family medicine. *Family Systems Medicine* 13: 379–89.

Launer, J. and Lindsey, C. (1997) Training for systemic general practice: a new approach from the Tavistock Clinic. *British Journal of General Practice* 47: 453–6.

McDaniel, S., Hepworth, J. and Doherty, W. (1992) *Medical Family Therapy.* New York: Basic Books.

McLeod, J. (1988) *The Work of Counsellors in General Practice.* London: Royal College of General Practitioners.

Nickless, R., Mathers, D., Fender, E. and Gamer, J. (1990) Can GPs counsel? [Letter] *British Journal of General Practice* 40: 478.

Penn, P. (1982) Circular questioning. *Family Process* 21: 267–80.

Rowland, N., Irving, J. and Maynard, A. (1989) Can GPs counsel? *Journal of Royal College of General Practitioners* 39: 118–20.

10 Inter-disciplinary collaboration for group therapy

Peter Thomas, Mary Costello and Susan Davison

Introduction

According to a recent survey by the Counselling in Primary Care Trust, 30 per cent of all the General Practices in England and Wales now employ counsellors. The counsellor's role is still evolving, depending to some extent on each individual's prior training and professional background, but there is no doubt that counsellors offer a service which is popular with patients and GPs.

Table 10.1 Counselling statistics for surgery

Year	Total	*Referrals* Male	Female
1988	37	18	19
1989	42	20	22
1990	48	22	26
1991	66	23	43
1992	81	29	52
1993	67	25	42
1994	81	20	61
1995	98	33	65
1996	95	28	67
1997	74	25	49
Total	689	243	446

McGregor (1993) in a survey of general practices in South London, of which the practice described here is one, found that there were fourteen counsellors employed in twelve practices. She found the counsellors were dealing with very heavy work-loads, spending 90 per cent of their time in face-to-face contact with their clients. They were employed for an average of eight and a half hours per week and at that time were able to offer each client an average of eight and a half sessions. Since that time pressure of work in this practice has increased further and six sessions per client is now the norm.

The advantage of employing a counsellor in general practice is that patients can expect a rapid response with minimal administrative red tape. Patients can be seen in a setting with which they are familiar and they avoid the possible stigma of attending local psychiatric services. Thomas (1993), in an exploration of patients' perceptions of counselling, found 85 per cent preferred to see the counsellor at their doctor's surgery than to be referred elsewhere.

Boot et al. (1994) found that,

> compared with patients who received usual advice from their general practitioners for acute problems such as relationship difficulties, anxiety and depression, those who received counselling from qualified counsellors working within the Primary Health care context showed greater improvement in psychological health as measured by the General Health Questionnaire.

Short-term counselling is most effective in helping people in crisis (Caplan 1964). Advantage may be lost when patients have to wait two to three months for an appointment with a counsellor, and even longer for their six sessions. GPs are often the first port of call in a crisis as their service is freely available and does not involve a waiting list. The range of presenting problems of patients referred for counselling by GPs in the practice for the year 1997 is summarized in Table 10.2. During the counselling assessment deeper issues may be uncovered which would indicate short-term therapy may not be an appropriate treatment. Boot et al. (1994) found that 9 per cent of patients counselled actually got worse, suggesting that in a minority of patients counselling quickly uncovered many more problems than the patient initially presented with, or caused previously hidden difficulties to come to the surface.

Speirs and Jewell (1995) found in their pilot study of two practices employing a counsellor that, '69 per cent of assessed clients were taken on for short-term counselling, whilst 25 per cent were referred to a more appropriate service'.

Thus, for a minority of patients the decision may be made to refer them onward to local psychiatric services. This may be the best use of scarce resources when local services are able to respond quickly and appropriately.

However, the patient may resist referral onward just at the point when he has developed the trust and summoned up the courage to let the counsellor know how bad things really are.

It was in response to these considerations that the authors decided to collaborate in setting up a psychotherapy group in general practice. Unlike the more usual counselling groups, which aim to gather together clients with similar problems, such as bereavement or depression, this group was to be set up on a slow-open, group analytic model with a view to allowing individual clients as much time as they needed to work through their emotional difficulties. The value of such groups is not in question (Dick 1983); it remained to be seen if such a group could function effectively in general practice, where special problems might be encountered. What follows is a report of our experience of the first six years of this group.

The practice and personnel

The practice is situated in South London and serves a largely working-class, multi-ethnic population. Deprivation indices, published by the Department for Education and Employment, rate the locality as the second most deprived area in the country, with an unemployment rate, in 1997, of 24.4 per cent and 51.4 per cent of people living in public housing. The surgery was originally a Victorian house and, with only three female principals, has a homely, intimate atmosphere. The GP (MC) joined the practice in 1991. She had a special interest in psychotherapy, especially groupwork, having worked for a year with both large and small groups in a psychiatric day hospital which boasted two group analysts. She had also attended the Institute of Group Analysis Introductory Course and had some experience of personal therapy. The counsellor (PT) is a UKRC Independent Registered Counsellor and is employed at the practice for eleven hours per week. He had already set up groups for bereaved clients in the practice. He was spending eight hours a week in direct work with clients. Together they approached the local psychotherapy unit to see if they could obtain supervision for their proposed group. A local consultant psychotherapist (SD) agreed to supervise the work. Additional funding to increase the counsellor's hours was obtained from the local Health Commission. The supervisor's time was a free good, this being seen as a 'service development'. The GP negotiated with her fellow principals that her time with the group would be sacrosanct. This meant she would have to stop the evening surgery early one day a week and was not available for emergencies during the time of the group. It was also agreed in principle that patients attending the group would see her colleagues rather than her for any concurrent physical problems except in an emergency when no other doctor was available.

Setting up the group

The group would consist of a maximum of eight clients and two conductors, meeting weekly one evening for one and a quarter hours at the surgery. The group normally has three, month-long, breaks around Christmas, Easter and August. The conductors allowed fifteen minutes at the end of each group to 'de-brief', explore the group dynamics and write up the case notes.

Entry to the group followed an initial assessment followed by six individual sessions with the counsellor. If during the course of treatment it became apparent that further help was needed and that the client might benefit from a group experience, the counsellor would explore the group option with them. An outline of the group was given at this stage and a discussion of the group boundaries. Eight members were prepared in this way and committed themselves to the group, although in the event one member failed to attend. The group option was declined by some clients. This type of preparation has reliably been shown to be of value in advancing group cohesion and reducing early dropouts (Bloch 1992).

It was decided to have a slow-open stranger group in which new members would be introduced as members left. Group members were requested to give the group four sessions' notice of leaving. All matters pertaining to the group remain confidential.

Our aim was to create a cohesive group which would enjoy a degree of security in which mutual challenge and confrontation could be tolerated.

Characteristics of group members

Overall, between May 1992 and July 1995, 22 clients were offered a place in the group. There were 10 men and 12 women and the age range was 24–62 years. The average was 34.5 years for women and 35.5 for men. Six were married, three separated, one divorced and twelve single. The majority of clients were Caucasian (13 were British Caucasian, 4 European). Ethnic minorities were British Afro-Caribbean (3), British Indian (1) and one Chinese.

The presenting problems were varied, including: anger management (3), depression/anxiety (5), problems with relationships (4), marital breakdown (2), difficulties at work (4), bereavement (1), low self-esteem (1), sexual difficulties (2). A degree of depression and difficulties with personal relationships were common to most people. During the six sessions of individual counselling it became clear that this group of clients had more complex and longer standing difficulties than average. Disclosure of childhood sexual abuse occurred in several cases.

Table 10.2 Presenting referral problems for 1997

Symptom	Total
Anger	3
Alcohol	1
Anxiety/PA	6
Bereavement	14
Depression	25
Eating disorders	2
Medical related	2
Relationships	11
Sexuality abuse	2
Work stress/unemployment	8
Total	74

Of the eight members who were originally offered the group, one never joined and three still remain. Fourteen clients have both joined and left the group. Six dropped out without completing the four weeks' ending contract, staying in the group for an average of three and a half months. Of these, four belonged to ethnic minorities, indicating that it might be more difficult to retain members of minority groups where the majority of the group were British Caucasian.

Of the eight members whose ending of group therapy was planned, four left because of work commitments, one joined another group and three felt they had resolved their difficulties. The average length of stay in the group was fourteen months.

The group process and supervision

Group analysis draws upon psychoanalytic, sociological and systems theory perspectives. From psychoanalysis it takes the setting and the boundaries, the Freudian unconscious, transference and counter transference, notions of internal object relations, unconscious fantasy, psychic defence, all of which manifest in current relationships. From the sociological perspective comes the view that the self and the mind are pre-eminently social constructs which only come into being and develop in a social context; self-knowledge comes from reflective intersubjectivity. Systems theory, applied to the social level, predicts that any group of people will tend to assign roles to one another and to fit in with one another's expectations so as to minimize conflict and dissonance, that is by accepting and projecting transferences within the group. The analytic work involves recognizing the patterns as they are repeated over time and enquiring into the unconscious assumptions and prejudices that sustain them.

Group members were encouraged to respect the time boundaries and to risk more open communication than was habitually theirs. The role of the conductors has been to maintain the setting and the dynamic administration in such a way as to further the work of the group. The nature of the relationship between the therapists, as well as each individually, attracted transferences and patterns of enactment which could be interpreted.

The group has moved through many different phases, as established members leave and new members join to replace them. A lot of work has revolved around endings, beginnings, and absence. Group members have become quite sophisticated in their observations of one another and have learnt to hold each other to task when difficult issues have to be confronted. On the whole, commitment to the group has remained high, although at times attendance became erratic, usually for understandable reasons (therapist absence due to illness, holiday breaks, introduction of new members etc.).

Supervision of the group work was offered fortnightly and has become less frequent as the therapists gained confidence. However it is important to note that both therapists brought considerable experience and relevant skills to the project. Supervision concentrated on technical issues, such as introduction of new members, attempts to retrieve potential dropouts and dynamic administration. Rather than using detailed process recording, the supervision sessions tended to focus on how each individual member habitually related to other group members and the conductors, in order to elucidate transferences and defensive fantasy. This proved a useful way of thinking about how an individual might become 'stuck' in the service of the group and what shared fantasies might be operating. As far as possible the therapists adhered to Foulkes' dictum that interpretation is only required when the work of the group has become blocked.

The clients' perspective

As Thomas stated in 1993, the consumer's voice is often silent. We decided to ask current group members to write their personal reflections of their experiences of being a group member within our group, with particular reference to 'the advantages and disadvantages of the group being within a general practice'. The selected members were chosen by the group members themselves, following repeated discussions within the group. PT brought the idea to the group and they decided that it would be appropriate for only those members who had experienced being in the group with both conductors to participate. This reduced the number of group members to four. They did not feel it would be appropriate to locate past group members. The group requested PT to provide them with guidelines as to appropriate headings and content, which were provided, together with a copy of the previously published article relating to the group (Thomas et al. 1997). Three of the members submitted written reflections within the agreed deadlines; these have been used below.

Each member produced their comments in a unique way, despite the guidelines. For the sake of clarity they are explored under certain headings.

1 Free versus private therapy

'I wouldn't have been in a position to have considered private counselling, so the question of choice was never an issue. To find there was an opportunity to have counselling within my GP practice, in which I have every confidence, was constructive and reassuring.' (A)

'I feel very privileged to have had the opportunity of free counselling. It is an excellent provision from this practice and shows the practice's commitment to mental health issues.' (B)

'I do question whether it is a good idea to have a group which has no fixed term, or at least an upper time limit. One group member has been going to sessions for five years, much to her own annoyance, and I wonder about the validity of this open-ended approach. What it does do, I suppose, is make you make up your own mind about when is the right time to leave.' (B)

'But a very important thing the group has taught me is that the world is not so black and white. It may sound trivial but it has been fundamental – I really do not seem to be as much of an obsessive perfectionist as I was before; I really don't seem to have to be right all the time.' (B)

2 Confidentiality and boundaries

'Being seen by other patients in the surgery wasn't an issue for me. There were a number of occasions when I'd bumped into other group members outside, which when I brought it up in the group, I'd found I'd broken group rules in various ways which threatened the confidentiality of group members. I remember at the time, I'd been quite surprised at the effect I had. On another occasion when I discussed an issue from the group with my GP (MC), which I brought back to the group, I was surprised by the great consternation it caused with other group members.' (A)

'The fact that the group is within the general practice means it is easily located for me. It can be embarrassing however. I dislike walking through a full waiting room to go upstairs to the group room. I wonder if an acquaintance or neighbour might see me. (The practice is just streets away from my house.) Once I had an eye problem and in the waiting room I met not one, but two group members. We sat next to each other and talked, in a very general way, not about feelings or group issues, but it felt rather uncomfortable. It reminded me of when I once walked home with a group member who lived nearby, and I wondered if one of my flatmates might see me and ask how I knew a 60-year old woman in the area! Being so much part of the locality means that the group and relations therein can sometimes feel a bit claustrophobic. I have never bumped into a group member other than at the practice, but I remember hoping I would bump into one specific member who had left very angrily – so that I could persuade her to come back!' (B)

3 Having individual therapy prior to the group

'Seeing the counsellor (PT) for an assessment session followed by 6 sessions seemed to be constructive and about the right amount of time for him to get to know the nature of my problems before embarking on group sessions. Also for me to get a feel of how he worked and whether a sufficient feeling of trust was there to feel there would be benefits from joining a group. As I had no previous experience of groups I didn't know what to expect, but that there would be some form of continuing to work on my problems with him was what mattered.' (A)

'This group, and my six individual sessions with Peter, constitute my second experience of counselling. But this is the first time I feel I have derived real benefit from the counselling, and it is my first experience of group therapy.' (B)

'I think it would be more difficult to go from individual to group therapy with the same counsellor if only a few members of the group had had the individual therapy; as it is, I feel like all the group members are in the same boat, all have had six sessions with Peter, he has spent the same amount of time with all of us.' (B)

4 The effects of a mixed group

'To try and maintain a balance of mixed ages, sexes, issues and ethnicity reflecting the world outside was an important structural element in making work within the group optimally effective. It must have been a difficult balancing act for the counsellor (PT) bringing in men given that they are less likely to consider that they need to address their feelings. Ethnicity seemed to produce a sense of embarrassment from white members.' (A)

'The group members are very diverse in many respects. To start with I found this interesting and also helpful: it was quite a surprise to me that

I could relate so closely to people so different from myself. However as the months have passed I have found this something of a stumbling block. There are people in the group who are waiting for major operations, who have suffered child abuse, who have been charged with child abuse, and sometimes the weight of this overwhelms me so that my problems just seem ridiculous. Then I get angry with myself, because I think, I have problems, I am here for a reason too.' (B)

5   The effects on personal relationships and health

'My main personal problems were to do with intimacy and trust in relation to men and gender issues in my work revolving around self-worth. The most useful insights were in the area of listening to group members turning over these issues. It was useful hearing group members' approaches to forgiving and how to move on. Lessons in how not to jump in to try to save people. To learn to listen, to hold back, to let others have their pain and their time. I'm more aware of others' needs, most importantly in my relationship with my daughter.' (A)

'The most marked physical effect of my time with the group has been my progress from almost complete insomnia and dependence on sleeping tablets to being able to sleep really well. I also developed a new attitude which enabled me to cope with a sudden onset of arthritis by putting my health before my work. I can now take pleasure in giving myself treats and sometimes time to relax.' (A)

'My physical health has increased noticeably since I started counselling.' (B)

'Maybe a major thing the group has taught me is that you don't have to be 100 per cent well to feel better – I feel better, I am no longer depressed, and I know how to recognize it if things slip again, and how to get help.' (B)

6   Issues related to the role of the GP conductor

'I feel my GP (MC), is very much aware of my mental health needs as well as physical. It feels as if I have a very personal relationship with the practice, that all my health needs are looked after there. I feel I can trust my doctor more knowing that she is so involved with mental health issues.' (B)

'MC was part of the group for my first two sessions, and then she left. We had quite a close relationship anyway, based on the fact that we got on very well but also the fact that she had been very involved in some physical health problems and also in my mental health problems. I therefore found her involvement in the group rather comforting – someone I already knew – and it also felt helpful that my GP should get to know me thoroughly. Interestingly, I have only seen MC once since she left – almost a year ago – and that was with the eye problem, and so I cannot comment on how our brief shared group time has affected our relationship. I am not running to her with every minor mental health problem – I discuss those in the group – but I feel very strongly that should I have serious mental health problems I could go to her immediately. I think however that if I had spent more than two weeks in the group with MC I would have found it more difficult. The fact that group members could not see MC as a GP while they were in the group would have been a major stumbling block, for my relationship with MC as a GP is one I value very highly.' (B)

'On the one occasion that I had to have medical treatment from the GP (MC), a circumstance agreed as being out of bounds, I had the interesting experience of her efficient medical professionalism benefiting me. After the incident where she had given me an injection, I found I was more open to being able to hear her contribution in the group and found her more helpful to my personal needs. On reflection, this experience was far more reassuring to me than her role as a facilitator in the group had been, about which I was at first subjective and uneasy.' (A)

'My interest in her (MC) professional and private life grew considerably once I'd joined the group.' (C)

'Something that used to upset me was when a group member would relay their visits with MC before they'd started the group. The special-sounding relationship they'd built, often after only a few meetings, seemed to me to have accelerated their entry into the group. As if MC had her favourites, I don't think MC colluded with this idea but I felt they'd been hand picked, and then there was me, the other one.' (C)

7 *The effect of moving from two conductors to one*

'It was interesting when MC left because we were really affected by it. We seem to have shelved the issue concerning when we feel ready to see MC again as a GP. Group members present at the time of MC's departure have dwindled and it seems unfair on other group members to stir it up. I don't know if I'll be ready to see her (MC) until I have left the group. In fact I didn't realize how affected I'd been until I wrote this and saw her recently. I was in a room with the practice nurse and MC burst in asking for something. I could only see her back, but was still excited by her presence. She turned round to look at me and showed absolutely no emotion. I was disappointed. It was our first encounter since she had left. It made me realize how important she was to me.' (C)

'I have to say that I kicked up a real fuss about having to write this. As if I was being unfaithful to the group.' (C)

'Since I have written it I am pleased. It has uncovered a lot of painful and valuable feelings I did not know that I had.' (C)

'It was slightly awkward for PT, and us, when MC left. A sort of power shift, and I wondered if this would make PT into a new power strength.' (C)

Discussion

Our experience in setting up and running a therapeutic group in general practice has demonstrated that it is logistically possible and has many desirable consequences. There were also some disadvantages.

The possibility of having a long-term, slow-open group, which has developed a culture of enquiry and respect for psychic reality and which patients from the practice can join, undoubtedly relieved some of the burden on the counsellor. Otherwise he felt he was offering an inadequate service to patients who clearly needed more than six sessions of individual counselling. Those patients who expressed an interest in joining the group clearly appreciated not having to be referred to the local psychotherapy services.

Concerns that were raised had to do with confidentiality and the possibility of meeting other group members outside the confines of the group. In some more settled and cohesive communities it might be more difficult to set up a stranger group from a single general practice. In this group two patients were living in the same block of flats.

The role conflict for the GP conductor of the group was considerable. It was not uncommon for her to be consulted in her role as GP by the partners, parents or children of group members which inevitably affected the dynamics. When group members themselves contrived to consult her for non-urgent physical problems they were obviously testing the boundaries of confidentiality both of the group and the GP consultation. This could be addressed as the group became more sophisticated.

More difficult to manage was the impact the GP's commitment to the group had on the workload within the practice. Conflict over time-management with her partners, especially when one was on holiday or sick, inevitably impinged on the group. There was no direct financial gain to the practice for the GP's time being spent in this way, which led the partners to question whether this was an appropriate service development within the practice. However, MC's awareness of group function and structure has improved the appropriateness of referrals and reduced possible collusion and splitting that invariably takes place in a general practice setting. It can also be said to have improved MC's understanding of the untouched depths of psychopathology within the practice population.

After four years the GP decided to leave the group to pursue other commitments; the experience gained in group processes has been used in other areas both within and outside the practice. This was experienced by all parties as a difficult loss and involved a prolonged period of grieving. Several members managed to consult with her, despite an agreed three-month cooling off boundary. This gradually diminished and now she is rarely consulted by any group member.

Overall the counsellor saw nearly twice as many women as men (see Table 10.1) and this imbalance has increased in recent years. This led to a gender imbalance in the group and may have resulted in some male patients being offered the group who were not ideally suited to it. Indeed, by not referring on some of the more complicated cases the choice of possible psychological interventions may have been unduly restricted for these people. The fact that female patients now have to wait for places in the group means that the speed of response advantage of this group over local psychotherapy services is compromised. Partly because of pressure of time, supervision was less frequent than would have been ideal.

The GP and counsellor were perceived in the group transference as a 'couple' with an intimate and exclusive relationship. Both felt that this transference was also expressed by members of the general practice personnel. An unexpected advantage, which could perhaps have been predicted, has been much closer working relationships, between GP and counsellor and between the GP's practice and the local psychotherapy unit. A concurrent development has been a fortnightly work-discussion group for local counsellors in general practice held in the psychotherapy unit which has allowed a fruitful exchange of ideas to develop.

The establishment of a long-term, slow-open, group analytic group is possible in general practice when the specific expertise is available. It allows for the psychotherapeutic treatment of patients with quite severe psychopathology in primary care, for whom six-session counselling is insufficient.

Some problems were encountered. For example it was not always possible to avoid role conflict for the GP group therapist who was occasionally consulted by group patients for physical ailments. The relatively small pool of potential group members may have been a contributory factor in the difficulty there was in engaging and holding men and ethnic minorities.

We offer this as one way in which local specialist psychotherapy services can support counsellors in primary care in providing a service acceptable to patients who prefer not to venture away from the familiar ground of their local surgery. It is however very important to plan and fund adequate prior training and supervision for the therapists.

REFERENCES

Aveline, M. (1984) 'What Price Psychiatry without Psychotherapy?', *The Lancet* (October): 856–8.

Aveline, M. and Dryden, W. (1993) *Group Therapy in Britain*, Oxford: Oxford University Press.

Baker, R., Allen, H., Penn, W., Daw, P. and Baker, E. (1996) 'The Dorset Primary Care Counselling Service Research Evaluation' [unpublished report].

Bloch, S. (1982) *What is Psychotherapy?* Oxford: Oxford University Press.

Boot, D., Gillies, P., Fenelon, J., Reubin, R., Wilkins, N. and Grays, P. (1994) 'Evaluation of the Short-term Impact of Counselling in General Practice', *Patient Education and Counselling* 24: 79–89.

Burton, M., Sandgrove, J. and Selwyn, E. (1995) 'Do Counsellors in General Practice Surgeries and Clinical Psychologists in the NHS see the same Patients?' *Journal of the Royal Society of Medicine* 88: 97–102.

Caplan, G. (1964) *Principles of Preventive Psychiatry*, New York: Basic Books.

Corney, R. and Jenkins, R. (1993) *Counselling in General Practice*, London: Routledge.

Dick, B. (1983) 'Outpatient Analytic Group Psychotherapy: A Ten Year Study of Outcome' in M. Pines (ed.) *The Evolution of Group Analysis*, London: Routledge (1993).

Howard, K., Kopta, S., Krause, M. and Orlinsky, D. (1986) 'The Dose–Effect Relationship in Psychotherapy', *American Psychologist* 41: 159–64.

Irving, J. and Heath, V. (1989) *Counselling in General Practice. A Guide for General Practitioners*, Rugby: British Association for Counselling.

Jenkins, G. (1995) 'Effectiveness in Counselling Services: Recent Developments in Service Delivery' [unpublished report].

Kendrick, T., Sibbald, B. and Hall, J. (1993) 'Distribution of Mental Health Professionals Working On Site in English and Welsh General Practices', *British Medical Journal* 307: 544–6.

Martin, E. and Mitchell, H. (1983) 'A Counsellor in General Practice: A One-year Survey', *Journal of the Royal College of General Practitioners* 33: 366–7.

McGregor, M. (now Venning) (1993) Poster presentation, *Collaboration in Care Conference*, London: St George's Hospital.

McLeod, J. (1992) *Counselling in Primary Care, The GP's Perspective*, Royal College of General Practitioners Clinical Series on Counselling in General Practice, London: College of General Practitioners Enterprises.

Medlik, L., Short, N. and Maskell, G. (1987) 'The changing role of psychologists in primary care', *The Practitioners*, 231: 224–7.

Myers, E. (1982) 'How to Screen for Group Therapy', *Pulse* 42 (16): 71.

Sibbald, B., Addington-Hall, J., Brenneman, D. and Freeling, P. (1993) 'Counsellors in English and Welsh General Practices: Their Nature and Distribution', *British Medical Journal* 306: 29–33.

Speirs, R. and Jewell, J. (1995) 'One Counsellor, Two Practices: Report of a Pilot Scheme in Cambridgeshire', *British Journal of General Practice* 45: 31–3.

Thomas, P. (1993) 'An Exploration of Patients' Perceptions of Counselling with Particular Reference to Counselling within General Practice', *Journal of the British Association for Counselling* 1: 24–30.

Thomas, P., Costello, M. and Davison, S. (1997) 'Group Work in General Practice', *Psychodynamic Counselling* 3 (1), 23–31.

Trepka, C., Laing, I. and Smith, S. (1986) 'Group Treatment of General Practice Anxiety Problems', *Journal of the Royal College of General Practitioners* 36: 114–17.

11 Evaluating clinical counselling in primary care and the future

Roslyn Corney

The need for evaluation

Now that counselling is available on the NHS, serious consideration has to be paid as to whether it is a legitimate use of NHS funds. As counselling is a new service, it is under greater scrutiny than treatments or therapies which have been in use for years, although a high proportion of other treatments in general practice have very limited evidence as to their clinical effectiveness (Light, 1991). In addition, counsellors in general practice may find that their work is particularly scrutinized as there are few visible signs of what has gone on in a counselling session and counsellors may find it difficult to give a full explanation of what they do. This is linked with the confusion that arises from understanding the difference between the individual work undertaken by a counsellor and the supportive and listening skills that other practitioners in primary care may use in their daily work with patients.

There are also issues over whether counsellors are the most appropriate category of workers to be dealing with the emotional and social problems of patients in general practice. Other mental health professionals may consider themselves to be more appropriate, including clinical psychologists and community psychiatric nurses. Would patients with depression and anxiety be better treated by professionals with a mental health background? Interprofessional rivalry has intensified now that GPs are major purchasers.

However, there are a number of other reasons why evaluative studies are essential. First, preliminary studies suggest that some patients may be helped more than others. In a time of limited resources, it is essential to focus on those individuals who can benefit most from counselling. Evaluative studies should aim to identify these patients.

Second, it is a common finding that there is greater variance in outcome in treated clients than in untreated controls, suggesting that some individuals may be possibly harmed by therapy. Evaluative trials should aim to identify those patients who may be harmed.

Third, there is a wide range of therapies, ranging from behavioural approaches to psychoanalysis. We urgently need to know which therapies benefit which patients most and which ones are most acceptable to patients.

Fourth, in terms of training and considerations of manpower, it is important to know what level of skills is necessary for benefit to occur. How much training and level of expertise is necessary for benefit to occur? This linked to all three prior questions; some clients may benefit most by the setting up of a self-help group, while the more seriously disturbed/damaged client will probably need skilful and knowledgeable handling.

Services can be evaluated by examining the input, throughput and output of a service (e.g. information on referral and who is referred, information on type of work carried out and information on closure). In addition, any evaluation should also examine outcome – whether the service actually improved the health or well-being of the patient or client. While both types of evaluation are necessary to measure the effectiveness and efficiency of a service, the measurement of outcome is much less frequently carried out in all branches of medicine. For example, hospital managers may collect information on waiting lists and the number of operations carried out but may find it difficult to give figures on how many patients continued to feel better one year after the operation or even how many had died.

The same is true in terms of evaluating counselling. It is relatively easy to measure the setting up of a counselling placement but much more difficult to investigate client outcome. Unfortunately both types of evaluation are necessary if we are to answer some of the more important questions, such as whether we are making the best use of the resources available for the treatment of emotional problems and distress.

Evaluating counselling has additional problems. Unlike the evaluation of a drug or a practical procedure, it is difficult to measure and assess the quality of the counselling. We do not know what are the 'ingredients' of counselling which are most likely to bring about change. With some distressed individuals, a brief session with a known and trusted GP or health visitor may be more appropriate than a longer period with a counsellor.

Subjective and anecdotal evidence

The recent increase in the number of GPs employing counsellors in general practice is proof that GPs want counselling services to be available to their patients and presumably perceive these services to be helpful. One of the most common changes made by fundholders in the South East Thames Region was the employment of counsellors (Corney, Kerrison and Tan, 1996a). A study evaluating a locality counselling service found that the majority of non-fundholders were also keen to refer patients to the counsellors involved (Corney and Falconer, 1997).

Users of psychiatric services repeatedly demonstrate their wish for counselling (Rogers, Pilgrim and Lacey, 1993). Counselling has been seen by population surveys to be the treatment of choice for depression (Priest et al., 1996), indicating that clients view it as an acceptable (or even preferable) alternative to medication.

Clients seen by the counsellor can be asked to give their views of whether the counselling helped. These views can be assessed by independent researchers interviewing the clients or by sending postal questionnaires. Clients' views can be important and valid sources of feedback. They may be helpful in clarifying which therapeutic methods are more acceptable to clients. Questions asked may also include service issues such as satisfaction with access, hours, waiting lists, reception procedures, and concerns over confidentiality etc.

The results of all studies of general practice clients' views (known to the author) suggest that a very high majority of clients find counselling helpful. For example, one study found that 44 out of 47 clients indicated that help was received (Waydenfeld and Waydenfeld, 1980). Another study of patient satisfaction found that 85 per cent of clients agreed that counselling should be available in general practice, 78 per cent would use the counselling service again and 84 per cent would recommend it to others (Anderson and Hasler, 1979). Numerous subsequent studies have yielded very similar results.

Accepting these findings as indications of outcome is problematic, however. Clients' subjective assessments of help received are not definitive evidence of outcome, as clients do not know what would have happened if they had not seen a counsellor. In addition, surveys of client satisfaction in general practice show consistently high levels, whatever the topic. These levels may be more a measure of previous expectations; patients may be happy with any extra help or time given. It is also possible that similar favourable reports would be obtained if clients were given the same amount of time by an untrained, warm and caring befriender or by a self-help group which could also offer practical assistance on a longer-term basis. Patients may find it very difficult to criticize a service, especially when arranged by a medical team upon which they rely. Alternatively, there may be some clients who will never be satisfied whatever help is received.

Difficulties in conducting clinical trials

Although there is overwhelming evidence that patients and their GPs appreciate counselling, this does not answer the question of whether counselling in general practice is more effective in bringing about improvement in symptoms or quality of life than 'normal GP treatment'.

It is not possible to give a simple answer as to whether counselling is effective. Paul suggested that, 'the question towards which all outcome research should ultimately be directed is the following: what treatment, by whom, is the most effective for this individual with that specific problem, and under which set of circumstances?' (Paul, 1967).

In medicine, randomized controlled trials (often called clinical trials) are normally undertaken in order to evaluate whether a treatment is effective or not. They are the widely accepted 'gold standard' for comparing and evaluating different treatments, although there are often considerable difficulties in carrying them out in general practice (Pringle and Churchill, 1995). In these trials, the outcome of one group of patients receiving the treatment is compared to the outcome of another group who either receive no treatment or treatment of another kind. Ideally, patients entering into clinical trials should be randomly allocated to the experimental group or the control group so that there are no initial differences between the two groups.

The need for a control group is crucial, as high proportions of patients with depression and anxiety (those patients most likely to be referred to a counsellor) will get better over time without outside help. Patients will normally be referred to a counsellor at a point when their problems are likely to be at their worst. This means that most patients are likely to show some improvement at a follow up interview, regardless of treatment. To show that counselling is effective, we have to obtain even better rates of improvement in those receiving counselling than those receiving other types of treatment or none at all. It is therefore often difficult to prove statistically that counselling is more effective, except by conducting trials with fairly high numbers of subjects.

The results of clinical trials of counselling in general practice are much more equivocal than subjective reports. However, clinical trials are extremely difficult to undertake and most studies evaluating counselling are flawed in some way, some more than others. It must be remembered that we are at an early stage in refining our techniques of evaluation. It is important to be aware of some of the difficulties involved so that we evaluate the quality of the studies themselves as well as the results found.

In general, there is a broad range of difficulties encountered when conducting an outcome study. These difficulties are sometimes termed 'threats to validity' (Lambert, Masters and Ogles, 1991). The internal validity of a study refers to the extent to which the researcher has controlled for the existence of alternative or competing hypotheses that could account for the data. A study high in internal validity would be one that was conducted under laboratory conditions with all variables closely monitored and controlled. The external validity of a study, on the other hand, refers to the degree to which its findings can be reliably and meaningfully generalized to other situations. Thus a study high in external validity would take place in circumstances as close as possible to naturalistic conditions. Unfortunately studies high in internal validity (such as clinical trials) are often low on external validity and vice versa. Some compromise is usually necessary.

One of the most major difficulties in conducting clinical trials is that of achieving a reasonable sample size and getting GPs to refer patients to the trial. GPs may not readily refer to a clinical trial if they believe that counselling is beneficial, as they may not wish to deny this treatment to their patients. In these cases, relying on GPs to refer may lead to an unrepresentative sample. For example, a GP with concerns of this nature may only refer those with very minor problems to a clinical trial.

There is also the difficulty of client motivation. In most trials, subjects have to agree to randomization and to accept the treatment to which they have been allocated. The motivation of patients to receive counselling is therefore often variable. Some patients may either refuse counselling (even when allocated) or refuse to take part in the follow-up assessments. Alternatively, clients referred to the control group may seek out and obtain alternative help from outside the study. Thus subject motivation and attrition is a considerable problem. It is for this reason that a number of researchers have suggested that patient preference trials are a more appropriate methodology. In these trials, patients can receive the treatment of preference or alternatively agree to randomization. Few studies of this nature have been attempted and need much larger sample sizes for statistical analyses.

In many trials, it is often difficult to decide what constitutes improvement. Is it better physical or mental health, a reduction in family break-up, a reduction in psychotropic drug prescribing or a reduction in GP consultations? Deciding on what constitutes improvement may involve a number of value judgements. What is regarded as a favourable outcome for one client may differ considerably from what is regarded as a favourable outcome for another.

The outcome measures used have also been criticised. They may be considered by some to be inappropriate or lack sensitivity and it is important that further developmental work is undertaken. In practice, most trials include multiple assessments of health status; personal measures (e.g. self-esteem measures) and social adjustment (e.g. relationships). This is likely to lead to a fairer trial of counselling than those trials with assessments focusing predominantly on health measures.

There are no hard and fast rules on when to carry out assessments of change. Some patients may improve rapidly but then relapse, others may take longer but stay well. Some therapists argue that the mental health of clients may need to deteriorate (when first facing their problems) before they can get better. Some clinical trials have been criticized in that the follow-up assessments have been undertaken too soon or too long after the intervention. The best solution to this dilemma is to follow up clients more than once, once shortly after cessation of counselling and again at least once at a later time.

Unlike clinical trials on drugs, no placebos are readily available; thus patients are aware of the treatment group to which they have been allocated. Usually the control group receives 'treatment as usual' or is allocated to a waiting list. It may be more appropriate to use a control treatment such as a befriender or an untrained listener spending similar amounts of time with the client.

There are also problems in that the treatment given is usually poorly defined. It is therefore difficult to assess what is actually causing any improvement. Although some trials use trained, regularly supervised therapists who use treatment manuals (for example, Klerman et al., 1987), these are not in the majority. On the other hand, there are concerns regarding the external validity of these trials. In practice, most clinicians carefully adapt and select the most appropriate interventions for each of their clients and would not find adherence to a theory-driven manual as most appropriate to bring about client change.

There is also the possibility that the clinical trial methodology may be more suitable to test some types of therapeutic interventions rather than others. It is possible that one of the reasons why cognitive behaviour therapy is shown to have most effect in many trials is that much of its focus is on reducing symptoms and the measurement of symptoms is commonly used as an outcome measure. The change brought about by psychodynamic therapy may be more difficult to detect using the standard outcome measures commonly used.

There are a number of other problems, including variance in ability between the counsellors or therapists, the quality of the patient–therapist interaction, as well as variance among patients. These are documented in more detail by Kline, 1992.

Evidence from clinical trials

The first clinical trial of counselling in general practice was carried out by Ashurst and colleagues. In this study, 726 patients aged between 16 and 65 from a health centre and a group practice were randomly assigned to counselling or to routine GP treatment (Ashurst and Ward, 1983). Patients were referred to the study if they had consulted their GP for what was termed a neurotic disorder. High proportions had been prescribed psychotropic drugs. The two counsellors generally favoured a non-directive approach and made use of progressive relaxation, supportive counselling, interpretative psychotherapy, transactional analysis, behavioural techniques, Gestalt and dream work. While a high proportion of the patients valued the help they had received, no striking differences in outcome (measured one year later) between groups were elicited, although it was felt by the authors that some individuals benefited considerably. One of the problems with this pioneering study was the question of client motivation. Not all the patients recruited into the study specifically wanted counselling help and this is likely to have reduced the effects of treatment.

Another study was carried out in Sydney, Australia, and it compared the outcome of three groups to which patients had been randomly assigned (Brodaty and Andrews, 1983). Patients were aged between 18 and 65 and had had persistent psychological symptoms for at least six months. In one group, 18 patients received eight weekly half-hour sessions of brief, problem-orientated psychodynamic psychotherapy from a trained psychotherapist. Another group of 18 individuals received eight weekly half-hour appointments with their family doctor (who had no specific training). The third group of 20 patients received no additional therapy. No differences were found between the three treatment groups in outcome scores measuring symptom severity, social dysfunction, physical disability or medication.

In a third study by Boot and colleagues (1994), patients referred to a counsellor improved much more than those receiving GP treatment and this difference was statistically significant. Those referred to the counsellor also felt more satisfied with the service and fewer were taking psychotropic drugs or were referred elsewhere. However, outcome was assessed using a questionnaire that is best used for screening, the General Health Questionnaire, and was measured only six weeks after initial referral to the study. There were also problems with the randomization procedure and subject attrition. For example, 192 patients were recruited into the study but only 108 (56 per cent) returned the follow-up questionnaires. In addition, although randomization should make the two treatment groups reasonably equal, 124 were referred to the counselled group and only 68 to the GP treatment group.

In a pilot study conducted by King and colleagues (1994), patients could choose whether to receive non-directive counselling or routine care from their GP. In spite of this element of choice, the 19 patients receiving counselling did not make any more improvement than the 5 patients receiving GP care alone. A further two-centre patient preference trial is now being undertaken by King and colleagues. In the current trial, patients can choose counselling, cognitive therapy or GP treatment or alternatively agree to randomization (King and colleagues, personal communication, 1997).

In a study by Friedli and colleagues, GPs were asked to refer patients to the study who were suffering from an emotional problem (Friedli et al., 1997): 136 patients entered the study. Overall, no statistically significant differences were found in outcome between the group referred to the counsellors and those referred back to the GP for routine treatment. However, in a *post hoc* analysis, the researchers included only those who were classified as cases on the Beck Depression Inventory (using a score of 14 or over). Under these conditions, those referred to the counsellor did improve more than those who were not ($p = 0.035$). The counsellors all used Rogerian non-directive counselling methods and undertook between one and twelve sessions over a twelve-week period. Depression, anxiety, other mental health disorder symptoms and social adjustment were measured by self-report at baseline, three months and nine months.

Hemmings conducted a study which included 188 patients. He did not find any statistical difference in outcome between a group referred to a counsellor and a group receiving routine GP advice (Hemmings, 1997). Patients with a variety of different problems and symptoms were included in the study. The three counsellors were trained using different models, but all exceeded the minimum requirement for the British Association for Counselling accreditation. Outcome measures took place at four and eight months and included measurements of interpersonal problems, clinical symptoms and self-esteem. Subsequent service use was also monitored, as well as prescribing patterns.

Trials of the counselling skills of other members of the primary care team

The effectiveness of the counselling skills of other members of the primary care team has also been studied. The results of one clinical trial suggested that health visitors given skills training in non-directive counselling could bring about an improved outcome in women diagnosed with postnatal depression (Holden, Sagovsky and Cox, 1989). Another study of nurse practitioners specially trained in interpersonal counselling found that counselled patients had significantly greater reductions in symptom scores than controls (Klerman et al., 1987).

In a study by Catalan and colleagues (1984), brief counselling by GPs was found to be as effective as drug therapy. In this study, patients were randomly assigned either to one group who received a prescription for anxiolytics or to another group who were given brief counselling by the GPs and no prescription. Improvement at one and seven months was similar in both groups. The authors suggest that such counselling need not be intensive or specially skilled and concluded that anxiety may often be reduced to tolerable levels by means of explanation, exploration of feelings, reassurance and encouragement. More recent studies from this group of researchers have found that brief problem-solving therapies given by research psychiatrists and trained GPs are as effective as the antidepressant amitriptyline and significantly more effective than placebo (Catalan et al., 1991; Mynors-Wallis et al., 1995).

Raphael conducted a study on women considered to be at risk for post-bereavement morbidity (1979). Significant lowering of morbidity was found in the group referred for treatment compared with the controls. Although the intervention was carried out by a psychodynamically trained psychiatrist, Raphael indicated that primary care team members such as community nurses had also been successfully trained to carry out the therapy.

Self-help packages may also have value in this area and need further study. One trial compared a stress self-help package administered by the GP with routine GP treatment (Kiely and McPherson, 1986). The authors found greater improvement at three months in those receiving the package and this group also visited the GP less often for psychological problems.

Trials of other mental health workers in primary care

Studies have also been conducted to evaluate the effectiveness of other mental health workers in primary care. As with counselling, the results are equivocal, with many studies showing only short-term effects. These studies have included psychologists, behaviour nurse therapists, social workers and community psychiatric nurses. While studies using psychologists have indicated improved outcome, reduced psychotropic drug prescriptions and fewer consultations with the GP, many of these effects were not long-lasting (Corney, 1993). However, a recent trial of brief cognitive therapy has shown a longer-term effect (Scott et al., 1997).

One study conducted on patients with major depression compared antidepressant medication prescribed by a psychiatrist; cognitive behaviour therapy (as given by a clinical psychologist); counselling and case work (given by a social worker); and routine care by a GP (Scott and Freeman, 1992). They found that all treatment groups had improved at sixteen weeks and that the clinical advantages of all the specialist treatments were small. However, patients positively evaluated the psychological treatments, especially social work counselling. The main problem with this study was the sample size of 121 patients, which is rather too small to find statistically significant differences in treatment effects.

A group of researchers conducted a meta-analysis of eleven British studies of specialist mental health treatment in general practice (Balestrieri, Williams and Wilkinson, 1988). In each study the outcome of treatment by a specialist mental health professional located in general practice was compared with the outcome of 'treatment as usual' by general practitioners. The main finding was that treatment by mental health professionals was about 10 per cent more successful than that usually given by general practitioners. Counselling, behaviour therapy, and general psychiatry proved to be similar in their overall effect. The influence of counselling seemed to be greatest on social functioning, whereas behaviour therapy seemed mainly to reduce contacts with the psychiatric services.

While the majority of clients believe that they have been helped, the majority of clinical trials on counsellors and psychologists have not shown a major effect of treatment, especially in the long term. The general lack of treatment effect may be due to the fact that high proportions of patients will improve, regardless of treatment received. It is the group of clients who will not improve without psychological help that need to be identified for future trials.

The more promising results demonstrating positive outcomes have been those studies conducted on specific client groups, such as those with postnatal depression or those at risk for post-bereavement morbidity.

There is also some tentative evidence, although inconclusive, of the value of problem-solving techniques and cognitive behavioural therapy in primary care. This is supported by the results of outcome studies on depression and anxiety conducted in other settings. In these studies, cognitive behaviour therapy has been found to be particularly effective (reviewed by Roth and Fonagy, 1996). These findings have led to many health authorities and trusts only funding counsellors in primary care who use these more directive techniques.

Cost-effectiveness and the use of services

Studies have investigated use of medical services and have used this as a measure of outcome as well as costs. A number of studies have indeed shown a reduction in visits made to the doctor after cessation of counselling in contrast with a period before (Marsh and Barr, 1975; Waydenfeld and Waydenfeld, 1980). These and other studies have found a reduction in the number of psychotropic and other drugs prescribed (Speirs and Jewell, 1995) or a reduction in referrals to psychiatrists after a counselling attachment had been instigated (Illman, 1983). These results have to be interpreted with caution, as it is likely that the client will be referred at a time of crisis in their lives when attendance is also likely to be high. The number of visits to the doctor might have reduced without the inter-vention of a counsellor as the crisis abated.

The use of medical services is important when considering costs. Studies have attempted to find out whether counselling is cost-effective by comparing the cost of employing a counsellor with the money saved by a reduction in the client's use of medical and other services.

The evidence for this is equivocal. Clinical trials have yielded very mixed evidence of the cost-effectiveness of the experimental treatment. Some trials have found that part of the salary of the worker can be met from savings (Robson, France and Bland, 1984) while others found that the specialist treatments were more expensive compared with routine GP care (Scott and Freeman, 1992).

Studies in the United States of America have yielded evidence of the cost-effectiveness of counselling. They have found that the use of psycho-therapy and behavioural medicine services can reduce use of medical services and this is why some health insurance companies have added psychotherapy to the list of services covered by their schemes. The Hawaii Medicaid Project (Cummings et al., 1993) found that targeted, focused psychological treatment produced a dramatic and significant reduction in the subsequent medical needs and medical resource consumption of a group of patients. This six-year study included patients with heart disease, hypertension, diabetes and even substance abuse. Similar clinical trials are needed in the United Kingdom, although it may be more difficult to show a reduction in costs as medical expenditure is generally much lower than in the States.

Qualitative research

Many researchers and clinicians consider that the use of clinical trial methodology, with its methodological constraints, is inappropriate for the study of counselling. For example, even if trials show an effect of treatment, they offer very little increased understanding into the processes involved in bringing about change.

Many researchers and research clinicians call for the need to adopt new models for research which more closely fit human behaviour, rather than the clinical trial which has been adopted from drug therapy research and the physical sciences. They suggest that the models used should be more similar to those used in anthropology and sociology which have tended to deal with some of the complex issues involved in human behaviour and culture.

Rather than reduce complex phenomena into quantifiable categories, qualitative research aims to capture the complexity of social phenomena in the concepts and theories that it generates. It also aims to take fully into account the ways in which these phenomena are expressed in that specific context.

Qualitative research is carried out using a variety of methods (Good and Watts, 1989). Most researchers indicate the need to use a variety of data collection methods from more than one source, including semi-structured and unstructured interviews; participant observation; non-participant observation; case material; and documentary evidence. Interviews are normally tape-recorded or videos made so that the precise details of conversations can be recorded and used. The particular questions asked are guided by preliminary ideas but should be made in an open ended way so that the respondent is free to answer according to how he or she personally feels.

The process of analysing data is rigorous and time consuming, involving a detailed system of coding and categorization. Analysis of the initial data obtained is used to direct the data collection at later stages. The final stage of the analysis consists of the development of a number of themes or categories enabling the material to be seen in a conceptual framework.

Qualitative studies can be undertaken in primary care settings. They can be used, for example, to investigate the process of change, in order to increase our understanding of what brings it about. These studies can be seen to be more relevant to practitioners who are constantly striving to develop their own skills in bringing about positive change in clients. For example, video- or tape-recording of the counselling sessions may be undertaken, supplemented by the counsellor making detailed notes after each interview. This could include the client's and the counsellor's perceptions of the problems presented, the plan of action, whether this was agreed with the client as well as the client's motivation to be helped. After cessation of counselling, details can be collected on the counsellor's perception of whether the client was helped, details of the therapy and any arrangements made for future involvement. In addition, detailed interviews conducted with the client and important others (e.g. relatives, carers, the GP etc) on their perceptions of improvement and the help received will shed further light on the process from all concerned.

Qualitative work or detailed analyses of consultations could also be used to examine whether counselling attachments have altered the behaviour and attitudes of GPs or other members of the primary care team. A great deal of this type of research remains to be done.

Case studies and the case control design

Case studies, defined by Bromley as 'an account of the person in a situation', are also of particular relevance and concern to the research practitioner. Case studies may take many different forms but normally are descriptive and include a causal analysis attempting to give an explanation of the observations found. Case studies may involve one or more individual persons, groups, or organizations but all involve 'singular, naturally occurring events in the real world . . . not experimentally contrived events or simulations' (Bromley, 1986). Other distinctive characteristics are that they are usually focused on a small number of units, they nearly always concern a span or time and they are about events taking place 'in vivo'. In case studies, there is an emphasis on the experience of those involved and this usually involves a smaller distance between researcher and the researched compared with traditional approaches (Orford, 1992). Thus a single case study may relate to the setting up of a counselling attachment or a detailed analysis of the counselling process within this setting.

Another type of case study which can be used in service evaluation is the single-case control design. In these studies, the individual client acts as his or her own control. Thus symptoms or problems experienced during a set period before counselling are compared with those experienced during a similar period after counselling. This type of study is commonly conducted by psychologists and cognitive behaviour therapists who obtain baseline ratings on symptoms over a period of time and then chart these ratings over the period of contact and again at a follow-up session some weeks or months later. While this is a fairly simple task with some disorders, for example, phobias or anxieties, it is much more difficult with more complex problems, including family and interpersonal situations. This type of study is also more appropriate when a problem-solving approach is adopted, with the therapist and client deciding on which priority areas need to be tackled.

Single-case studies can be carried out in routine clinical practice. While they are important in the refinement of a clinical technique, it is not always possible to generalize to a broader population. In addition, without a control group, it is difficult to prove that any benefit is due to the therapeutic technique employed.

Case control studies

Another methodology used to evaluate outcome is the case control study. With these studies, the outcome of one group of clients receiving the intervention is compared with another group who do not. For example, the outcome of clients referred to a service including an employed counsellor is compared with the outcome of clients referred to a service which does not. The difference from the clinical trial is that the participants are not randomly allocated to the intervention group or the control. These studies are often higher in external validity (i.e. more naturalistic) than clinical trials but lower in internal validity.

An example of this type of study was carried out by Martin and Mitchell (1983). They compared the outcome of a group of eighty-seven patients receiving counselling with a matched group of patients drawn from the age/sex register. They found no major differences in outcome between the two groups, although this was only measured in terms of attendance rate and psychotropic drug prescription. The controls were matched only according to their age and sex and not their social/psychological characteristics, so it is difficult to draw conclusions from the results.

This group of investigators also studied whether having a counsellor in the practice had altered GP behaviour (Martin and Martin, 1985). They investigated this by examining medical notes over a period of time. The notes of 300 patients who had been continuously registered with the practice since 1974 were randomly withdrawn from the files. The number of psycho-social problems and the number of prescriptions for psychotropic drugs recorded in the years 1975, 1979 and 1982 were noted. They found that the number of patients who had had a psychiatric diagnosis recorded in their notes during one year fell between 1975 and 1982, the number of prescriptions for antidepressant drugs also fell but the prescriptions for tranquillizers and sleeping tablets rose substantially. They hypothesized that the change in psychotropic prescriptions could have been due to the doctor becoming more willing to consider psychogenic problems as being precipitated by stress rather than a biochemical change. The reduction in patients being given a psychiatric diagnosis could be due to early attention to patients' emotional needs preventing later breakdowns. The authors concluded, however, that no major changes were detected over the seven-year period.

Studies by counsellors in practice

In addition, to the studies outlined above, all counsellors should consider that monitoring and evaluation is an important aspect of their role.

Evaluating one's work is an important part of an individual's professional development. It can also be used to develop and adapt the service.

These limited evaluations may be particularly worthwhile as they can aid future decisions regarding the best way to use the counsellor's limited time in the surgery. For example, an evaluation may find out that the consultative role of the counsellor (giving other team members support or advice regarding their patients) is as valuable as the counsellor seeing clients directly. Alternatively, an evaluation can suggest that running a group for clients (for example, a support group for those needing longer term help) means that more people can be treated than with individual work. Assessments may also yield information on the types of patients who seem to benefit most from seeing a counsellor as well as those who do not. Even a monitoring of the characteristics of patients who fail to attend may be helpful in developing future guidelines to GPs.

A number of studies of referrals have been reported in the literature which give guidelines on the type of information to collect (Marsh and Barr, 1975; Cohen, 1977; Meacher, 1977; Anderson and Hasler, 1979; Waydenfeld and Waydenfeld, 1980; Martin and Mitchell, 1983; Martin and Martin, 1985). Examples of forms that can be used and adapted can be found in Corney and Jenkins, 1993.

Counselling in general practice in the future

It is important that counsellors, counsellor trainers and GPs carefully consider the evidence collected so far. Counsellors need to consider their model of working and whether it is appropriate for their clients' needs in general practice. It is possible that non-directive individual work may not be the most effective way of working in general practice, although it may suit the counsellor trained in its use.

Counsellors should constantly monitor their own practice and give feedback to GPs on the suitability of clients referred and how their role fits into the team. It is only by a serious consideration of the counselling process that the most appropriate use can be made of a limited resource.

Counsellors also need to be flexible and adapt their way of working to fit in the setting. For example, studies have shown that long waiting lists are common and that these may contribute to an increase in non-attendance at the first appointment (Corney and Falconer, 1997). Counsellors with long waiting lists need to test out alternative models of working, such as keeping a short period of time each week for emergencies or assessment sessions. Simple changes, such as asking patients to make appointments via the receptionist (rather than being notified through the post) can sometimes reduce considerably the number of clients who fail to keep appointments.

One of the major advantages of primary care is that interprofessional collaboration can take place. Studies suggest that counsellors are more likely to work independently than other mental health professionals (Corney, Ward and Hammond 1991). Many do not discuss their clients with GPs or give any feedback apart from indicating that contact has been made. The counsellor needs to consider whether this independent model of working is appropriate for primary care. If a counsellor continues to work completely independently, many of the advantages of being placed in a GP setting are lost. Discussing clients and their needs will not only benefit the client (in most cases) but will increase the integration of the counsellor into the team.

Integration with other services and secondary care

There have also been concerns that the development of primary care services will lead to an increased fragmentation of mental health services. Employing workers directly, such as clinical psychologists or counsellors, can be an attractive option to GPs as they can have complete control over their activities. However, employed professionals are less likely to have contact with secondary care services and are more likely to work in isolation. This may be particularly true for counsellors (Tyndall, 1993; Corney, Ward and Hammond, 1996).

One way of encouraging integration is for counsellors to receive supervision through the local secondary care psychotherapy department. Others have suggested that counsellors become part of the clinical psychology services, so that counsellors and psychologists can work in conjunction rather than in competition (Miller, 1994). In any event, counsellors might find it valuable to have a base outside the team, possibly with other mental health professionals. This would encourage further integration and multidisciplinary working. It would also reduce isolation and might also mean that counsellors can work together to ensure reasonable conditions of service.

A closer integration with secondary care services may also assist the counsellor on whether to refer patients on to others (and when). A counsellor may be referred distressed and disturbed patients who may not benefit from therapy and may possibly be harmed. If counsellors receive support and backup from mental health professionals, they can learn to identify those clients who may be more appropriately treated elsewhere.

As many of the clients in primary care may have practical problems, it is also important that the counsellor has a clear understanding of the roles and resources of other workers in health and social care settings as well as those in the wider community. Counsellors need to be aware of other types of providers and personnel who may also be able to help their clients, such as social services personnel, community mental health teams, voluntary agencies and self-help groups.

Considering the needs of the practice as a whole

Another alternative to the present delivery of services would be for the practice and the counsellor to work in a much more proactive way. In addition to working with referred clients, counsellors could suggest that part of their role is to consider the psychological needs of the practice population as a whole and become involved in the development of a programme on how best to meet these needs.

Issues to be considered could include: how to identify clients in need of psychological help (possibly at an earlier stage of their problems); how to develop the psychological helping skills of all the primary care team members; when to refer patients on to counsellors and mental health workers, and to whom. The use of voluntary agencies and community groups can also be considered, to provide additional emotional support and practical help to patients.

The provision of individual counselling may also feature in this plan but the counsellor should also be active in considering alternative methods of working, such as group work. A complete concentration on individual work will mean that very few patients will be helped. Counsellors need to reconsider their roles and responsibilities in the practice.

More emphasis is necessary on the development of the communication and counselling skills of all the primary care team members, including nurses and doctors. Developing the skills of primary care professionals by increased training and consultation with mental health professionals may in fact be more effective for the patient group as a whole. Studies have shown that GPs' detection and management skills can be enhanced by training (Gask et al., 1987) and some of the most promising results described earlier have been obtained from the clinical trials of GPs and health visitors trained in counselling and problem-solving techniques.

The need for evaluation

This chapter should leave the reader in no doubt that there is still a great need for the further evaluation of psychological treatments in primary care at all levels. These should not only focus on evaluating counsellors and mental health professionals but also on the role of other members of the primary care team. There is a need for evaluative studies to find out the training needs, levels of skills, competence and expertise required by other personnel who use counselling skills as part their work. A variety of other therapies should be tested apart from individual one-to-one counselling, including group work, self-help packages, the use of volunteers and self-help groups. The needs of patients in primary care for emotional help and support will never be satisfied by the employment of counsellors alone.

REFERENCES

Anderson, S.A. and Hasler, J.C. (1979) Counselling in general practice. *Journal of the Royal College of General Practitioners*, 29, 352–356.

Ashurst, P. and Ward, D. (1983) An *Evaluation of Counselling in General Practice*. Final report of the Leverhulme Counselling Project. Report available from the Mental Health Foundation, London.

Balestrieri, M., Williams, P. and Wilkinson, G. (1988) Specialist mental health treatment in general practice: a meta-analysis. *Psychological Medicine*, 18, 711–717.

Boot, D., Gillies, P., Fenelon, J., Reubin, R., Wilkins, M. and Gray, P. (1994) Evaluation of the short term impact of counselling in general practice. *Patient Education and Counselling*, 24, 79–89.

Brodaty, H. and Andrews, G. (1983) Brief psychotherapy in family practice. A controlled prospective intervention trial. *British Journal of Psychiatry*, 143, 11–19.

Bromley, D. (1986) *The Case Study Method in Psychology and Related Disciplines*. Chichester: Wiley.

Catalan, J., Gath, D., Edmonds, G. and Ennis, J. (1984) The effects of non-prescribing of anxiolytics in general practice: controlled evaluation of psychiatric and social outcome. *British Journal of Psychiatry*, 144, 603–610.

Catalan, J., Gath, D.H., Anastasiades, P., Bond, S.A.K., Day, A. and Hall, L. (1991) Evaluation of a brief psychological treatment for emotional disorders in primary care. *Psychological Medicine*, 21, 1013–1018.

Cohen, J.S. (1977) Marital counselling in general practice. *Proceedings of the Royal College of Medicine*, 70, 495–496.

Corney, R. (1993) Studies of the effectiveness of counselling in general practice. In *Counselling in General Practice*, R. Corney and R. Jenkins (eds), London: Routledge.

Corney, R. and Falconer, S. (1997) Locality counselling projects: service evaluation report. Bexley and Greenwich Health Authority. [Unpublished report].

Corney, R., Kerrison, S. and Tan, G. (1996) Fundholding in South East Thames: a study of selected fundholders and non fundholders between 1991 and 1996. [Draft document submitted to the Primary Care Development Fund.]

Corney, R., Ward, E. and Hammond, J. (1996) *General Practitioners' Use of Mental Health Services: The Impact of Fundholding*. Final report to the Department of Health.

Corney, R. and Jenkins, R. (eds) (1993) *Counselling in General Practice*. London: Routledge.

Cummings, N., Dorken, H., Pallak, M. and Henke, C. (1993) *Medicaid, Managed Behavioural Health and Implications for Public Policy: A Report of the HCFA Hawaii Medicaid Project and Other Readings, Health Care Utilization and Cost Series*, vol. 2 [unpublished].

Friedli, K., King, M., Lloyd, M., Horder, J. (1997) Randomised controlled assessment of non directive psychotherapy versus routine general practitioner care. *The Lancet*, 350: 1662–1665.

Gask, L., McGrath, G., Goldberg, D. and Millar, T. (1987) Improving the psychiatric skills of established general practitioners: evaluation of group teaching. *Medical Education*, 22, 132–138.

Good, D. and Watts, F. (1989) Qualitative research. In *Behavioural and Mental Health Research: A Handbook of Skills and Methods*, G. Parry and F. Watts (eds), Hove and London: Lawrence Erlbaum.

Hemmings, A. (1997) Counselling in primary care: a randomised controlled trial. *Patient Education and Counselling*, 32, 219–230.

Holden, J., Sagovsky, R. and Cox, J. (1989) Counselling in a general practice setting: controlled study of health visitor intervention in treatment of postnatal depression. *British Medical Journal*, 298, 223–236.

Illman, J. (1983) Is psychiatric referral good value for money? *British Medical Association News Review*, 9, 41–42.

Kiely, B.G. and McPherson, I.G. (1986) Stress self-help packages in primary care: a controlled trial evaluation. *Journal of the Royal College of General Practitioners*, 36, 307–309.

King, M., Brosner, G., Lloyd, M. and Horder, J. (1994) Controlled trials in the evaluation of counselling in general practice. *British Journal of General Practice*, 44, 229–232.

Klerman, G., Budman, S., Berwick, D., Weissman, M., Damico-White, J., Denby, A. and Feldstein, M. (1987) Efficacy of a brief psychosocial intervention of symptoms of stress and distress among patients in primary care. *Medical Care*, 25, 1078–1088.

Kline, P. (1992) Problem of methodology in studies of psychotherapy. In *Psychotherapy and its Discontents*, W. Dryden and C. Feltham (eds), Buckingham: Open University Press.

Lambert, M., Masters, K. and Ogles, B. (1991) Outcome research in counselling. In *Research in Counselling*, C. Watkins and L. Schneider (eds), Hillsdale, NJ: Lawrence Erlbaum.

Light, D.W. (1991) Effectiveness and efficiency under competition: the Cochrane test. *British Medical Journal*, 303, 1253–1254.

Marsh, G. and Barr, J. (1975) Marriage guidance counselling in a group practice. *Journal of the Royal College of General Practitioners*, 25, 73–75.

Martin, E. and Martin, P.M.L. (1985) Changes in psychological diagnosis and prescription in a practice employing a counsellor. *Family Practice*, 2, 241–243.

Martin, E. and Mitchell, H. (1983) A counsellor in general practice: a one-year survey. *Journal of the Royal College of General Practitioners*, 33, 366–367.

Meacher, M. (1977) A pilot counselling scheme with general practitioners: summary report. London: Mental Health Foundation [unpublished].

Miller, R. (1994) Clinical psychology and counselling in primary care: opening the stable door. *Clinical Psychology Forum*, March, 11–14.

Mynors-Wallis, L., Gath, D., Lloyd-Thomas, A. and Tomlinson, D. (1995) Randomised controlled trial comparing problem solving treatment with amitriptyline for major depression in primary care. *British Medical Journal*, 310, 441–445.

Orford, J. (1992) *Community Psychology: Theory and Practice*. Chichester: Wiley.

Paul, G.L. (1967) Strategy of outcome research in psychotherapy. *Journal of Consulting Psychology*, 31, 109–118.

Priest, R., Vize, C., Robert, A., Roberts, M. and Tylee, A. (1996) Lay people's attitudes to treatment of depression; results of opinion poll for Defeat Depression Campaign just before its launch. *British Medical Journal*, 313, 858–859.

Pringle, M. and Churchill, R. (1995) Randomised controlled trials in general practice. *British Medical Journal*, 311, 1382–1383.

Raphael, B. (1979) Preventative interventions with the recently bereaved. *Archives of General Psychiatry*, 34, 1450–1454.

Robson, M., France, R. and Bland, M. (1984) Clinical psychologist in primary care: controlled clinical and economic evaluation. *British Medical Journal*, 288, 1805–1808.

Rogers, A., Pilgrim, D., and Lacey, R. (1993) *Experiencing Psychiatry: Users' Views of Services*. London, Macmillan.

Roth, A. and Fonagy, P. (1996) *What Works for Whom? A Critical Review of Psychotherapy Research*. New York: The Guilford Press.

Scott, A.I. and Freeman, C.P.L. (1992) Edinburgh primary care depression study: treatment outcome, patient satisfaction, and cost after 16 weeks. *British Medical Journal*, 304, 883–887.

Scott, C., Tacchi, M., Jones, R. and Scott, J. (1997) Acute and one year outcome of a randomised controlled trial of brief cognitive therapy for major depressive disorder in primary care. *British Journal of Psychiatry*, 171, 131–134.

Speirs, R. and Jewell, J.A. (1995) One counsellor, two practices: report of a pilot scheme in Cambridgeshire. *British Journal of General Practice*, 45, 31–33.

Tyndall, N. (1993) *Counselling in the Voluntary Sector*. Buckingham: Open University Press.

Waydenfeld, D. and Waydenfeld, S.W. (1980) Counselling in general practice. *Journal of the Royal College of General Practitioners*, 30, 671–677.

Index